ORGANIZING FOR COLLECTIVE ACTION

The Political Economies of Associations

SOCIAL INSTITUTIONS
AND SOCIAL CHANGE

An Aldine de Gruyter Series of Texts and Monographs

EDITED BY

Peter H. Rossi • Michael Useem • James D. Wright

Bernard C. Rosen, **The Industrial Connection: Achievement and the Family in Developing Societies**

Paul Diesing, **Science and Ideology in the Policy Sciences**

James D. Wright, Peter H. Rossi, and Kathleen Daly, **Under the Gun: Weapons, Crime, and Violence in America**

Walter I. Wallace, **Principles of Scientific Sociology**

Robert C. Liebman and Robert Wuthnow (eds.), **The New Christian Right: Mobilization and Legitimation**

Paula S. England and George Farkas, **Households, Employment, and Gender: A Social, Economic, and Demographic View**

Richard F. Hamilton and James D. Wright, **The State of the Masses**

James R. Kluegel and Eliot R. Smith, **Beliefs About Inequality: Americans' Views of What Is and What Ought to Be**

James D. Wright and Peter H. Rossi, **Armed and Considered Dangerous: A Survey of Felons and Their Firearms**

Roberta G. Simmons and Dale A. Blyth, **Moving into Adolescence: The Impact of Pubertal Change and School Context**

Carolyn C. Perrucci, Robert Perrucci, Dena B. Targ, and Harry R. Targ, **Plant Closings: International Context and Social Costs**

Robert Perrucci and Harry R. Potter (eds.), **Networks of Power: Organizational Actors at the National, Corporate, and Community Levels**

David Popenoe, **Disturbing the Nest: Family Change and Decline in Modern Societies**

John Mirowsky and Catherine E. Ross, **Social Causes of Psychological Distress**

James D. Wright, **Address Unknown: The Homeless in America**

Alice S. Rossi and Peter H. Rossi, **Of Human Bonding: Parent–Child Relations Across the Life Course**

G. William Domhoff, **The Power Elite and the State**

David Knoke, **Organizing for Collective Action: The Political Economies of Associations**

ORGANIZING FOR COLLECTIVE ACTION
The Political Economies of Associations

David Knoke

Aldine de Gruyter
New York

About the Author

David Knoke is Chairman of the Department of Sociology, University of Minnesota, and was a Fulbright Senior Research Scholar, Christian-Albrechts-Universitat, Kiel (1989).

Dr. Knoke was co-founder and acting chair of the American Sociological Association's Section on Political Sociology, served as newsletter co-editor, and is on the editorial board of *Administrative Science Quarterly*.

In addition to numerous journal articles, his most recent books include *Organized for Action* (with J. R. Wood, 1981), *Network Analysis* (with J. H. Kuklinski, 1982), *The Organizational State* (with E. O. Laumann, 1987), *Statistics for Social Data Analysis* (with G. W. Bohrnstedt, 2nd ed., 1987) and *Political Networks: The Structural Perspective* (1990).

ALDINE DE GRUYTER
A Division of Walter de Gruyter, Inc.
200 Saw Mill River Road
Hawthorne, New York 10532

Library of Congress Cataloging-in-Publication Data
Knoke, David.
    Organizing for collective action : the political economies of associations / David Knoke.
        p.   cm. — (Social institutions and social change)
    Includes bibliographical references.
    ISBN 0–202–30412–4
        1. Pressure groups—United States.   2. Associations, institutions etc.—United States—Political activity.   I. Title.   II. Series.
JK1118.K564   1990
322.4'3'0973—dc20   89–37782
                                                                        CIP

Printed in the United States of America
10 9 8 7 6 5 4 3 2 1

To Emma Naveaux Dunn and Dorothy Reiter Knoke

CONTENTS

PART IV. ORGANIZATIONAL POLITY

PART V. CONCLUSION

PREFACE

When President Bush's "thousand points of light" brighten the American political landscape, they illuminate tens of thousands of collective action organizations pursuing every aspect of community life from abused children and acupuncture to zoning and zoology. Citizen involvement in voluntary associations has been a staple of democratic theory since the founding of the Republic. That curious mixture of selflessness and self-interest which attracted and puzzled Tocqueville persists today in many guises. People join organizations to serve the public interest, to engage in sociable interaction, to obtain personal and group advantages. The associations may simultaneously be ends in themselves and vehicles for changing public policies. By pooling the small contributions from many individuals, organizations can multiply their scant powers many-fold. But, the collectivity may seek goals that conflict with the desires and intents of many participants. How to resolve this conundrum of the one and the many is the question at the core of all thought and research on collective action organizations. The answer requires a sustained theoretical and empirical inquiry into the structures and processes of a large sample of associations.

For this book, I constructed a theory of collective action organizations that seeks to account for the variations among them in internal and external political economies. By emphasizing that familiar term in a new context, I deliberately draw attention to the twin poles of power and wealth, around which individual and organizational strategies revolve. My theory is premised on the insufficiency of simple rational choice theories of social action and the necessity to incorporate normative and affective motivations, incentives, and objectives in any realistic explanation of concerted, coordinated behavior. It posits that the solution to the dilemma of group resources and social control lies in expanding the possibilities for democratic participation, by members in their organizations, and by organizations in their society. How useful this theory proves to be, both for its analytic insights, and as a guide to practical applications, remains for the reader to decide. I ask only that you approach this book with an open mind regarding the conceptual model and be tolerant toward the empirical findings. If you become even a little convinced by the argument, or at least dissatisfied enough to search for your own explanation, I will consider my efforts to have been worthwhile.

David Knoke

ACKNOWLEDGMENTS

The foundations of this book were launched in Bloomington, Indiana, in 1976 when I agreed to direct the annual sociology graduate research training seminar, Indianapolis Area Project, at Indiana University. The National Institute of Mental Health awarded me a research scientist development grant, and the National Science Foundation gave research funds to James R. Wood and me to collect data on members of voluntary associations in Indianapolis. Out of that collaboration came our book, *Organized for Action* (1981, Rutgers University Press). As the title of the present work suggests, it is very much a successor to that previous project, but expanded considerably in scope to cover the entire United States.

Many organizations and individuals over the past 15 years helped bring this project to fruition. Two research grants from the National Science Foundation (SES82-16927 and SES85-08051) provided the funds for the basic research collection. Two Sociology Program directors, James Zuiches and Joanne Miller, and the peer review panelists were unstinting in their support. The Indiana University Institute for Social Research and the University of Minnesota College of Liberal Arts gave generous blocks of time for data collection and analysis. A grant from the Russell Sage Foundation propitiously steered me to include the women's organizations in the sample. For data collection, the Indiana University Center for Survey Research, Kathryn Cirksena, Field Director, and the Minnesota Center for Survey Research, Rosanna Armson, Field Director, were indispensable. Especially important were research assistance provided by Richard Adams, Lois Kelly, and Denise Floe. The General Social Survey, directed by James A. Davis and Thomas W. Smith, and its Board of Overseers, chaired successively by Peter Rossi and Duane Alwin, permitted the inclusion of some important questions on its 1987 survey. The assistance of Lawrence Bobo and Thomas Guterbock in framing that module was invaluable. Of course, the project could not have succeeded without the willing participation of countless organizational leaders and members who provided the essential information about themselves and their associations' activities.

I was fortunate to encounter many colleagues over the decades who offered advice and criticism of drafts, provided platforms or forums for presentations, opened journal and book space for early reports, and otherwise bolstered my morale during this long process. Although they may not recognize their precise contributions, I thank Howard Aldrich, Ronald Aminzade, Samuel Bacharach, Jeffrey Berry, Richard Braungart, Paul Burstein, Nancy DiTomaso, William Form, Joseph Galaskiewicz, Patricia Gurin, Paul Hirsch, Bert Klandermans, Trev Leger, Bruce Mayhew, Bernard McMullan, J. Miller McPherson, Brint Milward, Norman Nie, David Prensky, Paul Reynolds, Kay Lehman Schlozman, Susan Stephens, John Sullivan, Louise Tilly, Michael Useem, Sidney Verba, Christine Von Der Haar, Jack Walker, David Whetten, James Wood, Christine Wright-Isak, and many anonymous referees and reviewers. My debt to these fine scholars is substantial, and I have striven to repay it in part by emulating the high quality of research and writing found in their own works. As always in these endeavors, the forbearance of the two women who mean the most to me in the world, Joann and Margaret, is appreciated.

PART I

INTRODUCTION

1

UNLIMITED FREEDOM OF ASSOCIATION

There is only one country on the face of the earth where the citizens enjoy un-limited freedom of association for political purposes. This same country is the only one where the continual exercise of the right of association has been intro-duced into civil life and where all the advantages of which civilization can confer are procured by means of it.

Alexis de Tocqueville
Democracy in America
Vol. II, p. 115 (1945)

In 1983, opponents of Maine's annual one-day moose hunt succeeded in plac-ing a referendum on the ballot to ban the sport. At the urging of the state's wildlife and fisheries department, the North American Wildlife Federation dis-tributed 200,000 copies of a brochure explaining that, far from decimating the moose population, the hunt actually produced a healthier herd by culling out weak and sick animals. Although a majority of voters polled just 2 months before the election favored eliminating the hunt, the brochure apparently changed enough opinions so that the referendum was defeated by a 2-to-1 margin.

Recent innovations in electronic word processing have radically altered newspaper and magazine publishing technologies, reaching well beyond the composing room into the advertising and editorial departments. Remote per-sonal computers and phone transmissions now allow race tracks, funeral homes, and police stations to dump news copy directly into a publisher's com-puters, bypassing journalists altogether. Strikebreaking activity becomes harder to detect when reporters can work outside the office and send in copy electronically. Alarmed at the threat of job losses, The Newspaper Guild's 1985 national convention delegates unanimously called for increased vigilance by TNG locals. "Adequate jurisdiction and coverage clauses" must be negotiated in bargaining-unit contracts, to protect union members against employers contracting work to freelancers, forcing employees to use their personal home computers without adequate reimbursement, and accepting remotely transmitted copy from news sources.

As the immigration reform bill struggled through years of congressional debate, an American Society of Engineering Education spokesman testified at one of the innumerable subcommittee hearings. Primarily an association for teachers and graduate fellowships, the ASEE observed an increasing shortage of college engineering faculty. One short-term solution would be to permit foreign nationals to teach in American colleges immediately after receiving their Ph.D.'s, instead of returning home for two years as then required. The ASEE testimony convinced the immigration bill's congressional sponsors to modify the provisions eventually enacted into law in 1987.

In celebration of the nation's 200th anniversary, Bikecentennial, a bicycle trip planning organization, was born. Within a decade it grew to more than 20,000 members whose annual $18 dues gave them access to organized cross-country bike tours, discounts on books and merchandise, a free copy of the *Cyclists Yellow Pages,* subscription to the bimonthly *Bike Report,* voting rights to elect Bikecentennial's board of directors, and assurances of "an effective voice in bicycling matters." With a $60,000 foundation grant, the association mapped more than 15,000 coast-to-coast miles of "quiet, scenic secondary roads" for its tour members.

These episodes—easily multiplied a thousandfold—illustrate the wide diversity of purposes and activities pursued by collective action organizations. This book provides a theoretical and empirical account of the political economies of American associations. Elements for a comprehensive theory lie scattered across diverse disciplines such as sociology, political science, organization analysis, business management, social work, labor economics, recreation and leisure studies, and law. The common threads stitching these strands together are people's decisions to become involved in a collective activity, the organizing efforts of association leaders, resource exchanges within and between organizations, the provision of incentives to participants, collective decisions on the allocation of group resources, and the pursuit of political goals in the larger society. Extracting a multilevel conceptual model from these elements and testing its implications with data from numerous American associations comprise the focal point of this book. This chapter lays the background for the specific research questions raised in subsequent chapters. It begins with an analytic definition of the collective action organization.

What are Collective Action Organizations?

Examples of collective action organizations abound. They range from a neighborhood block club trying to halt property decay to an elite committee of elder statesmen seeking international security through a stronger national defense. They pervade every functional subsystem of society: ceramic manufacturing trade associations, consumer food-buying cooperatives, municipal garbage labor unions, polar exploration societies, ballet promotion councils, fellowships of religious athletes, leagues of amateur bass fishermen, self-help groups of displaced homemakers, confederacies of civil libertarians—the list is endless. At latest count, the Gale Research Company's *Encyclopedia of Associations,* which does not tabulate locally based organizations, listed more than 20,000 American national associations fitting a reasonable description of a collective action organization (Koek and Martin 1987). Some of these associations are not membership groups (e.g., clearinghouses, research institutes, nonprofit foundations). However, the vast majority consist of voluntary affiliated natural-person (or organizational) members, all presumably sharing a common interest in the stated collective action goals the association seeks. For convenience, the terms "association" and "organization" are used interchangeably throughout this book to indicate "collective action organization."

Collective action organizations seek nonmarket solutions to individual or group problems. A person joins an association to enjoy benefits and satisfactions that can only be obtained by interacting with others having similar interests. The contrast between a clinic delivering paid professional therapy to patients and a group of substance abusers meeting to support one another's struggles with their addictions is obvious. Less evident is a trade association of widget-manufacturing companies. Although the companies buy and sell goods with suppliers and customers, their association is not itself a for-profit business. It is a voluntarily supported entity that tries to pressure the federal government and courts to arrange favorable conditions for the industry's economic operations: lower taxes, fewer environmental regulations, import protection, weaker unions, and so on.

As with all organizations, collective action organizations' purposes are limited. Some may encompass goals that can be met mainly inside the organization (e.g., Alcoholics Anonymous, a Saturday night barbershop quartet). Others must interact with persons and organizations in the external environment (e.g., the United Auto Workers, the local parent–teachers association). Whenever services are readily provided by a government or are available to individuals through purchases in the marketplace, a collective action organization is redundant and superfluous. Thus, sewage disposal and shoe repair rarely become the purpose of voluntary associations. But neighborhood crime patrols and alumni club vacation packages *do* compete effectively with governmental or profit making providers in some areas. A collective action organization's existence depends upon the perception by potential participants that some advantages will be gained by cooperation with others—whether these benefits accrue directly to individuals or to the collective whole.

Collective action organizations maintain their formal boundaries by designating specific criteria for membership status and by controlling the movement of persons across these boundaries. Members are rarely paid for their involvement, but are usually required to make some contribution of personal resources—financial or time-and-effort (the Red Cross considers a single blood donation sufficient)—to the collectivity in order to remain a member in good standing. Sometimes the dues amount to substantial sums; for example, professional societies and labor unions sometimes charge hundreds of dollars. Although affiliation is voluntary, many associations formally prevent some categories of persons from joining (e.g., those lacking proper education credentials in a professional society). Most expel members for misconduct or failure to pay dues. But, some organizations, needing to present the world with an image of broad popular support, may list withdrawn members on their rosters as still-active participants. Others may conveniently count episodic supporters and passively interested constituents who could be called on only in exceptional circumstances for financial or political sustenance. Does a $2 contribution to the heart disease door-to-door fund drive really confer affiliate status on a donor? Because claimed membership size can be a critical resource, collective action organizations find it advantageous to manipulate these figures.

Many national associations are wealthy enough to employ full- or part-time staff, but such executive, managerial, professional, and clerical participants are formally subordinate to the membership. These employees presumably conduct the organization's daily business under authority granted by the membership, usually delegated through elected officers or a board of directors. In a collective action organization the mass membership has at least formal rights to select leaders, and, indirectly through those leaders, to sanction organizational decisions. Thus, the National Geographic Society is not a genuine association, since its 10 million "members" are really just magazine subscribers. Similarly, the YMCA's "members" are actually fee-for-service clientele, while voting is restricted to a small circle of laymen, nominated by local branch boards of managers, who ritually ratify the board's chosen successors (Zald 1970, p. 93).

Collective action organizations usually have mechanisms for mass membership involvement in internal decision making. Nomination and election of officials, appointments to committees, referenda on policy issues, and periodic meetings and conventions are well-known devices that allow interested members to voice their opinions and exert some control over the overall direction of association affairs. Every association displays the formal trappings of democratic governance in constitutions or bylaws. Their actual practices may fall far short of such desiderata however, as the grass-roots members of some major American labor unions well know. Still, participatory democracy remains an ideal both expressed and implemented to varying degrees in almost all associations.

To summarize, collective action organizations (1) seek nonmarket solutions to particular individual or group problems; (2) maintain formal criteria for membership on a voluntary basis; (3) may employ persons under the authority of organizational leaders; and (4) provide formally democratic procedures to involve members in policy decisions.

Associations can be illuminated in contrast to other familiar social formations (Knoke and Prensky 1984). Primary groups, such as social circles, friendship cliques, and families, pursue highly diffuse purposes and maintain vague criteria for affiliation (Who belongs in the inner crowd at the Southview Junior High?). At the other extreme, work organizations, such as government bureaucracies and private-sector corporations, impose rigidly hierarchical authority systems on their participants. Their employees' livelihoods depend on financial compensation for full-time work in the organization. The employment contracts in firms and bureaus stipulate an exchange of wages and salaries for participants' labor power, allowing them few rights to collective decision making (but see recent debates over "industrial democracy"). The assembly line workers at the Chrysler plant have no say over the company's investment and production decisions. Nor do nurses, orderlies, or even most physicians exert much control over the policy directions of the hospitals in which they work. Nonemployees coming into contact with work organizations are considered external "suppliers," "customers," or "clients" (welfare recipients, county prisoners), who also lack authority rights.

Just as association members retain constitutional authority over their officers, so do stock owners over private enterprises, and voters over elected governments. In practice, however, the average participant's power relative to the managing officials in all three types of organizations may be so diluted as to render problematic his or her influence on organizational decision making. The potential for minority control and abuse of collective resources remains as much a threat in nominally democratic associations as in more overtly hierarchical firms and bureaus. Later chapters examine some of the consequences of variations in organizational governance.

Centrality of Associations in Society

In his functional analysis of modern society as a complex interlocking set of subsystems, Talcott Parsons conceptualized three basic forms of social organization that develop through processes of differentiation and pluralism:

markets, bureaucracies, and associations (Parsons 1969, pp. 51–55). These "structuring principles" perform the basic adaptive, goal attainment, and integrative functions, respectively. Associations, by which Parsons seemed to have in mind chiefly professional societies of doctors and lawyers, help to integrate both markets and bureaucracies through simultaneous political and solidary actions:

> The democratic association, then, both as underlying the authority of governments and in private sectors, is a political entity, but not only that. It is grounded in the solidarities of various kinds and levels of associational "communities" which, with their initially normative "definitions of the situation," function in ways that are at least to a considerable degree independent of collective decision making and enforcement mechanisms (Parsons 1969, p. 13).

By straddling the public and private sectors, associations knit together the diverse institutions of modern civil society that threaten to come unraveled when each actor pursues a narrow self-interest. In Parsons' wont, associations perform the benign service of fostering a consensual normative order and conferring authority upon society's leaders. One need not embrace harmonious functionalism to recognize that associations also have the capacity to further pluralize an already refractory society. In vigorously pursuing their members' narrow self-interests, collective action associations often constitute formidable "organizational weapons" for combat against opposing groups. The term is Selznick's (1960) label for the Bolshevik party, but it is apt for the American Medical Association's fight against Medicare, the National Association for the Advancement of Colored People's struggle to end segregation, and the Sierra Club's effort to delay the Alaska pipeline. These contradictory qualities of collective action organizations—of promoting internal unity and external conflict—pervade theoretical analyses over the years.

To structure the large theoretical literatures on collective action organizations, three broad paradigms are elucidated in the following sections: (1) the problem of societal integration; (2) the problem of organizational governance; and (3) the problem of public policy-making. My review of these perspectives lays the foundation for the new theoretical synthesis and empirical analyses that follow.

The Social Integration Problem

As Western nations began industrial expansion, from the mid-eighteenth century on, the transformation from capitalist agricultural to factory modes of production swept away the traditional hierarchies of communal society. Urban crowding, unemployment, poverty, and crime created physical deprivations on a vast scale. Rebellions periodically racked the old regimes as democratic and socialist forces challenged the premises of the aristocratic political order. New social institutions—prisons, police forces, poorhouses, mental hospitals, schools, political parties, labor unions, and self-help associations—emerged to cope with the turmoil. The agony of Europe, and to a lesser extent America, foreshadowed the upheavals in twentieth century developing nations. The sufferings of destitute working classes began to stir "the Social Question" in the minds of political elites and social theorists: what brought about the distressful condition of ordinary people and what could alleviate it? (See Rossides 1978, p. 234.) The importance of social organizations that could reintegrate the fragmented social order figured prominently in the analyses of major theorists such as Durkheim, Simmel, and Tocqueville. A harkening after the imagined *gemeinschaft* of bygone eras permeates this paradigm.

Emile Durkheim's master concept of *anomie* explained social disorder as a result of abnormal functioning of the division of labor that destroys organic solidarity within a population. Class wars, industrial strife, suicides, crimes against property and persons all flourish when the division of labor fails to coordinate properly the functional activities of individuals (Durkheim 1933, pp. 353–95). As a solution, Durkheim proposed "corporative organizations," akin to medieval guilds or modern syndicates. Based on occupations and professions, these groups would exercise moral force by subordinating their members' special interests to the general good. For the corporations' members, group attachments would overcome the social atomization and alienation of the modern division of labor:

> That is why when individuals who are found to have common interests associate, it is not only to defend those interests, it is to associate, that is, not to feel lost among adversaries, to have the pleasure of communing, to make one out of many, which is to say, finally, to lead the same moral life together (Durkheim 1933, p. 15).

The reconstituted corporative organizations, in turn, would integrate and mediate relationships between the individual and the remote, impersonal national state:

> A nation can be maintained only if, between the State and the individual, there is intercalated a whole series of secondary groups near enough to the individual to attract them strongly in their sphere of action and drag them in this way, into the general torrent of social life (Durkheim 1933, p. 28).

By diversifying authority among the major economic interests of society, political pluralism and individual liberty are preserved. Hegemony by a "hypertrophied" state is averted (Durkheim 1951, p. 389; also Durkheim 1958).

Georg Simmel elaborated the theme of "freely chosen association" as the source of freedom and individualism in modern society (Simmel 1955, p. 130). In his famous geometric image of concentric and intersecting circles, each person acquires a social personality to the extent that "his pattern of participation is unique; hence the fact of multiple group participation creates in them a new subjective element" (Simmel 1955, p. 140). The more numerous the groups to which a person is attached, and hence the more distinct social statuses he or she occupies, the less potential for any one group to dominate and control that member in a comprehensive way. Like Durkheim, Simmel saw the modern proliferation of group affiliations as compensating for the alleged loss of primary social bonds that had integrated traditional societies. From the confusions and conflicting claims of diverse group affiliations, a new type of social cohesion emerges:

> Thus, the creation of groups and associations in which any number of people can come together on the basis of their interest in a common purpose, compensates for that isolation of personality which develops out of breaking away from the narrow confines of earlier circumstances (Simmel 1955, p. 163).

Although Simmel discussed group affiliations in general terms, he clearly included the many formal associations existing beyond the primary group level. By focusing on microlevel social interactions, however, Simmel had little to say about the ways that groups integrate persons into the larger social, economic, and political institutions.

Alexis de Tocqueville, on the other hand, made several astute observations about the contributions of formal associations to the national integration of the young United States, beginning with his famous aphorism that "Americans of all ages, all conditions, and all dispositions constantly form associations" (Tocqueville 1945, II p. 106). In democratic societies, all citizens are independent, feeble, and powerless. In early nineteenth century America, the small federal government could not carry out the "vast multitude of lesser undertakings, which the American citizens perform everyday, with the assistance of the principle of association" (Tocqueville 1945, II p. 108). To get things done in the decentralized American political system, people had to act on their own initiative. By working cooperatively in associations, democratic citizens created local communities that promoted their individual and collective interests (Pope 1986, p. 64). In effect, the layer of intermediate organizations between the individual and the state retarded the centralization and bureaucratization of government administration. It acted as a bulwark against the tyranny of the majority.

Civil associations—by which Tocqueville meant groups primarily concerned with intellectual, cultural, and social goals—preserve civilization against barbarism; that is, against the disappearance of individual liberty and freedom. Like Durkheim and Simmel, Tocqueville saw voluntary organizations as enhancing the individual's social bonds, multiplying the sources of social identification, and preventing the social atomization that is inherent in democratic society's leveling tendencies. But Tocqueville also assigned important functions to political associations (parties and factions having explicit political goals), viewing them as crucial protection against mass revolution.

He saw a "natural and perhaps necessary connection" between civil and political associations. The former facilitated the latter, but in return "political association singularly strengthens and improves associations for civil purposes" (Tocqueville 1945, II p. 115). Political association integrates local communities with the national society. It "makes the love and practice of association more general, it imparts a desire of union, and teaches the means of combinations to numbers of men who otherwise would have always lived apart." Political organizations are "large free schools, where all members of the community go to learn the general theory of association" (p. 116). This civic education function of associations is a central theme in theories of societal democracy discussed below.

Concerns about secondary groups and associations that mediate between citizens and the state took on a special urgency for mid-twentieth century political analysts who witnessed the rise of communist and fascist dictatorships. Whenever social conditions approximate a "mass society"—where populations and elites directly manipulate one another—unconstrained social and political movements can erupt and eventually be captured by totalitarian extremists (Kornhauser 1959). When social bonds weaken, people lose their grip upon their social identities and the norms that govern their behaviors. Social control in the pluralist sense of self-regulation by social groups disappears, to be replaced by repressive social control from central authorities (Janowitz 1978, p. 28). Without a strong stratum of intermediate groups, individuals can relate to the larger society and state only through inclusive nationwide structures. This situation approximates Simmel's concentric circles that expose the individual to total domination from the highest level. In contrast, strong and diverse secondary associations induce "multiple proximate concerns" (Kornhauser 1959, p. 76) that diffuse the potential for massification and extremism.

Overlapping group memberships check the aggregation of power among elites, and extensive crosscutting group affiliations discourage the superimposition and intensification of rancorous social conflicts (Coleman 1957; Dahrendorf 1959, pp. 213–215). The familiar assertions of Durkheim and Tocqueville, that work associations and community organizations could socially integrate the citizenry and counterbalance the bureaucratic power of the state, were echoed by Nisbet (1953, pp. 49–50) and Kornhauser (1959, pp. 76, 229–31). Halebsky summarized this thesis:

> Intermediate groups have provided not only the historic basis of societal integration but have also defined the individual's place in the community, have helped instill community moral standards, and have constituted the focus of individual participation and the basis for the satisfaction of individual needs (Halebsky 1976, p. 37).

Quite a load for such fragile social organizations to bear! In order for societal freedom and liberty to prevail, intermediate groups must be autonomous and substantially self-governing. Such criteria naturally led theorists to consider the processes of organizational governance.

The Organizational Governance Problem

The fundamental issue in organizational governance is the distribution and legitimation of power among a collectivity's participants. The presumed tension between democratic and bureaucratic principles [most striking in Robert Michels' 1949 hypothesis of an inevitable "iron law of oligarchy"] is itself ironic, in view of bureaucracy's historic link to democratic movements. The theory of societal democracy, elaborated in the next section, emphasizes political equality through formal institutional practices such as periodic contested elections, written constitutions, and citizen participation in collective decision making (e.g., Parsons 1969, pp. 51–55). Popular demands for equality before the law and for protection from arbitrary judicial and administrative decisions encouraged the creation of bureaucratic authority. Bureaucratic administration emphasized regulation by impersonal rules and recruitment by merit of officials from all social strata (Weber 1947, pp. 329–41). Standardized operating procedures evolved: certification of appointees' education credentials, hierarchical supervisory structures, regularized career promotions, and decision appeals procedures. But, as bureaucracies institutionalized formal equality, the societal authority of bureaucratic officials expanded, along with growing potential for abuses (Bendix 1962, p. 437). Even within nonbureaucratic organizations, where "collegial" or "amateur" forms of direct governance initially prevailed, the principle of immediate democracy became "technically inadequate, on the one hand in organizations beyond a certain limit of size . . . or on the other hand, where functions are involved which require technical training or continuity of policy"(Weber 1947, p. 415). Once factions had arisen within an organization on a permanent basis, self-governing direct democracy broke down and was replaced by self-perpetuating bureaucratic administration.

Michels' pessimistic prognosis ("who says organizations says oligarchy") assumed that organization leaders enjoy inherent structural advantages vis-à-vis lower level participants: superior technical and managerial knowledge, control over the formal means of communication, superior political skills, as well as power conferred by the incompetence, indifference, and apathy of the masses (Michels 1949, pp. 72, 88–89). Furthermore, once ensconced in power, the logical imperatives of the rulers—to maintain and aggrandize their power— assures that this active minority will pursue collective policies favoring their personal interests. This loss of power by the mass of participants was unremarkable in firms and government bureaus, which did not claim to operate on democratic principles. (See Bacharach and Lawler 1980; Pfeffer 1981; and Mintzberg 1983, for recent analytic efforts to specify the nature of organizations' internal power cleavages, coalitions, and conflict processes.) Michels' startling insight was his allegation of oligarchy even in purportedly democratic organizations such as labor unions, worker's cooperatives, and the German Social Democratic Party.

The oligarchy hypothesis subsequently attained the stature of a universal condition in large complex organizations. Empirical studies in numerous contexts repeatedly detected persistent leadership cliques within unions, trade associations, professional societies, fraternal organizations, and other types of associations (Kerr 1957; Harrison 1959; McConnell 1966, pp. 119–27, 152; Truman 1971, pp. 139–55; Schmidt 1973; Meister 1984, p. 146; Nyden 1985; Benson 1986). The International Typographical Union, with its famous two-party system for contesting elections, was interpreted as the deviant specimen that proved the general rule (Lipset *et al.* 1956, p. 464). In most organizations, the absence of an effective, organized internal opposition inevitably permitted an incumbent administration to monopolize the organization's political resources. Ironically, the entrenchment of bureaucracy ultimately eliminated the very democratic forces that historically gave it life.

To dismiss democratic principles of governance as a complete fraud is too cavalier. It is true that direct self-government becomes impossible in any sizable organization. That an active minority is indispensable says little about the conditions under which an oligarchy emerges. Several factors particularly seem to encourage a leadership clique whose interests diverge from those of the membership.

1. A small number of members who provide a disproportionate share of the organization's resources, as in a trade association (Levitan and Cooper 1984).

2. Legal restraints on the membership's ability to exit voluntarily from the organization, as in unions that enforce a closed shop situation.

3. Associations whose members are split along ideological lines into opposing factions that fight for control of the administrative machinery, as in a political party with left and right wings. These conditions seem conducive to an oligarchy that invariably disregards many of its members' interests in conducting collective affairs.

Democratic governance seems more sustainable under a contrasting set of conditions:

1. Structural safeguards that encourage leadership turnover and member participation in decision making, such as contested elections, limited tenure in office, extensive committee work, use of policy referenda.

2. A sophisticated, highly educated mass membership that will not defer to leaders on the basis of claimed skill and expertise, as in a professional society.

3. The absence of fundamental disagreements between leaders and members about basic collective goals. When no significant disagreements arise, oligarchy will not produce policies that differ from those of a democratic regime.

Private association governance rarely experiences substantial cleavages of interest between the rulers and the ruled. Rather than adversary organizations, they are primarily unitary democracies (McConnell 1966, p. 141; Mansbridge 1980). Dissenters are more likely to keep silently loyal or to exit and launch their own organization than they are to remain and fight against the majority's will (Hirschman 1970; Salisbury 1969). Thus, unity of purpose within an organization empowers it to undertake effective collective action to attain its goals.

Rather than inevitable, oligarchy governance appears to be problematic under varying social conditions. American national associations exist within a political culture that highly values democratic norms:

> If corporations, churches, and the various organizations lacking membership in any realistic sense are excepted, the overwhelming number of the remainder are founded on a conception of authority which derives from the democratic ethos of the surrounding culture. In most, membership has a defined meaning, and the will of the membership provides the basis of authority (McConnell 1966, p. 134).

The pervasive American ethos of popular sovereignty molds every institution in the direction of participant control.

> In summary, the significance of the "democratic mold," which affects all
> ciations and to some degree almost all organizations in our culture is of [   ]
> mental importance in the process of group politics. It has a profound relationship
> to the problem of unity—not only the cohesion of the particular association, but
> as well the unity of the society of which it is a part. Associations in our culture
> are expected to be "democratic" (Truman 1971, p. 138).

Conceivably, this democratic ethos simply provides one more institutional myth behind which a Michelsian inversion of values proceeds unchecked (Meyer and Rowan 1977). More plausibly, these cultural norms nourish a genuine substance behind the democratic facade. The voluntary nature of association affiliations (labor unions aside) compels the leadership's attention to the membership's interests. Because leaders must continually mobilize both material resources and constituency support from the mass membership, they cannot capriciously flout its interests. [Just as elected officials in the larger society, the leaders must cultivate member support by providing both sufficient services and frequent policy successes to satisfy their members' cravings and demands.] The competent operation of an organization's internal political economy is a critical requirement for leaders to generate support for collective actions. Member involvement in decision making comprises a basic governance mechanism that confers legitimacy and creates commitment. Scott *et al.* referred to this condition as political rationality: "Political rationality requires gathering the support to implement decisions by making payoffs to—or otherwise gaining the consent of—those constituents who dominate the organization"(Scott *et al.* 1981, p. 136). For leaders to ignore the membership and to pursue a private self-aggrandizing agenda is to court eventual mass defections that would decimate the leaders' privileges. Even the Teamster bosses' excesses finally caught up with them after a generation of pension fund abuses. In a normative climate of democratic values, association leaders' interests in self-preservation necessitate their authentic adherence to democratic governance principles.

To summarize, collective action organizations are founded on the premise of democratic member control. Ideally, officials must attend to and be responsive to members' concerns. Thus, intraorganizational politics are encouraged, and the reciprocal exercise of influence between ends and means poses recurrent dilemmas. For an association to be effective in the instrumental sense, the formal control apparatus of bureaucracy may be indispensable. However, bureaucracy imperils democracy if it distances ordinary members from direct involvement in decision making. The more detached the members become, the less obligation they feel to support the collectivity, and ultimately the less successful the organization is. Further, democratic participation is a valued end in itself that many organizations seek to sustain at the cost of lessened goal efficiency. For example, many women's rights associations seek to redistribute power and wealth in the larger societal institutions, but would consider their victory hollow if won by autocratic, nonparticipatory means (Freeman 1979; Mansbridge 1986). The uneasy coexistence of bureaucratic and democratic principles within collective action organizations must alert the empirical analyst to these critical dimensions of internal association politics.

The Public Policy-Making Problem

Collective action organizations are key concepts in pluralist or group theories of societal politics and government (Bentley 1908; Latham 1952; Rose 1967; Truman 1971; Lowi 1979). This perspective, beginning with Albion Small (Small and Vincent 1894), depicts society as composed of many social groups, none of which are able to dominate politically nor claim to represent the Rousseauist national will (or "public interest"). Instead, a constellation of group forces comprises the dynamic pressure group system that interacts through various political processes, including competitive elections, incremental group negotiations and bargaining, and legislative lobbying. The fundamental unit of analysis is the "interest group," defined as "any group that, on the basis of one or more shared attitudes, makes certain claims upon other groups in the society," most importantly including the government (Truman 1971, p. 33; see equivalent definitions by Salisbury 1975, p. 177; Berry 1984, p. 5; and Bayes 1982, pp. 15–17). Janowitz offered a typical pluralist depiction of economic interest groups pressuring elected officials to obtain public policy decisions that favor their narrow interests:

> In the absence of an operative democratic socialist ideology in the United States, there have come to exist voluntary associations of economic entrepreneurs, industrial managers, professionals, and trade unionists. All, except a handful, are prepared to bargain but without aspiring to rule. These voluntary associations operate on the principle that the elected political representatives will define the collective or public interest as each presses narrowly for its presumed economic self-interest. In reality, these organizing principles cannot be applied without important components of collective social responsibility, but these are derivative, implicit, and secondary (Janowitz 1978, p. 302).

Intergroup conflicts are adjudicated under the benign auspices of a neutral state, which determines and implements decisions that are collectively binding on the entire society. Thus, public policy-making is the result of many social group forces, exerted by collective action organizations, that reach equilibrium in a decentralized but consensual democratic polity.

The pluralist paradigm of collective influence rejects any nonparticipatory conception of societal democracy. Elitist notions that restrict members of a democracy to choosing among alternative candidates are suspected of seeking to constrict liberty (Riker 1982). For example, Joseph Schumpeter (1943) treated democracy as an institutional method of voting for leaders, who must then be left alone to govern without interelection pressures from the populace. The electoral majority can control leaders only by the sanction of loss of office at periodic contested elections. This elitist disapproval of popular involvement in day-to-day policy decisions reflects fears of a mass society, as discussed above, in which political elites are subjected to irrational manipulation by the crowd.

In contrast, the theory of participatory democracy argues that self-government requires a citizenry continually engaged in efforts to shape public policies:

> In strong democracy, politics is something done by, not to, citizens. Activity is its chief virtue, and involvement, commitment, obligation, and service—common deliberation, common decision, and common work—are its hallmark (Barber 1984), p. 133).

Citizen participation has the critical function of creating and maintaining the democratic polity. It develops the individual attitudes and psychological qualities essential for representative democracy to flourish in the national state (Pateman 1970, p. 42). Local arenas of participation—which include grass-roots political parties, industrial workplaces, and voluntary organizations—offer people practical experiences in developing democratic skills and procedures: "the more individuals participate the better able they become to do so" (Pateman 1970, p. 43). The civic education functions of civil associations were remarked upon by Tocqueville long ago. Rather than threatening to destroy a delicate equilibrium, mass participation is an indispensable ingredient in sustaining democratic norms and processes. For democratic populists, collective action organizations perform the dual functions of politically socializing their members and of acting as aggregative interest groups in the polity (Parsons 1969, p. 339).

The pluralist paradigm stands in sharp contrast to various elite and class conceptions that view the national state as dominated either by bureaucratic organizations or capitalist classes [see Knoke (1981b) and Alford and Friedland (1985) for overviews of these approaches]. These paradigms generally ignore interest groups as irrelevant, or relegate them to subordinate importance (e.g., Mills 1956). They see effective political power as monopolized by active minorities within the national executive departments, or by an inner circle of business politicians beholden to the classwide interests of capitalism (e.g., Domhoff 1978, 1983; Useem 1984). The interests of ordinary citizens go largely unrepresented or are actively thwarted by the collective policy decisions that result from this antidemocratic system. In several ways, the elite and class paradigms are versions of Michels' organizational oligarchy translated to the national scene. In assuming a priori that citizens have little impact on public policy-making, the theories discourage empirical research on the impact of popular opinion through collective action organizations (see Burstein 1985).

Two traditions that *do* attempt to grapple with the problem of group involvement in public policy-making occur in sociology and political science. As in the societal democracy paradigm, both acknowledge the centrality of social organizational processes in the understanding of effective political influence. The investigation of social movements focuses on the interface between civil society and the polity, while the study of interest group lobbying concentrates on the relationship of private- and public-sector organizations within the polity. Together, these two approaches form a useful context in which to examine the political functions of collective action organizations.

Variously labeled the resource dependence, resource mobilization, or political process models (Gamson 1975; McCarthy and Zald 1977; Tilly 1978; McAdam 1982), the sociological social movements literature shares a common concern for preexisting conditions and contexts that enable disenfranchised populations to become politically aroused. (Political scientists also contributed to this debate, in developing a stability-disruption-protest model of group processes; see Greenstone 1979). As noted above, the mass society theorists argued that protest activity originates in the absence of intermediate groups that constrain political actions within conventional channels. In contrast, the social movements analysts argued that preexisting social groups relations are essential before discontented challengers can articulate their grievances to the authorities:

> According to our mobilization model, the broad factors within a population affecting its degree of mobilization are the extent of its shared interest in interactions with other populations, and the extent to which it forms a distinct category and a dense network. Outside the group, its power, its subjection to repression, and the current constellation of opportunities and threats most strongly affect its mobilization (Tilly 1978, p. 81).

The success of the American civil rights movement of the 1960's, for example, is attributed to the creation of community social support systems involving black colleges, churches, and local NAACP chapters, within the context of favorable dispositions from the federal government and national mass media (Morris 1984; also McAdam 1982). Social movement organizations (SMOs) are formal complex organizations that identify with and seek to implement the goals of a broad social movement (McCarthy and Zald 1977, p. 1218). They perform several strategic tasks, including "mobilizing supporters, neutralizing and/or transforming mass and elite publics into sympathizers, achieving change in targets" (p. 1217). They are a subset of all collective action organizations, as defined in this book. As formal organizations, SMOs are subject to many of the constraints that shape the viability of other organizations. Indeed, Gamson identified centralized organizational power structures and formal bureaucratic features—constitutions, formal membership rosters, internal structural divisions—as vital elements in an SMO's successful policy influence:

> Bureaucratic organization provides a solution to the first problem of combat readiness—a cadre of reliable workers with coordinated tasks. . . . Centralization of power is an organizational device for handling the problem of internal division and providing unity of command (Gamson 1975, p. 108).

Thus, social movement theories contribute to an understanding of the collective influence problem by pointing to critical resource and social structural conditions that all collective action organizations must confront. Their limitation lies in their concentration on challenging groups that operate outside the polity's boundaries and that therefore must engage in unconventional political strategies having a low probability of success.

The political science approach to interest groups, on the other hand, attends to those organizations that already have made the successful transition from challenger to polity member (Tilly 1978, p. 53). The participants in a national policy domain consist of "all consequential organizations that have responsibility for directing, coordinating, or otherwise controlling the creation and distribution of domain values" (Knoke and Laumann 1982, p. 257). The core actors in any policy domain are public institutions and private sector collective action organizations that are capable of exercising influence over the outcome of public decisions. Some observers characterize these policy domains as "subgovernments," "iron triangles," or "cozy triangles" (Ripley and Franklin 1976), because public officials and interest groups routinely consult and collaborate on legislation. Others profess to find greater domain permeability by outside policy activists, forming a loose expert "issue network" (Heclo 1978; Gais *et al.* 1984). In either case, executive departments, legislative committees, local governments, corporations, business associations, labor unions, professional societies, public interest groups, and other collective action organizations constitute the core players in national policy domains (Laumann and Knoke 1987).

Whether the American national pressure group system is evolving toward the more corporatist structures that characterize several European polities seems doubtful. In those nations, participation in major policy decisions is restricted to a small number of "peak" capital and labor associations. They enjoy monopolistic access to the inner councils of government in return for maintaining hierarchical domination over their memberships (Lehmbruch and Schmitter 1982; Streeck and Schmitter 1985). The consequence is a high degree of coordinated economic planning between government bureaus and private corporations, with labor bringing up the rear (Williamson 1985). For a variety of historical reasons, corporatist modes of intermediation did not catch on in the United States (Wilson 1982). Nor does the decentralized structure of American national policy-making seem likely to disappear soon, despite the increasingly intimate relationship between public and private power over the past half century, and not withstanding the Reagan welfare rollbacks. Instead, the present pressure group system, in which autonomous collective action organizations pursue their diffuse goals through perpetually changing coalitions, continues to muddle along.

When investigating the policy process, the question becomes, "What do organized groups do in order to influence public decisions?"(Salisbury 1975, p. 206.) The most frequent mode of group government interaction is lobbying—the attempt to secure specific policy decisions or appointment of government personnel through tactics such as "[i]nitiating a lawsuit, starting a letter-writing campaign, filing a formal comment on a proposed regulation, talking face-to-face with a congressman or bureaucrat"(Berry 1984, p. 6). Other methods include testifying at hearings, working in coalitions with other collective action organizations, contributing to electoral campaigns, direct-mail fundraising, busing in constituents to contact their congressmen, and efforts to shape the public policy agenda through public relations (Kingdon 1984, pp. 61–64; for a comprehensive list see Schlozman and Tierney 1986, p. 150).

Many of these activities can be carried out by small professional staffs, but others rely on a group's leaders mobilizing their mass membership for direct action to influence public policymakers. The collective action organization's size, cohesion, and financial resources, as well as the nature of its organized opposition, are critical to successful mobilization. While many of the actors engaged in lobbying are mass membership associations, others are nonmembership institutions, such as corporations and public interest lobbies (Salisbury 1984; Schlozman and Tierney 1986, pp. 49–51). These organizations often possess larger resource stocks and greater political expertise than do the membership organizations, giving them the dominant position within the policy process. At present, policy researchers understand only crudely how the resources obtained by institutional and collective action organizations are transmuted into public policy decisions. What kinds of resources, under what circumstances, yield how much system output? Some form of political exchange seems to occur, but identifying and measuring these quantities proves exceptionally difficult [see Laumann and Knoke, 1987, Ch. 13 (with Kim), for an attempt to estimate a simple exchange model in our national energy and health policy domains]. Much theoretical and empirical work lies ahead in linking the actions of individual collective action organizations—both SMOs and conventional lobbying groups—to collectively binding policy decisions.

Conclusion

The preceding overviews of three theoretical paradigms for collective action organizations define the tasks of this book. Each approach addresses a basic issue in the political economy of associations. The problem of societal integration concerns the ways that people are tied to organizations and the ways that organizations connect their members with the larger society. The problem of organizational governance considers how individuals become unified collectivities capable of acting in a coordinated manner. Finally, the problem of public policy influence involves interactions among public and private interest groups to formulate the binding decisions under which we all must live.

These three problems must not be seen as competing, mutually exclusive paradigms that can guide detailed empirical investigations of collective action organizations. None are developed with adequate rigor to permit definitive tests of key propositions that would allow a researcher to choose the approach that best explains the situations of contemporary associations. More importantly, each paradigm examines essentially different levels of analysis—the individual, the organizational, and the systemic (Knoke 1986). In effect, they largely talk past one another rather than directly confronting the same aspects from opposing angles. Their value for empirical inquiry lies in their potential for sensitizing the researcher to the many distinct dimensions of complex sets of social relationships.

For example, understanding how persons decide to participate in a community association requires different theoretical concepts and measures from those focused on explaining how several organizations form a coalition to fight for a legislative initiative. The dynamics of choice in both cases involve different constellations of variables and their interactions. To reduce the task to a choice between social integration, internal governance, or policy-making paradigms risks a simplification that would distort a complex multilayer reality. Micro- and macrolevel phenomena are undoubtedly connected, but in tortuous ways that most existing social theories have not explicitly addressed (Coleman 1986a). This book undertakes that task by drawing inspiration from the three paradigms in constructing a testable theory of the political economies of collective action organizations. Themes and insights from the paradigms are woven into this new theory that seeks to bridge all levels of analysis. Rather than engaging in the futile effort to test the vague assertions of each approach, the goal herein is to synthesize their best components into a coherent and comprehensive account of the structures and processes of American collective action organizations. This ambitious project combines massive original data sets, sophisticated analytic techniques, and boldly imagined theory construction.

Plan of the Book

This section concludes with brief summaries of the remaining chapters:

Chapter 2 introduces the central question of how individuals make decisions. The rational choice approach favored by economists and positive political theorists overemphasizes utilitarian calculation and ignores conformity to social norms and affective bonds among group members. A synthesized approach is offered that combines all three decision-making elements.

Chapter 3 presents an integrated model of organizational political economy that bridges the microlevel of individual decisions and the macrolevel of collective social action. It addresses the question of how organizations acquire control over members' resources and allocate them to various goals.

Chapter 4 describes the data sets used in the book and presents a basic profile of American national associations and their members.

Chapter 5 describes the sources of funds for different types of collective action organizations and the budgetary allocations of these resources. The importance of organizational goals and external environments is examined.

Chapter 6 analyzes the incentive systems of collective action organizations. It shows how the formal goals sought by a group constrain the types of inducements available to members.

Chapter 7 continues the incentive system investigation from the members' viewpoint. Reasons for joining and contributing to the association, interest in types of incentives, and the services lobbying trade-off are analyzed.

Chapter 8 looks at the governance structures—authority and influence—within national associations and some of the factors that account for these arrangements.

Chapter 9 provides a comprehensive analysis of personal and organizational factors the generate member involvement in their collective action organizations. The importance of incentives, governance structures, and interest in policy issues for both psychological attachments and internal participation are estimated with multivariate models.

Chapter 10 turns to external political influence activities, first looking at individual members' involvements and then at the organizations' mobilization efforts, particularly the factors shaping the efforts of collective action organizations to influence the federal government.

Chapter 11 returns to the basic themes of the beginning. It discusses how this book illuminates fundamental problems of collective action organizations. In addition, it speculates on their implications for theories of individual and social choice, the significance of public and private goods as incentives, the impact of governance practices, the functioning of association political economies, and the future of democratic participation in America.

PART II

THEORY AND DATA

2

CHOOSING COLLECTIVE ACTION

Collective action is a recurrent problem for citizens of democratic societies. In a complex political economy, where huge organizational entities are the prime movers, individuals can realize significant advantages only by coordinating their actions with one another, by pooling their resources. In doing so, however, the group members experience a loss of power to the organization. In effect, they trade personal control over their resources for the "multiplier effect" of collective action (Coleman 1973). Whether a collective action organization can maintain its members' support depends on the elements that enter into individuals' choices about involvement in the group. This process applies to all types of organizations, but is especially problematic for associations that cannot financially compensate their participants for their involvement.

Collective action organizations are social systems comprised of two interdependent components—the individual member and the institution. Although there are important research issues relative to each component, the linkages between the two produce the most theoretically significant questions (Coleman 1986a). How do the organization's structures, such as its provision of incentives and its governance system, constrain the behaviors of its members? How do the choices that people make about their involvement affect the system's functioning? The most appropriate meta-theoretical stance toward these questions is methodological individualism. Neither a global holism (Mayhew 1980) nor a psychological reductionism (Homans 1964), methodological individualism views social phenomena as reciprocal relations between individuals and collectivities (Brodbeck 1958). A genuinely methodological individualist explanation integrates a broad range of factors, from "beliefs, action and intentions of individuals on the one hand, to the constraining properties of social wholes on the other''(James 1984, p. 176).

The critical theoretical task is to uncover the reciprocal causation between collective properties and individual behavior, without reducing or aggregating one to the other. Hence, an essential first step is to inquire into the process by which individuals decide to become involved in collective action organizations. Typical decisions relative to this process include what amounts of personal resources to contribute, what intensity of psychological commitment to make, and how extensively to participate in organized activities. Three theoretical perspectives address these issues: rational choice, normative conformity, and affective bonding. All three conceptualize individual behavior as purposive actions aimed at achieving some goal or objective desired by a person. However, each approach emphasizes distinctive decision-making elements. Rational actor models specify the utilitarian calculation of costs and benefits from alternative choices. Rational decision making poses a dilemma for collective action organizations that offer only public goods as inducements for their members' resource contributions. Normative conformity models stress the internalized expectations that people have concerning fair and equitable behavior, independent of the realization of personal interests. Finally, affective behavior models underscore the emotional component of behavior intrinsic to individuals' identification with social groups. Reviews of the research literature suggest that while each approach has some merit, none furnishes a completely adequate explanation of how individuals decide to become involved in collective action organizations. This chapter concludes with a synthesized model that blends components of all three approaches.

Rational Choice Models

Rational choice or subjective expected utility models have a long pedigree in the social sciences, beginning in neoclassical economics (Stigler 1950), developing in statistical decision theory (Savage 1954), spreading into political science (Harsanyi 1955), and entering sociology, mainly in exchange theories (Homans 1961; Blau 1964; Heath 1976). Becker argued that the economic explanation of human behaviors, based on ''the combined assumptions of maximizing behavior, market equilibrium, and stable preferences . . .'' is applicable to all human activity, from fertility to crime (Becker 1976, p. 5). Similarly, Coleman's (1975) purposive action theory is premised on actors whose behavior can be viewed as an ends–means rationality.

Rational actor models are perhaps the simplest and most elegant, but not necessarily the most realistic, of individual decision explanations. At their heart lies an assumption that each person possesses a utility function imposing a consistent order among all alternative choices he or she faces. She or he always chooses the alternative with the highest (maximum) utility. If the choice is uncertain, the person selects the alternative with the highest expected utility. That is, the utility of each alternative is weighted by the person's subjective expectation of what outcome will occur if that alternative is chosen. Rational choice behavior purposefully relates individuals' actions to their goals, whatever those goals happen to be (Riker and Ordeshook 1973, p. 12). It also requires the "heroic assumption" that persons possess complete knowledge about, and ability to compute and compare the consequences of, each alternative (Simon 1983, p. 293). Experimental evidence strongly indicates the infeasibility of such complex subjective calculations (Kahneman *et al.* 1982).

Rational choice under certainty involves first calculating costs and benefits for a set of alternative action outcomes, then selecting that alternative with the highest expected value. The value a person places upon each outcome (goal) is determined outside the rational choice process. The model is unconcerned about whether a person's goal is to eat a chocolate mousse, to find a cure for cancer, or to win the New York City marathon. With goals taken as givens, a rational action model tries to explain how people make choices among alternative actions that have different likelihoods of producing those goals.

The certainty situation can be described formally with just two possible actions, each of which is connected to a specific known outcome. The rational person performs the following calculus:

$$E(A_1) = B(O_1) - C(O_1)$$
$$E(A_2) = B(O_2) - C(O_2)$$

where $E(A_i)$ is the expected value of choosing alternative i, $B(O_i)$ is the benefit enjoyed from the outcome i, and $C(O_i)$ is the cost incurred in attaining that same outcome. If $E(A_1) > E(A_2)$, then the rational actor chooses the first alternative, thus maximizing likely benefits. A person's ability to make such calculations depends on a clear, unambiguous connection between alternatives to be chosen and their resulting outcomes. The classic marketplace, in which neither buyers nor sellers can alter prices by their individual actions, typically has such a structure. The prices (costs) of alternative goods and services are known to potential customers. Payment assures (usually) that the commodities (benefits) will be handed over to the customer. Thus, the rational shopper can readily calculate his or her net satisfaction from each transaction. Given preferences among alternative goods and a fixed amount of resources (a budget), a rational person can readily calculate how to maximize utility across a series of purchases. This simple model underlies the analysis of consumer behavior in economics. Friedman's (1953) well-known essay argued that economic actors do not even need actually to perform such calculations, simply to behave *as if* they do.

Uncertainty pervades real-life situations where ambiguous connections exist between actions taken and outcomes created. Many of the outcomes sought by collective action organizations are public policies; that is, changes in the state of affairs in the larger society. Yet, the processes by which an association produces public-policy outcomes from its members' resource contributions is not as straightforward as in market transactions. Other policy-oriented organizations seeking opposing outcomes complicate matters. A person's actions cannot lead with certainty to a result with known utility. Instead, expected values for alternative choices must be calculated by weighing the subjective probability that a given action will produce the valued outcome. For example, an association may try to pass the Equal Rights Amendment by investing its resources in a public education campaign or by directly lobbying state legislators. A convinced feminist, faced with the possibility of contributing funds to two organizations such as the League of Women Voters or the National Organization for Women, might perceive higher and lower probabilities of successful ERA passage based on use of the public relations or the lobbying strategy. Her decision about which group to contribute to then hinges on her subjective calculations about which action would yield the highest chance of ERA passage.

In formulating rational choice under uncertainty, the notation used by Riker and Ordeshook (1973, pp. 48–53) is helpful. They combined both benefits and costs of an outcome into a single utility measure, $U(O_i)$, which may take on positive or negative values, depending on the net balance of benefits and costs. Under conditions of risk, the calculation of expected value for two alternatives becomes:

$$E(A_1) = P_{11}(O_1)U(O_1) + P_{12}(O_2)U(O_2)$$
$$E(A_2) = P_{21}(O_1)U(O_1) + P_{22}(O_2)U(O_2)$$

where $P_{ij}(O_j)$ is the probability that by choosing the action i the outcome j will result. (The two probabilities in an equation must sum to one; for example, when the outcome is passage or failure of a piece of legislation.) After the sophisticated rational actor makes both calculations, she chooses that action $(A_1$ or $A_2)$ with the highest expected value. (Note that whenever each of the two alternatives leads to only one outcome, this process reduces to the choice under certainty conditions considered above.)

Choice under uncertainty better approximates many actual situations in which people face alternatives whose consequences are unclear, such as speculating in the stock market or deciding on which candidates to vote for in an election. Is Bush or Dukakis more likely to enact my preferred national defense policy? The uncertainty formulation is a reasonable approximation for an individual contemplating whether to relinquish control over personally held resources (time, money, participation) to a collective action organization that seeks to produce a public policy valued by him or her. Because the effectiveness of the organization's efforts is not certain (i.e., the policy might not be obtained), the rational person must decide whether contributing the resources to the group or spending them on other activities (a different group or personal consumption) will yield the higher expected value.

Self-interest is *not* an essential element in rational actor models, although it is often thought to be (e.g., Harsanyi 1969, p. 518). A person can choose rationally to maximize expected utility even if the valued outcome is not a personal gain. For example, a parent may contribute to a conservation club to preserve wilderness lands for her unborn grandchildren's enjoyment (Mitchell 1979; Godwin and Mitchell 1982). In the extreme form, rational action might be undertaken to benefit strangers; such altruistic individuals are often called saints. Obviously, the rational actor model does not allow *every* action to be considered rational choice, simply by assuming that any decision is the result of the highest utility among all alternatives. Such an assumption reduces the theory of rational action to a tautology that is untestable (see Olson 1965, p. 160, fn. 91). Nor is complete information essential. Rather, people can act on limited knowledge and information about the options open to them (see the "satisficing" or "procedural bounded rationality" version developed from cognitive psychology principles by March and Simon 1958; Simon 1983, 1985).

The essence of rational choice models is that people choose after assessing the probable gains and losses in well-being (their own and others') from a set of alternative actions. When an actor makes choices without carrying out such calculations, the decision cannot be considered rational under the concept used here.

The Public Goods Dilemma

Both the power and insufficiency of rational choice models come into sharp focus when applied to collective action organizations. The most prominent exemplar is Mancur Olson's classic, *The Logic of Collective Action* (1965). He analyzed situations in which individuals must decide whether or not to contribute toward a cooperative effort to produce a public good, a situation frequently found in many collective action organizations. In the political economy literature, the concept of *public goods* has a precise meaning. They "are enjoyed in common in the sense that each individual's consumption of such a good leads to no subtraction from any other individual's consumption of that good" (Samuelson 1954, p. 387). That is, "they must be available to everyone if they are available to anyone" (Olson 1965, p. 14). Many collective action associations try to persuade the government to produce public goods—such as tax rates, election reforms, import tariffs, professional status, or the right to own personal firearms—from whose enjoyment nonmembers cannot be excluded. Collective political actions, such as lobbying and publicity campaigns, are basic strategies of such organizations to secure public goods. While several other dimensions of public goods can be designated, such as subtractability and measurability, the nonexcludability feature is the main consideration here.

In contrast, *private goods* are consumed individually. Their methods of production allow a collectivity to restrict these benefits to persons possessing property rights; that is, to those people with membership standing (Riker and Ordeshook 1973, p. 245). Typical examples include an organization's newsletters and magazines, information services, group travel and insurance programs, workshops and seminars, and social activities such as parties and picnics. Collective action organizations vary in the mixtures of incentives that they offer to their members, with some associations concentrating solely upon direct services, and others offering both services and public-policy lobbying efforts. The remarkable explosion in American advocacy groups in the past quarter century created literally hundreds of these mixed political economies at the national level (Schlozman and Tierney 1983; Berry 1977, 1984; Salisbury 1984). An organization's reliance on mixtures of public and private goods as incentives for member contributions depends largely upon whether its collective objectives can be provided by itself (e.g., a stamp collectors' club) or whether they also require some external authority's decisions (e.g., a farm commodity association). In the latter case, an organization must allocate some portion of its collective resources to external influence activities, which may serve as a public-goods inducement to the group's membership.

Although Olson's treatment involved some detailed mathematical relationships, his basic conclusion is simply stated: Even when all interested group members would gain benefits from production of a public good, the members may fail to make adequate contributions toward its production if the organization relies solely on the value of the public good to induce member contributions.

Olson's conclusion seems to derive from two principles embedded in the rational actor model. First, members' shares of the public good are so small, particularly in large groups, that the amount of resources they will rationally contribute (i.e., where benefits must exceed costs) will also be minuscule (pp. 64–65). Therefore, the ability of any one person's actions to affect the probability that the public good will be produced is virtually nil and it is irrational for one to pay any of the costs of producing the good. This postulate may be called the "Principle of Imperceptible Effect." Olson distinguished further among groups according to their "size" (pp. 48–50 lists three types). He stated that in small groups, a rational member might take on the costs of providing some level of the public good if her personal gain outweighed the cost of production (pp. 22–36). Historically, many American public interest groups were launched by funds from wealthy sugar daddies, not from many small contributors (Walker 1983). However, Olson believed the total amount of the public good was still likely to be "suboptimal," given the interest in the good among all group members. Olson has been taken to task for his treatment of the group size effect (Riker and Ordeshook 1973, pp. 69–77; Frohlich *et al.* 1971, pp. 125–50; Smith 1976), but that hypothesis is not critical to this book.

A second concept is the "Free Rider Principle" (see also Buchanan 1968, p. 89). Because rational actors always try to maximize their gains (or minimize their losses) from any decision, the best decision is to contribute nothing toward the public good. If the other group members produce the good anyway, no one can be excluded from enjoying it, by definition. By paying nothing toward the creation of the good and spending her resources elsewhere, the rational person will achieve the maximum expected value from such resources. However, since all other group members perform the same cost–benefit analyses, no one will decide to contribute toward the public good and none will be produced. (This is the "strong" version of the free rider principle. A "weak" version states only that the resources will be less than optimal given the group's interests in the public good.) Realizing this dynamic, any rational person must conclude that only a sucker would contribute to a public good organization. She must judge the probability to be very small that the good will be produced even if she were to make a contribution proportionate to her interests and resources. The rational decision on both counts leads a person to withhold resources from the organization. In technical terms, the free rider problem stems from a reluctance of individuals to fully express their true demands for the collective good (Brubaker 1975). The ability to conceal one's real interests from others leads to a strategy of understanding the value of (and hence the willingness to pay for) the public good by the interested individual. Rational choice models evoke a strong undercurrent of cynicism and manipulative behavior.

Olson's major insight into the dynamics of collective action organizations was the apparent necessity for such groups to induce member resource commitments for collective goals by means other than the utility of the public goods themselves. He suggested two types of *selective incentive* mechanisms: coercion and positive inducements (pp. 50–51, 133). Such incentives do not operate indiscriminately like public goods, but are made available to members contingent upon their contribution to the collective action. *Coercion,* or negative sanctions, takes forms such as compulsory membership in unions, compulsory participation in picket lines during strikes, and threats of excommunication from a church or revolutionary party. Coercion redraws organizational boundaries (holding members in or throwing them out) and hence changes the excludability aspect of the public good. For example, a compulsory shop means that nonunion members cannot take advantage of negotiated wages as they can at an open shop. Coercion works on a rational actor by raising her costs for alternatives to supporting the public good.

Positive inducements reward members only when they contribute toward the public good. As private goods (i.e., what is consumed by one member is not available to others), positive inducements act upon a rational person's calculus by raising the benefit component of the public good alternative relative to other possible actions. Olson believed that without positive inducements, many large groups could not obtain resources from members to be applied to producing their public goods goals. By offering a private good with certainty of delivery to a group member only upon contributing to the public good (typically by paying membership "dues"), the member's utility gain would outweigh her loss (including the opportunity costs encountered by not spending the resources on other public or private goods). Thus, an organization's efforts to produce public goods are reduced to a "by-product" of their members' rational pursuit of private goods (Olson 1965, p. 132–35).

As an economist, Olson sprinkled his book with illustrations from economic collective action organizations—labor unions, farm cooperatives, industry groups, taxpayer associations. His conception of the individual benefit from a public good, such as a wage, a tax rate, or a market price, drew heavily from marginal utility analysis. The gain to a group member from the public good depends upon the proportion of the group's total interest the member controls (for example, the percentage of acreage that a farmer harvests, or a company's sales share of a market; p. 23). (Olson appeared to misunderstand a "pure" public good, where each individual's utility is equivalent to another's, since the good yields the same benefit to each person regardless of how many others partake of it; see Samuelson 1954.) In Olson's examples, cost–benefit calculations are facilitated by the easy conversion of public goods into monetary prices (although utility is *not* identical to price). When utility is not readily expressible in monetary terms—as in collective action organizations that pursue noneconomic goals—the capacity of rational actors to perform the essential calculations may be seriously impaired (see Harsanyi 1969, for an argument that rational choice models must attempt to extend motivations beyond economic self-interest).

Olson wrote only half a dozen pages on noneconomic groups, and seemed doubtful whether his model truly applied to such organizations (1965, pp. 158–

65). At one point he argued: "Logically, the theory can cover all types of lobbies," including noneconomic groups such as those with "social, political, religious, or philanthropic objectives" (1965, p. 159). Then he exempted philanthropic and religious lobbies (p. 160), as well as lost-cause groups consisting of persons with "a low degree of rationality" (p. 161) and mass social movements whose adherents are "psychologically disturbed"(p. 162). Olson appeared to recognize that motivations other than rational cost–benefit calculation may lead persons to contribute to collective action organizations. Rather than subsuming these motives under rational choice through a tortured logic and thereby making his theory "no longer capable of empirical refutation" (Olson 1965, p. 160, fn. 91), he preferred to restrict severely the types of collectivities to which his by-product theory applies.

In the past two decades, considerable efforts were poured into refining Olson's theoretical insights (Brubaker 1975; Smith 1976; Fireman and Gamson 1979; Oliver 1980; Runge 1984; Oliver *et al.* 1985; Bendor and Mookherjee 1987; Oliver and Marwell 1988). Among the modifications proposed were: imperfect information, the selective inducement aspect of collective goods, and entrepreneurial emphasis on nonmaterial benefits (Moe 1980, pp. 18 and 142–44); elaboration of the property space of utilitarian incentives (Zald and Jacobs 1978); the differential side effects of positive and negative incentives for collective action (Oliver 1980); the importance of leadership in fostering decision-maximizing behavior (Leibenstein 1980); and the primacy of collective bads and the costs to the individual of not contributing to collective actions (Mitchell 1979). Many theorists were more concerned with qualifying the rational choice process than with conceptualizing alternative motives. Other theorists argued that Olson's analysis is more widely applicable to organizations that offer mainly public policy goals as inducements to join, such as Common Cause (Salisbury 1975; Berry 1977; Moe 1980) or trade associations (Staber and Aldrich 1983). But these modifications still maintain the central thrust of Olson's economic rationality approach: individual decision making is a cost–benefit calculus weighing the values of selective private goods incentives against the public goods produced by an association.

Research Evidence on Collective Action

Empirical tests of hypotheses drawn from Olson's collective action theory were inconclusive. Chamberlain's (1978) experiments with college students found strong evidence of the group size–suboptimal provision hypothesis, but no support for free riding. Marsh's (1976) interviews with members of the Confederation of British Industry showed that many member firms made little

use of the CBI's services. Yet they believed that their public goods benefits were greater as members than as nonmembers. Though the firms' conclusions were "irrational" in Olson's terms, Marsh felt the benefits and costs
involved were too low to "impel them to the rationality threshold"(Marsh
1976, p. 271). Moe (1980, pp. 201–18) analyzed survey data from members
of five large economic associations that engaged in legislative lobbying. He
found that the associations' extensive packages of economic services:

> . . . are widely used and valued by members, and they typically have greater
> inducement value than politics . . . [but] it is still true that a good many mem-
> bers join for political reasons—and, in fact, except in the Printers, most of the
> respondents in each group indicate that politics plays a pivotal role in their deci-
> sion to maintain membership (Moe 1980, pp. 217–18).

Similarly, Tillock and Morrison (1979), using survey data from Zero Population Growth, showed that many members willingly contributed to the organization in the absence of selective incentives. In a reply, Olson argued that
selective incentives were indispensable, given the fact that many people with
interests in population control did not join ZPG. On the other hand, Mitchell,
using membership data from several environmental interest groups, argued that
"private goods supplement the public goods and bads incentives that have a
powerful motivating force of their own"(Mitchell 1979, p. 121). Further, Godwin and Mitchell (1982) fitted six decision models to samples of persons living
in an Oregon coastal commission's jurisdiction, and to mail survey data from
members of five national environmental groups. They found that free riding
was present in decisions to join public interest groups, to participate in their
internal affairs, and to contact public officials. However, the rational choice
formulation needed to be extended to incorporate norms of fairness and the act
of taking others' happiness into account (see also the exchange between Hardin
and the two authors in the same issue). Oliver (1984) discovered that persons
active in their Detroit neighborhood associations were more pessimistic than
token members about their neighbors' willingness to make contributions. She
concluded that active members accept their neighbors' free-riding: if others are
unlikely to produce a collective good, one must either provide it herself or do
without. Thus, in small organizations where individual contributions *do* make
noticeable differences, the community pessimists allow others to accrue benefits based on their efforts.

Survey data from New York City and Hamburg, West Germany, residents
found no relationship between material selective incentives and participation in rebellious political actions (Muller and Opp 1986). However, respondents' interests in public goods significantly increased their aggression against
authorities. Similarly, the principal incentive to participate in the West Ger-

man antinuclear movement was "preference for the collective good or the cost of the collective bad (in the respondent's perception), in particular the perceived personal threats by nuclear power stations"(Opp 1986, p. 106). Normative factors—protest norms and expectations by reference persons—also affected protest behavior, as did pleasure in protesting, a form of psychological gratification. A time series analysis of factors affecting aggregate membership levels in three American national associations (American Farm Bureau Federation, League of Women Voters, and National Association of Home Builders) found that, contrary to Olson's conclusions, people joined in response to collective benefits, especially when the group interests were threatened by external political and economic conditions (Hansen 1985).

Perhaps the most damaging empirical critique of the Olson model was Marwell and Ames' field experiments on the free rider problem (1979, 1980, 1981; also Alfano and Marwell 1981). They asked high school students to allocate $5 in tokens between a private good with a fixed interest rate and a public good having higher rates of return depending upon the amounts contributed by the other group members. Contrary to Olson's free rider hypothesis that either suboptimal or no investment in the public good would be made, two thirds of the subjects invested half their tokens, while only 13% invested nothing in the public good. Although the optimum investment point was not reached, the strong free-rider hypothesis was clearly refuted. Postexperimental debriefing of subjects suggested that normative expectations of fairness accounted for much of the subjects' behavior.

> . . . [N]ormative factors such as fairness seem to have strongly influenced economic decisions. It appears that subjects see the claims of groups for public goods as intrinsically normative in nature and their participation in the provision of goods as at least one major goal to be weighed in their matrix of motives (Marwell and Ames, 1979, p. 1359).

Intriguing as the Marwell and Ames' findings are, their external validity remains to be demonstrated on behaviors of adults in real collective-goods associations.

Taken together, these studies challenge the credibility of rational decision processes as a comprehensive explanation for collective action. The results point to a complex relationship between public- and private-goods inducements offered by organizations, and heterogeneous motivations among members responding by contributing to collective action. The pure subjective expected utility-maximizing egocentric actor does not fare well in the real world. Equity norms, interpersonal attachments, and political influence objectives are significant in the decisions of many participants.

Several conceptual schemes have suggested other bases of member motives and organizational incentives that cannot be reduced to utilitarian cost–benefit calculi: the instrumental-expressive dichotomy (Gordon and Babchuk 1959); Clark and Wilson's (1961) famous material-purposive-solidary incentive typology; Kanter's (1972) instrumental-affective-moral components of utopian commune commitment; Etzioni's (1975) utilitarian-normative-coercive bases of organizational compliance and his plea for a multiple-utility conception incorporating both pleasure and morality obligations (Etzioni 1986); the importance of solidarity and moral principles (Fireman and Gamson 1979); and Knoke and Wright-Isak's (1982) rational choice, normative conformity, and affective bonding motivations. These typologies share a common recognition that members vary enormously in their preferences for and responses to a diversity of incentives offered by collective action organizations. The list of plausible motivations is limited only by the imagination. For example, Moe (1980, p. 113) mentioned in an offhand way "altruism, belief in a cause or ideology, loyalty, beliefs about right and wrong, camaraderie, friendship, love, acceptance, security, status, prestige, power, religious beliefs, racial prejudice." Silver (1974, pp. 64–65) depicted a revolutionary's "psychic income" to motives such as "sense of duty to class, country, democratic institutions, the law, race, humanity, the rulers, God, or a revolutionary brotherhood as well as his taste for conspiracy, violence, and adventure." Clearly, with many possible motives for behavior, a complex and unmanageable model can quickly result. Reducing such complexity to simple calculi of net benefits minus costs distorts reality and ignores organizations' capacities to tailor their inducements to fit the diversity of members' interests.

To steer a course between the extremes of unimotivational theories and the laundry-list approach, the following sections examine two alternative explanations of behavior—normative conformity and affective bonding. Together with rational action, they form the basis of a synthesized model that accounts for individual decisions to become involved in collective action organizations.

The Normative Conformity Model

If economics is the province of rational choice theory, sociology is properly the domain of the normative conformity model. A norm is a "prescribed guide for conduct or action which is generally complied with by the members of a society" (Ullman-Margalit 1977, p. 12). People acquire norms through social learning, imitation, and pressures for conformity and against deviation. Compliance with norms depends on people's belief that such norms are indispensable for the proper functioning of society, rather than on coercion or instrumental calculation of costs and benefits. People frequently verbalize the norms concerning the behaviors they expect others to adopt. People typically conform their behaviors to these obligatory standards because they have internalized them as right and proper, not because they fear punishment for violating them. Norms concerning fair and equitable treatment guide people's interactions in many social situations (Schwartz 1977). The hypothesis that group norms induce conforming behavior is central to most versions of role theory, although programmatic research on the causes of nonconformity is difficult to find (Biddle 1986, p. 80).

Discussion of the influence of norms on social behavior would be deficient without mentioning the work of Talcott Parsons. His voluntaristic theory of action was created to answer the Hobbesian problem of social order (Parsons 1937, pp. 89–94) by assuming socialized, rational individuals. Social action combines elements of voluntary individual will and collectivism represented by the internalization of social norms. The basic analytic unit of the theory is the *unit act:*

> In the unit act there are identifiable as minimum characteristics the following: (1) an end, (2) a situation, analyzable in turn into (a) means and (b) conditions, and (3) at least one selected standard in terms of which the end is related to the situation (Parsons 1937, p. 77).

Action occurs within a framework of normative regulation, which partly determines the ends sought and which sets constraints on the means people use to pursue these ends. The standards, or norms, by which the means and ends are articulated are action elements that exhibit "sentiment attributable to one or more actors that something is an end in itself" (Parsons 1937, p. 75). In this model, action is "an effort to conform with norms." The internalization of normative patterns of the common culture and individuals' conformity to these patterns, with their ambivalent psychological reactions to strain, were subsequently formulated as an explicit theory of human motivation by Parsons and Shils (1951). As Warner (1978, p. 1321, fn. 5) pointed out, Parsons later included in his definition of the normative the criteria of "moral obligation" and the taking of an end in itself of socially oriented (and socially imposed) definitions of the desirable. The concept of moral obligations to conform to shared values is, of course, the seminal element in the sociological writings of Emile Durkheim, one of Parsons' major sources of influence.

In contrast to the utilitarian tradition from which he departed (Parsons began academic life as an economist), the social action theory conceives of behavior as primarily, but not solely, guided by norms. Enforced by formal and informal sanctions, a social system's normative prescriptions and proscriptions for behavior are internalized jointly among the system's actors. Although internalized shared symbolic directives ("oughts") are invisible in real terms, they are in fact more consequential for social behaviors directed toward desirable ends than are more visible external material directives. Thus, social action for Parsons cannot be reduced to a deterministic reflex of material conditions as it is, for example, in some Marxist or behavioral psychology theories. Like rational actor models, the normative actor model is an explanation of behavior as purposive rather than determinative. The main difference is that for the rational actor, interests (individually oriented conceptions of desired states) rather than norms (socially oriented conceptions of desired acts) are the central element in decision making.

At the analytic level, the normative actor is not devoid of nonmaterial constraints upon her behavior, since through the internalization of social norms other actors interpenetrate one another in the sharing of symbolic beliefs. Unfortunately, some critics interpreted Parsons as proffering an overly socialized view of human action (e.g., Menzies 1977). Allegedly, normative internalization allows for no autonomous, voluntaristic choices because supraindividual constraints fully determine those actions that superficially seem to be freely chosen. This interpretation of Parsonsian action theory is inaccurate, as Alexander's (1978) essay on the formal and substantive voluntaristic sources of Parsons' theory made clear. By synthesizing the individualist and collectivist traditions of social theory, Parsons sought to preserve individual decision-making autonomy vis-à-vis the material elements of the situation. Hence, social action must be seen as *both* instrumental and normative, with the former preserving its deterministic quality and the latter its voluntary nature:

> Individual action is ordered by the patterning of normative symbols and by the organization of material constraints. Yet, since normative patterns are internalized, a significant cause of any action rests with the willed behavior of the concrete individual (Alexander 1978, p. 183).

Apparently, Parsons used both individualist and collectivist paradigms to assert that action is constrained at the analytic level, while preserving actual individuals' freedom to pursue interests as persons come to define those interests. If this interpretation of Parsonsian action theory is accurate, the apparent theoretical incompatibility of a purposive rational actor model and a deterministic normative actor model is false.

As a legacy from the halcyon days of structural functionalism, the normative actor model was applied to many empirical social behaviors. Efforts to understand deviant behavior—delinquency, crime, mental illness, sexual activity, religious heresy—were a particularly important focus of normative actor models (e.g., Cohen 1955; Cloward and Ohlin 1960). Small group experimental studies also suggested that instrumental norms provide the basis for conforming behaviors (Santee and Van Der Pool 1976; Thelen *et al.* 1981). However, few studies explicitly pitted the explanatory power of the normative actor against the performance of the rational actor model to account for the same behavior.

Normative components were important in a model that predicted individual behaviors from subjective intentions that was developed by Icek Ajzen and Martin Fishbein (1980). Their effort grew from preceding discoveries of low covariations between measured attitudes and behaviors. They argued that attitudes are only one important determinant of behavior. They reconceptualized behavior as a result of intentions to act, which in turn were an additive function of (1) attitudes toward the behavior, (2) normative beliefs about and motivations to comply with the behavior, and (3) the relative importance of attitude and subjective norm. All other social and psychological influences on intentions were posited to operate through their effects on these three components (Fishbein 1967, p. 490). Thus, the Fishbein model contains elements of the rational actor model combined with the normative actor model. Importantly, effects operate independently of one another. Through exposure to the beliefs about legitimate actions held by other people, an individual is socialized to internalize the normative standards prevailing within her social system. These influences affect a person's behavior apart from the utility calculations made about action and regardless of personal normative considerations. The additive requirement of the model implies that even when the utility of an act and its probability of a successful outcome is high, the behavior may not occur if normative beliefs constrain the commission of the act.

In numerous empirical tests, Fishbein and Ajzen generally found that the normative components of the equation often produced larger values than the attitude toward the behavior. Intentional actions such as weight loss, occupational choice, family planning, consumer decisions, voting, and alcoholism treatment appeared to be explained well by their model (Ajzen and Fishbein 1980, pp. 102–242; see also Muller's 1979 survey results on aggressive political participation). The experimental findings argue for an explicit incorporation of normative components into realistic individual choice explanations.

The Affective Bonding Model

In contrast to the extensive theoretical work concerning rational choice and normative conformity as motives for individual decision making, until recently relatively little sociological analysis was devoted to the affective basis of behavior. Antecedents may be found in passing mentions by Simmel (1950, p. 410–11) and Weber, who wrote that "action is affectual if it satisfies a need for revenge, sensual gratification, devotion, contemplative bliss, or for working off of emotional tensions (irrespective of the level of sublimation)" (Weber 1978, pp. 24–26). This satisfaction of needs is anticipated before the action and indicates the actor's orientation to the objects of action. Thus, while affective action may be nonrational, or even irrational, it remains purposeful, although the connection between ends and means may lie buried at some unconscious level.

Sociologists have only recently begun to incorporate work from the psychology of emotions, but emotional processes seem likely to prove an important component in the understanding of social behaviors (Shott 1979; Hochschild 1979; Scheff 1983). Many treatments of emotions begin by attempting to link physiological and psychological arousal states to social meanings. Bodily changes are labeled as emotions under the mediation of cultural, structural, and other factors. The social constructionist and positivist approaches to emotion analysis differ on the relative importance accorded to biophysiological and social determinants of emotional labeling (Kemper 1981). However, as Denzin cautioned, "Behavior becomes emotional only when it is so interpreted by the person and brought into self-interactions"(1983, p. 404). Thus, emotions are best studied sociologically, as episodes involving interactions between selves and others, rather than as privately created experiences.

In analyzing individual decision making from an emotional perspective, the most relevant element would seem to be emotions involved in role taking. To the extent that members of collective action organizations experience distressful emotions due to inappropriate role performances, or satisfying emotions upon successful performance, they may become emotionally motivated to contribute toward collective activity. Responding to collective action situations is partly an identification process in which the membership role is internalized along with specific affective bonds both to other members and to the symbolic representation of the group as a whole. The resulting sense of "oneness" between person and group strengthens the member's motives for contributing personal resources to the organization. Some collective action organizations may formally encourage affective attachments among the participants, by means such as holding frequent social activities for face-to-face interactions. In other groups, opportunities for members to experience emotional responses are incidental to transactions with the organization or its agents. Harold Lasswell pointed to the centrality of emotional engagement in forging political cohesion in groups:

> Now people who act together get emotionally bound together. This process of becoming emotionally bound is dependent on no conscious power. . . . This reinforces the perceptions of similarities and supplies the dynamic for the identification process. Even the negative identification is a tribute to the extent to which the affective resources of the personality become mobilized in human contact (Lasswell 1977, p. 185).

The importance of interpersonal affective bonds also appears in recent writings about social movements and collective action. Wilson and Orum (1976) and Fireman and Gamson (1979) both stressed the importance of group solidarity based on network ties to relatives, friends, co-workers, and significant others. Such affective bonds within a movement's constituency boost the propensity of group members to respond favorably to appeals for collective action. Several empirical studies of religious groups (Stark and Bainbridge 1980; Snow *et al.* 1980; Heirich 1977) and of utopian communes (Kanter 1972; Zablocki 1980) concurred on the importance of solidarity for recruitment and commitment to the collectivity. The problem of group cohesion, particularly under threatening circumstances, is more effectively solved using affective commitments produced by strong emotional bonds than by either rational calculation or normative conformity. "The tenacity with which many communes cling to life, despite high rates of failure and of membership turnover, cannot easily be explained in terms of their members' individual self interest" (Zablocki 1980, p. 249). While most collective action organizations fall far short of the total self-investment required by communes, their reliance upon affective processes cannot be ignored.

To conclude, the theoretical and research literature on rational choice, normative conformity, and affective bonding suggests the diversity of motivational processes in people's decisions to commit their personal resources to collective action organizations. These diverse studies imply that no *single* motivation suffices to explain individual decision making. In the next section, a synthesized motivation model combines all three approaches as distinct components.

A Synthesized Motivational Model

A predisposition/opportunity perspective on individual motives and organizational inducements was proposed by Knoke and Wright-Isak (1982), drawing on sources cited above. The fundamental expectation is that individual members of collective action organizations are motivated (predisposed to act to attain valued goals) by three general decision-making processes:

1. *Rational Choice.* Cost–benefit calculi that maximize the individual's expected utility.
2. *Affective Bonding.* Emotional attachments to other persons and groups.
3. *Normative Conformity.* Adherence to standards of conduct grounded in socially instilled values about principled behavior.

Neither affective bonding nor normative conformity motivations can be reduced to rational choice cost–benefits, except by a tortuous logic that renders the latter concept universal and, therefore, useless for empirical work.

These three motivations are presumed to affect jointly basic decisions about an individual's involvement in collective action: whether to join an association, whether to remain a member, how much to participate in collective actions, and what amount of personal resources to contribute to the collectivity. The initial assumption is that each component independently affects these behavioral decisions, yielding the general multimotivational specification:

$$D=f(R) \cdot g(A) \cdot h(N)$$

That is, a person's involvement decision *(D)* is the result of three functions —*(f)*, *(g)*, and *(h)*—of each of three motivational predispositions to act— *R* (rational choice), *A* (affective bonding), and *N* (normative conformity). The greater a person's predisposition on each type of motive, the higher the probability of involvement in the organization. Beyond this general specification, theoretical or empirical guidance about the functional forms (*f, g,* and *h)* of the relationship between motives and decisions are lacking. Complex and nonlinear processes (e.g., exponential, logarithmic, threshold effects, feedback loops) may complicate the relationships. However, the relevance of this conceptualization for this book lies not in estimating directly the impact of motives on behavior, but in generally understanding how members respond to organizational incentives. To do this, we must conceptualize how organizational incentive opportunities mirror individual motivational predispositions. The next chapter presents a political economy theory that emphasizes these macro-micro linkages.

Conclusion

Individuals choose their involvements in collective action organizations on the basis of their rational cost–benefit calculations, their desires to conform to group norms, and their affective ties to the collectivity. Emphasis on one of these dimensions of choice to the exclusion of the others results in an incomplete and distorted explanation of why people contribute their resources and commit themselves to associations. All three processes must be simultaneously taken into account in any thorough examination of the relations between individuals and their organizations. From a genuine methodological individualist perspective, understanding the individual choice process is essential to explaining how an organization constrains its members' behaviors and how these behaviors shape the system's functioning.

In terms of the three broad theoretical paradigms discussed in Chapter 1, the motivational model has greatest bearing on the problem of social integration. The bonds between persons and institutions continually strengthen or weaken during routine encounters with other participants, especially those in authority positions. Whether such interactions deepen a person's attachment to a collectivity or repulse potential supporters depends in great measure on which motives propel a person into a situation. People who seek only utilitarian gratification are most likely to find that their needs can be met in a variety of market exchanges. However, plunking down hard cash for goods and services is not conducive to the buyer's sincere sympathy with the seller, all merchandising hokum about "brand loyalty" notwithstanding. Whenever utilitarian motives are unaccompanied by emotional or normative needs, only tenuous links between people and institutions can be sustained. Because formation of affective bonds and fulfillment of normative principles requires enduring interactions with specific individuals and groups, they are essential for forging strong and stable social obligations that integrate persons into larger social formations. By concentrating at the most microlevel of analysis, the multimotivational model offers a framework for answering the question of how social integration in a complex industrial society can be achieved.

3

A THEORY OF ASSOCIATION
POLITICAL ECONOMY

To become more than a conceptual scheme or a mindless accumulation of social facts, research on collective action organizations must be guided by theoretical concerns. This chapter presents a new synthetic theory of association political economy that is tested in the remainder of the book. The next section describes the necessary elements of a scientific theory. These criteria are then applied to develop a theory of collective action organizations that involves both micro- and macrolevel phenomena. Formal definitions of theoretical concepts and their expected relationships are stated here in, but operational measures of variables and empirical tests of these theoretical relationships are depicted in appropriate places in succeeding chapters.

A collective action organization's political economy is not a unitary structure or process, but the intersection of several components, each operating according to its own set of social forces. For convenience of exposition, these components are broken down into external environment, internal economy, internal polity, and external polity. The theoretical task in this chapter is to explicate the general conditions that produce variations in the forms of these components across the population of American national associations. That is, what basic properties of associations and their members affect these fundamental structures and processes? The theoretical propositions expressing these relationships are cast in a simple bivariate covariation form that allows subsequent tests of their validity.

Theoretical Requirements

The principles of scientific theory have been debated for years by philosophers of science and theoretical practitioners (see Freese 1980). The view presented in this section draws from various participants in this debate, but, as a synthesis, it undoubtedly will fully satisfy no one. The only reason for this preliminary exercise is to spell out explicitly the criteria for theory construction used in this book, so that the aims and procedures become transparent and open to criticism.

A scientific theory is a set of interrelated statements, or theoretical propositions, that account for the observed regularities in some phenomena. A theoretical proposition consists of any natural language statement that links two or more concepts, or terms, in a clear and unambiguous relationship (Hempel 1966, p. 71). The theoretical structure connects several such propositions that share common concepts, using generally accepted rules of logic. Ideally, the formal structure of a theory is an axiomatic-deductive sequence of propositions (Braithwaite 1955, p. 22), perhaps capable of being expressed in mathematical or symbolic logic terms. Short of that ideal, a theory must take an unambiguous and internally consistent form. That is, the conclusions obtained are fully determined within the system, and conclusions obtained from one part of the structure do not contradict conclusions from another part (Willer 1967, p. 10).

A theory may be stated in causal form. Causal propositions assert that changes in the value of one concept are associated with changes in the value of another concept, and can produce the change without changes by other theoretical concepts (Stinchcombe 1968, p. 31; Blalock 1969; see Heise 1975, p. 12 for a formal definition of causality). Taken as a whole, a theoretical structure is a "mechanism" that accounts satisfactorily for the nature of the included phenomena, whether by explicitly causal or merely associative relationships among the concepts. Theory provides a systematic explanation, or rationale, for some empirical observations, resulting in a deeper understanding of the matter at hand. No single theory can fully explain any given reality. Instead, it aims to represent limited aspects of the phenomena to be explained.

An analytic, or nominal, definition of a theoretical concept is created by narrowing the original meanings of a term used in common discourse. Through stipulating the special meaning that a term has within the theory, the concept gains precision and clarity (Hempel 1966, pp. 85–86). A theoretical definition identifies completely those properties or attributes of a phenomenon that are relevant to the explanation sought by the theory. A theorist may stipulate whatever aspects of a concept seem most important to the task at hand, while ignoring other potential features as irrelevant and useless. Thus, concepts have specific meanings within the context of a given theory, which may not be equivalent to their meanings in other theories. The inability of social scientists to agree on their theoretical definitions is a major source of controversy and confusion for research.

Formal theory construction is not an end in itself. To be useful in scientific research, theoretical propositions must be linked to the empirical phenomena that they purport to explain. This connection is made by operational defini-tions, or bridging principles (Hempel 1966, p. 72), that specify a detailed set of procedures for measuring the theoretical concepts in observable events. If a theory is to become testable with empirical data, hypotheses about the rela-tionships to be observed should be derived through logical procedures and rules of correspondence from the core theoretical propositions. To create the necessary strong connection between concepts and operational measures (vari-ables), the analytic definitions should be stated in terms that readily lend themselves to operational translation. Thus, when variables are substituted for concepts, the resulting empirical statements retain an isomorphism with the theoretical propositions. Some analysts refer to the operational representation of a theory as its *model* (Braithwaite 1955, p. 90; Willer 1967, p. 15; Harre 1976, p. 16). An operational model establishes a tight identity with the formal theoretical structure so that empirical observations serve directly to validate the theory.

An empirical test of a theory's consequences consists of comparing the op-erational hypothesis with empirical observation. If these consequences encoun-ter negative evidence, then the theory is falsified (Popper 1959; Lakatos 1970). It must be either modified to take account of the discrepancy or rejected out-right. One possible modification that retains the theory despite negative out-comes is alteration of the theory's scope, or domain of applicability, by specifying that set of conditions under which the theory has not been found false (Walker and Cohen 1985, p. 291). However, if the empirical conse-quences are true, the theory gains credibility, which increases as alternative theoretical formulations are eliminated (Stinchcombe 1968, p. 53–54). With the accumulation of successful test outcomes over an increasingly wider range of empirical phenomena, the scope of the theory may generalize to the point where its propositions can be called "laws" (Braithwaite 1955, p. 9; Shye 1978, p. 3).

This cursory review lays out the criteria for constructing a theory of asso-ciation political economy. Analytic concepts are defined below using terms suitable to empirical observation. Expected relationships link together key

concepts. Schematic diagrams depict the overall patterns of theoretical connections among terms. The result is a theory about some of the basic structures
and processes of collective action organizations and their members, whose empirical validation absorbs the remainder of the book.

Scope and Overview

The political economy theory of collective action organizations explains
certain aspects of national mass membership associations in the late twentieth
century United States. It may apply as well to the organizations of other advanced industrial liberal democracies, but because data from those nations
were not available for empirical tests, the theory's relevance to those societies
remains undetermined. Its usefulness for early capitalist and for nondemocratic
societies, such as the U.S.S.R. and less developed nations, is doubtful but
likewise untested.

The theory concerns two intertwined systems that coordinate the acquisition and allocation of resources—both material and symbolic—that are essential for the continued functioning of an association. The organizational
economy specifies how sets of incentives induce members and external constituents to contribute their time, money, and effort to the group. The organizational polity relates the governance structure for reaching collective decisions
about the allocation of resources to various group goals. The theory is also
concerned with how the association directs its collective resources toward the
realization of public-policy decisions enacted by political authorities outside
the organization.

Following the principles of methodological individualism, the political
economy theory focuses research attention on both the micro- and macrosocial
levels of behavior: (1) How do organizational constraints shape the decisions
of individuals? (2) How do individuals' intentions and actions combine to affect organizational behaviors? Both questions assume that peopleare purposive
social actors whose decision-making processes incorporate the three motivational components (rational choice, normative conformity, and affective bonding) discussed in Chapter 2. The questions further assume that the social
system of a collective action organization consists of interdependent individuals, but that it exhibits properties which are not simple aggregations of member characteristics. A major theoretical task is to specify the mechanisms both
within and across the micro- and macrolevels of analysis.

The following sections expand upon the conceptual and relational aspects of
the political economy theory that was first developed by Knoke (1985). Later

chapters elaborate on these fundamental terms and review earlier research findings that bear on the relationship between these aspects. The measures used to operationalize and test the theoretical propositions are also described in later chapters.

Environments and Organizations

The basic objects of inquiry in the political economy theory are organizations and persons. A *collective action organization* is a goal-directed, boundary-maintaining, activity system (Aldrich 1979, p. 4), most of whose participants do not receive financial compensation for their involvement. Neither the goals, boundaries, nor types of activities should be considered fixed and unchanging. The relative paucity of paid participants distinguishes associations from other formal organizations such as firms, nonprofit organizations, and government agencies (Knoke and Prensky 1984). For some purposes an organization may be conceived as a unitary "natural person" having legal standing (Coleman 1974), but the central thrust of the political economy model is to analyze the organization in terms of its various component structures.

At the microlevel, collective action associations are comprised of two basic types of participants: members and leaders. *Members* are individual natural persons (or organizational representatives in the case of associations composed of other organizations) whose involvements are not excluded, limited, or subject to conditions: "a party to a closed social relationship will be called a 'member'"(Weber 1947, pp. 139–40). The exits and entries of persons across an organization's boundaries are enforced by the actions of specific individuals, namely the association's elites or authoritative leaders. Thus, *leaders* are organization members who have acknowledged rights to act as agents or fiduciaries for the collectivity. Leaders are usually identified by a title and a job description that stipulates the special tasks for which they are responsible. Thus, presidents, chairmen, treasurers, and boards of directors are typical association leaders. In addition to controlling the integrity of the organization's boundaries, leaders may be heavily engaged in the routine operations of daily business or in setting long-term policy directions for the group. In the concept of the organization as a unitary actor vis-à-vis external bodies, a leader typically serves as its representative. In some organizations a particular person, usually titled the executive director, serves as an administrative officer under an employment arrangement spelling out the limits to his or her ability to act without authorization from the political leaders.

Resources are any means or facilities that a collective action organization finds useful in functioning. The importance of resources for organizations resides in their applicability to achieve collective tasks, whether internal or external. In other words, resources are the bases of social power. This usage is clear in Nuttall *et al.*'s (1968, pp. 352–53) definition of a resource as "anything which allows one actor to control, provide or apply a sanction (positive or negative) to another actor." Rogers (1974, p. 1425) called these instrumental resources, distinguishable from infraresources: "attributes, circumstances or possessions that must be present before the appropriate instrumental resources can be activated or invoked." Examples are information and available time to participate. In the political economy theory, resources encompass both instrumental and infraresources used by people and organizations in getting others to act favorably to achieve their purposes. (For efforts to typologize various kinds of power resources, see Clark 1968, pp. 57–67; Laumann and Pappi 1976, p. 188; and Ornstein and Elder 1978, pp. 69–70.)

Among the many individuals and organizations outside an association's boundaries *constituents* maintain a special relationship. They are nonmembers who are favorably disposed toward the collective action organization's purposes and activities. They are potential sources of support for the group, whether in the form of financial contributions, material resources, or moral and psychological commitments (McCarthy and Zald 1977). Constituents are not only a source of detachable resources, they also comprise the primary pool of potential members who may be recruited across the organizational boundaries under appropriate circumstances. Other categories of external persons and organizations—such as beneficiaries, bystanders, and opponents—may interact with the association, but they are not considered of major theoretical importance in the political economy model. Governmental authorities, however, are included below.

No organization is an island; all must operate within larger physical and sociocultural settings that may affect their well-beings and performances. An *environment* is everything outside an organization's boundaries that can affect inputs and outputs of the organization (Bidwell and Kasarda 1985, pp. 33–34; Aldrich 1979, pp. 56–74). Thus, environments include the constituencies noted above, and also involve interorganizational relations and other macrosocial conditions. For example, population changes, technological innovations, and political trends may constrain or facilitate an association's ability to recruit supporters, acquire useful resources, and adopt formal internal structures. The productivity of the national economy, the legal codes regarding tax-free contributions, and the labor force distributions of potential participants all affect the resources available to an association from its constituents and members. Among many possibly relevant environmental dimensions, two distinctions are especially significant: information environments and resource environments (Aldrich 1979, pp. 110–111). The complexity and uncertainty of information about external conditions affects organizational activities through the ways that it crosses boundaries and is processed into collective decisions. Success or failure in the competition with other organizations for control of scarce resources may spell the difference between prosperity, survival, or disappearance (Yuchtman and Seashore 1967).

The theoretical concepts defined above are sufficient to specify several basic propositions about the expected relationships between a collective action organization and its external entities. Figure 3.1 schematically represents these connections as information and resources flows among macro- and microlevel components. The relationships are depicted as unidirectional; that is, from the external units to the organization. Reciprocal effects are not considered in the present theory, although a genuinely open-system perspective recognizes that organizations may alter their environments (Scott 1987, p. 20). The diagram shows the organization as an undifferentiated set of formal structures and individual member orientations (beliefs and actions). Subsequent propositions break down the internal organization into its components.

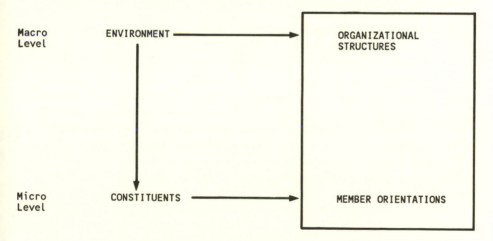

Figure 3.1 Relationships Among External and Organizational Components

Proposition 1: The richer the environment, the more discretionary resources there are available to a collective action organization's constituents and members.

Proposition 2: When members and constituents control more discretionary resources, they increase their contributions to the organization.

These propositions assert that organizations may more readily acquire essential resources when external conditions create "slack," or unused resources that the association can tap. Munificent environments offer an organization greater access to resources than do lean environments, but such conditions may also attract more competition. As a result, over time resources may become scarcer and harder to acquire without developing more efficient organizational strategies and structures.

Proposition 3: Environmental uncertainty and complexity generate unstable flows of information to constituents and members.

Proposition 4: Unstable flows of information reduce member and constituent support for and contributions to the organization.

Proposition 5: The more complex and uncertain an organization's environment, the more bureaucratic its administrative structure.

The rapidity, complexity, and unpredictability of changes outside the organization may create severe problems of adaptation not faced by organizations that operate in placid, dependable environments. As hypothesized in Proposition 5, one response to such turbulence is to change internal organizational structures and processes to cope with these environmentally induced problems.

Proposition 6: The greater the similarities between constituents and members, the stronger the constituents' support, the larger their contributions, and the greater the likelihood they will become members.

Constituent and member similarities can occur along three dimensions: (1) holding equivalent positions in larger social institutions, such as occupations or ethnic identities; (2) having strong ties in interpersonal social networks; and (3) sharing attitudes favorable to the purposes and activities of the organization. Congruence between an organization's members and its external constituents enhances the group's access to constituents' resources, including the ultimate step of bringing these supporters inside the association boundaries.

The Internal Economy

The internal economy of a collective action organization is concerned with the acquisition and allocation of resources. Resource mobilization means to gain significant control over assets that the organization did not previously control (Etzioni 1968, p. 388). Constituent and member contributions, in the form of dues and assessments, typically provide the bulk of the association's income. But money is not the only useful resource: members can also provide their organization with labor power, psychological commitment and identification, information and expertise, access to various targets, and even the simple legitimation conferred by publicly listing their names on the membership roster (Perrow 1970). In the absence of any other personal resources, members can always contribute their bodies in the form of mobilizable protest and direct confrontation to be used by organization leaders in negotiations with targeted authorities (Lipsky 1970). Although some evidence exists that resource contributions exhibit multidimensionality (Knoke and Wood 1981; Knoke 1981a, 1982, 1988), for present theory construction purposes, resources will be treated as undifferentiated and varying along a single continuum from lesser to greater amounts.

Incentive systems are sets of valued inducements under the organization's control that are provided to participants in exchange for support and resource contributions to the collectivity. Organization leaders offer three generic types of incentives:

1. *Utilitarian.* Private goods in the form of direct services to members that are consumed on an individual basis.

2. *Social.* Jointly coordinated social and recreational activities whose enjoyment is restricted to the membership.

3. *Normative.* Primarily public goods that require collective efforts to influence governmental policymakers. These incentives are also key elements in the organizational polity.

The parallel between association incentives and the member motivations discussed in Chapter 2 is evident and intended: utilitarian services appeal to rational choice motives, social-recreational activities elicit involvement on the basis of affective bonding, and normative incentives attract people with strong normative conformity predispositions.

A person's involvement in a collective action organization depends upon his or her interest in the particular inducement combinations offered by the organization. An *interest* is a conscious, subjective preference for the possession or usage rights to some object or activity. Interests vary in magnitude from large positive to large negative values. To say that a person is interested in an incentive implies a willingness to work toward realization of that inducement, including exchanges of less-valued objects. Schlozman and Tierney's (1986, pp. 14–37) excellent discussion of the interest concept pointed out that assessing self-interest as simply self-consciously held preferences can be problematic. People may lack information about the larger social causes and consequences that affect their life situations. Outside observers (including researchers) may be able to impute objective interests to social actors that they do not consciously hold; for example, that unemployed workers have interests in expansionary macroeconomic policies. However, the task of imputing interests to hundreds of organization members on dozens of issues based on scant evidence is too formidable for the present study. Hence, only the expressed interests of respondents will be used.

Organization goals are conceptions of desired end states toward which an organization and its participants orient their actions. Because associations' goals, like individual motives, are so diverse in their specific forms, discussion becomes manageable only by classifying goals under three general headings:

1. *Member Servicing:* All goods and services primarily of a material nature delivered to participants for their personal consumption. Examples include recreational clubs' social activities, trade associations' information research programs, unions' grievance procedures, fraternal organizations' insurance and travel plans, professional societies' research journals and employment services.

2. *Legitimation:* Acceptance by the general public and by relevant elite organizations of an association's right to exist and to pursue its chosen affairs.

3. *Public-Policy Influence:* Getting governmental authorities to apply *their* resources to instigate changes in laws and practices that will improve the situations of the organization's members as well as nonmember beneficiaries.

Not every collective action organization seeks to satisfy these three types of goals to the same degree. One theoretical task is to account for the relationship between organizational goals and member incentive interests.

In general terms, any *organizational structure* is a relatively stable pattern of relationships among social positions. The rules of conduct attached to the positions indicate the rights and obligations for interaction among the incumbents. The particular content of interactions among positions determines the nature of the structure. Interactions involving basic policy decisions comprise the governance structures, considered in the next section. The *administrative structure* of a collective action organization is its arrangement of roles and rules for conducting the ongoing routine business of the collectivity. The administrative structure typically involves paid employees distributed into the more or less internally differentiated form of a bureaucracy—specialized, standardized, formalized, decentralized, hierarchical systems of coordination and control (Scott 1987, pp. 24–26; Aldrich 1979, pp. 9–13). A basic function of the administrative structure is to create and operate the incentive system.

Figure 3.2 shows the expected relationships among the theoretical concepts involved in the internal economy. Administrative structure, organizational in-

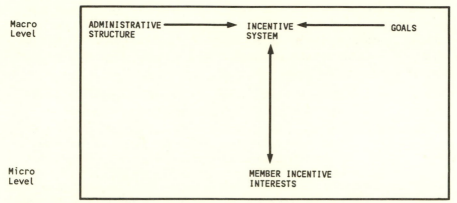

Figure 3.2   Relationships Among Internal Economy Components

centive systems, and organizational goals are all macrolevel phenomena linked to the microlevel interests of members through inducements offered by the organization in exchange for people's commitments and resource contributions.

> *Proposition 7:*   Organizational incentive systems are constrained to be congruent with organizational goals.

This congruence between goals and incentive systems arises in part because some types of goals are significant inducements to members, especially public-policy objectives. A further source of consistency is members' rejection of certain inducements as incompatible with the organization's overarching principles. For example, most participants in a stamp collection club would not consider suitable a collective effort to change the President's policy toward Nicaragua. Although the tendency to congruence between goals and incentives is substantial (Etzioni 1975, p. 14), the consistency should be less than perfect because some types of inducements, such as sociable interactions among members, are inherently compatible with a variety of goals.

> *Proposition 8:*   The more heterogeneous an organization's goals, the more diverse its incentive system.
>
> *Proposition 9:*   The greater the environmental complexity and uncertainty, the more diverse an organization's incentive system.
>
> *Proposition 10:*   A more bureaucratic administrative structure operates a more diverse incentive system.
>
> *Proposition 11:*   The more resources an organization controls, the more diverse its incentive system.

The four propositions above emphasize connections of the incentive system to the external environment and internal macrolevel structures. The underlying principle is that simple conditions require only simple incentive systems, while environmental and organizational complexity induce corresponding needs for complex incentive arrangements. An essential ingredient that allows an organization to maintain complex structures is large amounts of resources acquired through incentive transactions.

Proposition 12:   Organizations that operate more complex incentive systems attract members with heterogeneous interests in incentives.

Proposition 13:   The more intensely a person values an incentive offered by a collective action organization, the greater the contribution that person will make to the organization in order to receive the incentive.

The two preceding propositions assume that different individuals may value different types of inducements and that an organization may appeal to these diverse interests by offering a variety of incentives. The theory makes no attempt to explain why persons desire particular inducements, but takes their interests as given though not necessarily fixed. That is, members may change their "tastes" for particular incentives as a result of their experiences in the organization and elsewhere. Reasons for joining may not be the same as reasons for remaining involved.

Proposition 14:   Organizations that operate diverse incentive systems acquire larger contributions and stronger support from their members than those that do not offer diverse incentives.

Proposition 15:   The stronger the congruence between member incentive interests and organization incentive offerings, the higher the membership support and resource contributions.

A basic consistency or congruency between member incentive interests and organization incentive offerings arises from the leaders' efforts to discover inducements that elicit strong membership involvement. To the extent that the system appeals to the full array of members' desires, the organization will succeed in mobilizing larger quantities of essential resources.

The Internal Polity

Acquiring collective control over resources is only half the function of an organization's political economy. The essential task of its internal polity is to make binding decisions that allocate collective resources to the organization's goals. Choices among goals are reflected in many specific actions taken by the organization: proportions of the annual budget allocated to various categories;

new programs undertaken and old ones dropped or expanded; leaders elected or administrators hired to manage daily business; and efforts to influence the public-policy decisions of external authorities.

A collective action organization's *governance structures* are the means for making and implementing collective policy decisions about goals and resource allocations. A policy decision is simply the collectively binding choice among alternatives for a specific action by an organization. Relocating the national association headquarters, promoting the organization's charitable activities, publishing a new journal, hiring a Washington lawyer to lobby on a piece of pending legislation—each decision commits collective resources to one line of action to the exclusion of alternative uses. Governance structures are the distributions among organizational participants of formal authority and actual influence over such decisions. Governance structures are more concerned with broad policy directions than with the daily routines handled by the administrative structure. Rules for aggregating members' policy preferences are spelled out in constitutional authority arrangements as well as in the informal influence practices among members and leaders. A fundamental dimension of governance structures is the extent to which power to make decisions is concentrated in the hands of a few leaders or widely dispersed among the rank-and-file membership. Centralized governance structures restrict members' access to decision making, while democratic structures enable members to legitimate and constrain leaders' actions as agents of the group.

At the microlevel, an individual member's *policy interest* is a preference for a specific collective action to be taken by the organization, or for a policy decision to be made by external actors at the urging of the collectivity. A person has an interest in a policy to the extent that one outcome of that policy has greater symbolic or utilitarian value to him or her than another outcome (Coleman 1975, p. 81; Shubik 1982, p. 90–91). Under the multidimensional model of individual choice described in Chapter 2, the intensity of a member's policy interests can motivate his or her efforts to influence the outcome of collective decisions. However, members will differ in the preferences they hold for member servicing, legitimation, and public-policy influence goals. An organization's collective decisions about resource allocations among these goals are not always inducible from simple knowledge of each member's preferences for general and specific objectives. Analysts must probe into the structural arrangements that give some participants greater influence than others over collective decisions.

The structure of *policy communication* among organization participants is a basic mechanism for aggregating policy preferences from micro- to macrolevels. Given the democratic ethos of most collective action organizations, the transmission of policy information is bidirectional rather than operating predominantly from the top down, as in work organizations. Relatively stable patterns of information exchange continually inform participants about the limits of feasible policy decisions. Members inform leaders about their preferred policy directions while leaders attempt to persuade members to support their initiatives. Thus, frequent policy communication is a critical process for translating individual preferences into collective policy decisions.

An important function of the internal polity is stimulating member involvements in collective actions. *Member involvements* consist of individuals' participation in and psychological orientations toward the organization. They may take varying forms, such as contributions of time and money, participation in group activities, and intense psychological commitment to the collectivity. The importance of these involvements lies in the organization's need to tap members' individual talents and energies to carry out many of its collective decisions.

Figure 3.3 shows the expected relationships among the theoretical concepts involved in the internal polity. Organizational structures and governance structures are macrolevel phenomena linked to the microlevel policy interests of members and their involvements, either directly or through the policy communication processes occurring at both macro- and microlevels

Proposition 16:   Collective action organizations develop democratic governance structures under conditions of large size, complex incentive systems, nonbureaucratic administrative structures, multiple organizational goals, and greater environmental complexity and uncertainty.

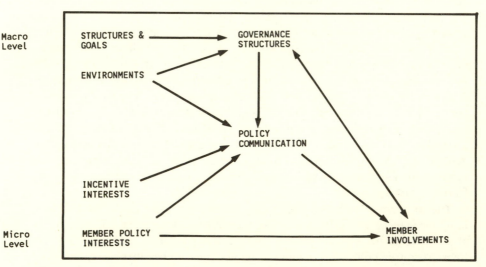

Figure 3.3 Relationships Among Internal Polity Components

This proposition places organizational conditions as antecedents to governance structures. The underlying principle is that a democratic polity is most likely to emerge when complex conditions require accommodation to multiple sets of interests and objectives. In contrast, simple and uniform conditions are more compatible with an oligarchic form of governance.

Proposition 17: The more intense members' interests in organizational policy issues, the greater their communication interaction.

Proposition 18: Organizations with more democratic governance structures generate higher rates of policy communication.

Proposition 19: Smaller size, absence of bureaucracy, environmental complexity and uncertainty, and stronger member interests in incentives stimulate a greater rate of communication on policy issues.

The frequency with which organization members interact on policy matters is a function both of their individual interest in these issues and of the governance structures that enable them to gain access to the decision-making process. Figure 3.3 depicts policy communication as *both* a micro- and a macrolevel concept, reflecting its dual aspect as an organizational structural property created from interactions among individual members. Thus, propositions 17, 18, and 19 should hold true at both the micro- and macrolevels of analysis, as well as for cross-level (contextual) relationships.

Proposition 20: Higher levels of policy communication, stronger member interests in policy issues, and more democratic association governance structures produce more member commitment to and participation in organizational affairs.

As shown in Figure 3.3, three factors directly affect the level of member commitments to and participation in organizational activities: organizational governance structures, member policy interests, and communication about policies. Macrolevel factors such as bureaucracy and goals, and microlevel variables such as member incentive interests, are expected to affect member involvements indirectly through these processes.

The External Polity

Collective action organizations that pursue legitimation and public-policy influence goals must interact with institutions outside their boundaries. The political mobilization process, which brings under collective control and coordination the resources for realizing such external influence objectives, comprises the final set of concepts and propositions in the political economy theory. The concepts and propositions below are intended only for associations that seek to influence government policy decisions.

A collective action organization must create the necessary *political capacity* for engaging in external political activities. Some resources must be allocated to social positions to monitor the political scene for threats and opportunities. For example, lobbyists can be put on retainer and a system established for alerting members to impending legislative decisions. An organization with more political capacity thus has greater potential for timely intervention whenever a specific situation arises relevant to its interests and goals. To transform this potential into actual collective action requires a *mobilization effort,* during which leaders attempt to arouse the members' actions toward external political targets. Mobilized efforts include coordinated phone and letter campaigns, protests, and demonstrations, as well as more conventional electoral campaign assistance and in-person presentation of policy views. Thus, when successful, the organization's mobilization effort stimulates *external activity* by members, under the control and direction of its political leadership.

The target of an organization's mobilization is an *authoritative decision* by persons or organizations outside the association who possess legitimate power to make and enforce policy decisions that are binding upon the organization, its members, or its beneficiary constituencies. Typically, these authorities are elected and appointed government officials, legislatures, and courts, but they also may be private sector firms or even other collective action organizations. In most influence situations, a collective action organization is not alone in seeking to shape the authoritative decision. Other groups, both *opponents* and *coalition partners* of the collective action organization, interact with the authorities in the complex public-policy decision-making process. The interactions among these groups hold the key to the decision ultimately made.

The final set of expected relationships among theoretical concepts in the external polity appears in Figure 3.4. The following propositions connect macro- and microlevel phenomena of the organization to policy interactions occurring in the larger political arenas with which the organization tries to influence public-policy decisions.

Proposition 21:   The more complex an organization's structures and environments, and the more important its public-policy goals, the greater the political capacity it develops.

Creating capacity to influence public-policy decisions requires substantial resource allocations, which are easier to acquire in associations that have large formal administrative, governance, and incentive structures. Only organizations that have strong public-policy goals are likely to allocate resources to develop political capacity.

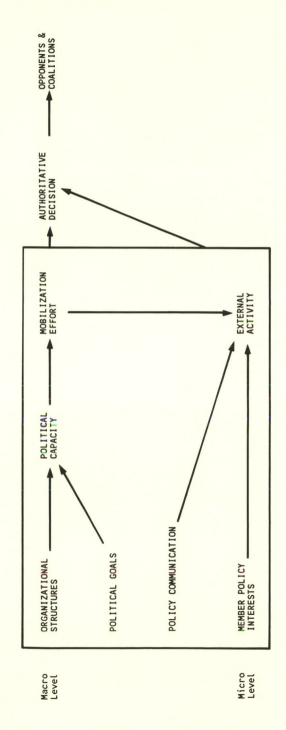

Figure 3.4 Relationships Among External Polity Components

Proposition 22:   Organizations with public-policy goals and greater political capacity are more likely to mobilize their members' policy ef-
forts.

Proposition 23:   The members of organizations with political goals, high political capacity, and strong mobilization efforts are more likely to
engage in external influence activities.

Proposition 24:   When members have strong interests in policy issues and high
rates of policy communication, they are more likely to engage
in external influence activities.

Participation in external activity follows from the organization leaders' efforts
to coordinate their members' involvement, but also requires that individuals
have a personal interest in the issues. As with commitments and participation
in the internal polity, the frequency of policy communication provides a critical mechanism linking micro- and macrolevel processes.

Proposition 25:   The fewer opponents an organization faces, the greater its success at influencing public-policy decisions.

Proposition 26:   Organizations that mobilize resources from their members for
political effort have greater success at influencing public-policy
decisions.

Proposition 27:   The more coalitions that an organization builds with other
groups, the greater its success at influencing public-policy decisions.

These propositions presume that public authorities in a liberal democracy are
responsive to pressures brought to bear on them by organized interest groups.
Their decisions reflect, in part, the relative weight of influence resources applied by the contending sides of the issue.

Testing the Theory

The propositions in the political economy theory of collective action organizations take the form of probabilistic covariations among pairs of variables.
They imply that under specified conditions, certain outcomes will occur in a
significant proportion of cases. The propositions are not cast as universal laws,
that is, statements in which all cases, past and future, are deduced without
exception from initial conditions. Rather, the phenomena to be explained are
expected to occur on less stringent grounds. The nondeterministic, or stochas-
tic, nature of these propositions does not make the political economy theory
any less of an explanation (Hempel 1966, p. 68). The propositions presented

above are designed to explain observed relationships among organizational and individual behaviors and attitudes. Explanation is holistic; that is, the propositions should not be tested in isolation. While no single one of these predictions is monumentally revealing, their combined quality gives the theory great value in understanding collective action organizations. The failure of a single relationship to be consistent with the data is not reasonable ground for rejection of the entire theory. The data to be examined may offer confirmatory evidence for the validity of the theoretical propositions. Counterinstances may be sufficiently severe to call for revision of portions of the theory. As research evidence accumulates in favor of or against the theory, progress will be made toward an explanation that more faithfully mirrors social reality. Only future research that addresses these same relationships can confirm the results of this book, thus further strengthening the theory, or disprove them, thereby weakening the theory.

Conclusion

Associations range from small hobby clubs without external connections to national "peak" business associations and labor unions that maintain complex webs of interaction with hundreds of constituent and authoritative organizations. The theory of association political economy presented above is intended to account for variations in significant structures and processes across this population of organizations. The theoretical propositions connect external environments and constituents to internal structures and members' orientations toward the organizational economy and polity. For groups with government policy influence goals, the output is the mobilization and application of collective resources aimed at influencing authoritative decisions. The propositions are stated in a simple covariation format whose functional forms (linear, exponential, logarithmic, additive, interactive) are left unspecified. In the following chapters, the analytic concepts are measured using data from samples of collective action organizations and members, and tests of the theory's validity are made. Not every proposition has appropriate data available for meaningful tests, nor does every analysis bear directly upon the theory. Some are merely descriptive statistics or explorations of side issues. However, the empirical assessment of the association political economy theory is the core task for the remainder of the book. As each portion of the theory is examined empirically, implications of the results relevant to the paradigms of social integration, internal governance, and public-policy influence are discussed.

4

A PROFILE OF AMERICAN ASSOCIATIONS

No one knows the exact number of collective action organizations in the United States. Unlike our decennial censuses of people and of manufacturing firms, complete tallies of American voluntary associations have never been conducted. Even rough estimates of this population are hampered by prior conceptual problems. What constitutes a collective action organization for research purposes? Should all state and local chapters of a national organization be counted as separate units, or should affiliates meet some standard of political or financial autonomy? Should organizations restricted to a local territory, such as a neighborhood, be considered equivalent to national organizations having millions of members? Does a collective action organization whose members are other organizations, such as a trade association, carry the same weight as an organization whose members are all individuals, such as a labor union? Every empirical study makes explicit or implicit decisions of these sorts that effectively define the organization populations to which its findings can be generalized.

Two basic approaches are feasible in designing a sampling frame within which to study collective action organizations. The first begins by drawing a representative survey sample of people from a population and asking them to give the names of all the organizations to which they belong. Larger organizations are more likely to contribute more members, but for a system of substantial size (such as the entire United States), the likelihood is small that any specific organization will be mentioned more than once. If individuals' reports about their organizations' sizes are reasonably reliable, a weighting scheme can be constructed to take into account the probabilities of every organization's appearance in the individual sample. This "hypernetwork" sampling design (McPherson 1982) thus permits a representative set of organizations to be identified through people's membership ties. The drawback to this procedure is the high cost of drawing a sufficiently large individual sample and screening respondents for the relatively small numbers of association memberships held by the average adult. At any time, perhaps one third of adults belong to no formal voluntary organization, and only one third hold membership in more than one association, not counting churches (Verba and Nie 1972, pp. 41–42; Olsen 1982 p. 128; but see Walker and Baumgartner [1989] for somewhat higher estimates based on a more liberal criterion of "affiliation"). The amount of active participation is even lower, since many of these memberships are nominal.

The alternative research design begins with an existing enumeration of collective action organizations and proceeds to draw a representative sample. Subpopulations could stratify the sample to permit separate estimates for distinct "domains of study" (Kalton 1983, p. 24). The obvious advantage of this design is the enormous savings in using an enumeration compiled by someone else. The equally clear disadvantage lies in whatever limitations in coverage and accuracy that were created by the original compilers of the population listing. For the present study, with its limited funds, the benefits of a secondary enumeration design outweighed the costs of a hypernetwork approach. Fortunately, several reasonably complete listings of American national associations were available, although their omissions of nonnational organizations prevents generalization of results to the full collective action organization population.

The National Association Study

The National Association Study (NAS) is two interconnected surveys, each using different sampling frames, as described in this section. The first survey consists of telephone interviews with leaders of 459 national associations, drawn from five strata and representing 13,000 American national organizations. The second survey used the first sample as a framework to draw a subset of 35 organizations from which samples of members were randomly selected. Questionnaires were filled out by 8746 members of 35 professional societies, recreational organizations, and women's associations. Thus, the two surveys not only permit analyses at the organizational and the membership level, but also cross-level (contextual) analyses.

Telephone Survey of National Organizations

The first step in drawing a sample of national associations was to compile an enumeration from existing secondary sources. Three compendia were used to assemble lists of national associations, classified into five strata. These categories were trade associations, professional societies, labor unions, recreational associations, and all others. The three directories used were:

- *National Trade and Professional Associations of the United States. 18th Annual Edition* (1983) Craig Colgate, Jr. and Roberta L. Fowler, eds. Washington: Columbia Books.

- *National Recreational, Sporting and Hobby Organizations of the United States. 3rd Annual Edition* (1981) Craig Colgate, Jr. and Laurie A. Evans, eds. Washington: Columbia Books.

- *Encyclopedia of Associations. 18th Edition* (1983) Denise Akey, ed. Detroit: Gale Research Company.

The Gale encyclopedia was the most comprehensive work, listing some 17,000 organizations, compared to 5700 and 2800 names listed in the two Columbia Books volumes. However, the Gale company included a substantial percentage of organizations, perhaps one quarter of the listings, that do not qualify as national membership associations, such as clearinghouses, research units, nonautonomous departments of associations, foreign organizations, government units, and some purely local associations. It further classified associations under 17 ad hoc categories, ranging from agricultural through veterans' organizations, which made aggregation into more substantively meaningful categories essential. Thus, the compilation of a master list of American national associations used the two Columbia Books volumes as the basic guide, with a supplement of "other" organizations drawn from the Gale encyclopedia.

The unique feature of the Columbia Books directories for this project was their identification of each association's annual budget. Both volumes had appendices that listed budgets by broad categories, thus allowing disproportionate samples to be drawn within these strata. Because the great majority of national associations tended to be small in terms of membership, resources, and formal structure, an oversample of large associations was necessary to obtain sufficient sample units at the upper range of variation. For the trade and professional associations, the division between large and small was a $250,000 annual budget, while for the recreational associations, the cutoff point was set at $100,000. In all three categories, the large-budget organizations accounted for about one fifth of the stratum population, and the small-budget associations the remaining four fifths. The labor union population at the national level was so small (192 national organizations) that subdivision was not warranted.

A complication to using both the Columbia Books directories was their inclusion of a few associations in both volumes (e.g., trade associations that manufacture sporting goods, and associations of coaches or athletes). To remedy this overlap, all organizations appearing in both books were assigned uniquely to one stratum before sampling.

Three categories—trade, professional, and recreational—were split into large and small sizes, using the budget criterion described above. The result were the eight sampling strata shown in Table 4.1. In practice, application of the criteria meant that the Columbia Books directories were used exclusively to identify the associations in all strata except the residual Other Associations category. Any association in the Gale encyclopedia not listed in the two Columbia Books directories was assigned to this heterogeneous fifth stratum. Any organization that was not a membership group was eliminated, as was any group in the residual category with fewer than 100 members.

These procedures identified a total of 13,013 national associations of all types. Table 4.1 shows the estimated numbers of associations in the eight sampling strata and the proportion of the total population in each stratum. These frequencies demonstrate that a simple random sample of the entire population would have resulted in very few labor unions and few large associations, but a huge number of "other" types.

In January and February 1984, telephone interviews were sought with informants from random samples of 50 to 60 associations in each of the eight sampling strata. Completed interviews were obtained with 459 association informants, while 36 were refused. Another 48 remained uncompleted at the end of the field period, while 53 names were determined to be missing cases. The latter had either become inactive or been absorbed by another group, or their associations had changed into for-profit organizations or were not mass membership groups. Two response rates are shown in Table 4.1. The first is based on inclusion of uncompleted cases in the denominators, while the second uses only definite decisions (refusals plus completions) as the case base. The overall response rate lies somewhere between 84.5 and 92.7%. Table 4.1 also displays the number of completed interviews and the two response rates for each of the eight sampling strata. The rates with incompletes included are somewhat lower for the last four strata because a shorter field period was available. The organizations data must be weighted, to adjust for disproportionate sampling rates, whenever analysis requires the various sampling strata to be combined for an overall population estimate.

Survey of Association Members

The second phase of the NAS sampled a subset of national organizations with individual mass members and mailed self-administered questionnaires to random samples of their memberships. Three sampling strata were used: professional societies, recreational clubs, and women's associations [see Knoke (1989a) for comparisons across these three categories]. Using the data on membership size, associations in each of these strata were listed in descending

Table 4.1. Response Rates by Sampling Strata for National Association Telephone Survey

Sampling Strata	Organization Population	Proportion of total	Number of interviews	Rates (%)with Incompletes:	
				included	excluded
1. Trade Associations					
Large	790	.061	60	98	98
Small	2,713	.208	49	89	91
2. Professional Societies					
Large	381	.029	57	89	92
Small	2,436	.187	52	88	95
3. Labor Unions	192	.015	60	73	83
4. Recreational Associations					
Large	268	.021	67	89	99
Small	1,433	.110	60	82	95
5. Other Associations	4,800	.369	54	73	90
Total national associations	13,013	1.000	459	85	93

order by total number of members. Sample organizations were selected proportional to size to fill quotas of 24 professional, 15 recreational, and 8 women's organizations. Letters were sent to the national leader of each association, inviting him or her to participate in the project in return for data sharing. Of the 24 professional societies, 20 permitted membership samples to be drawn, 2 refused, and 2 did not maintain a nationally centralized mailing list. Of the 15 recreational organizations, 9 participated in the project and 6 refused. Six of the eight women's associations participated. Given the differential numbers and refusal rates among the three types of associations, somewhat larger membership samples were drawn from each recreational and women's organization.

More than 14,000 questionnaires and postpaid return envelopes were mailed to randomly selected addresses from each organization's membership list. A cover letter explained the purpose of the study and promised confidentiality of the respondent's identity. At the end of 4 weeks, a second questionnaire packet was sent to persons who had not yet returned a completed one. Ultimately 8746 completed questionnaires were returned during the field period, which ran from September 1984 to May 1986. After subtractions for improper addresses (returns by the post office), the overall response rate was 61.6%. The average response rate for the professional society members (66.4%) was somewhat higher than for the recreational (59.7%) and women's association (58%) members. Only 3 of the 35 organizations had response rates below 50%.

The stem-and-leaf chart in Figure 4.1 shows at a glance all the response rates for the organizations. The digit to the left of the vertical bar represents the "10's" place or decile, while each digit to the right represents the "1's" digit (rounded) for a different organization. Putting together the left digit with one of the right digits shows the percentage response rate for one organization. Thus, two organizations had response rates of 84%, and one had 79%. The diagram reveals that a large majority of associations attained completion rates above 60%, but two groups fell below 40%. Both of these organizations apparently had not maintained up-to-date membership listings, to judge from the substantial number of questionnaires returned by the post office without forwarding addresses. At least one of the two groups had had an inactive national office for more than a year prior to the survey.

A Descriptive Overview

This section presents a descriptive overview of the organization and membership samples. Subsequent chapters test theoretical propositions about the political economies, but the purpose here is simply to show the range of variation in some of the major explanatory variables. These measures—organiza-

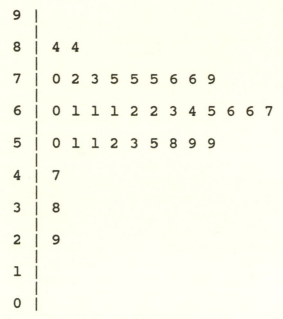

```
9 |
  |
8 | 4 4
  |
7 | 0 2 3 5 5 5 6 6 9
  |
6 | 0 1 1 1 2 2 3 4 5 6 6 7
  |
5 | 0 1 1 2 3 5 8 9 9
  |
4 | 7
  |
3 | 8
  |
2 | 9
  |
1 |
  |
0 |
```

Figure 4.1. Stem-and-Leaf Chart of Questionnaire Response Rates by Organization

tion size, administrative structure, goals, and environments—frequently serve as independent or control variables in the theoretical analyses. Hence, some brief attention here to their distribution should help to establish the context for their later use. Because the American national association population is so heterogeneous, some simple comparisons are made across the four main subpopulations defined by the sampling design: trade associations, professional societies, labor unions, and recreational groups. While neither the trade associations nor the labor unions were used in drawing the membership samples, they are both significant segments of the entire collective action organization population. As such, their contrast with the professional societies and recreational groups should prove illuminating.

Organization Size

One standard measure of organization size is the total number of participants. For most associations, a tally of individual members is sufficient. However, trade associations typically involve other organizations, some of which are quite large in terms of *their* sizes (e.g., number of employees). For example, the American Petroleum Institute has only 225 "members," yet includes the major oil corporations whose combined employees number in the millions and whose total assets amount to hundreds of billions of dollars. Of course, the API's own resources are only a small fraction of its members', albeit much larger than those of most trade associations. Since definitive methods do not exist for equating people with organizations, in this book the size indicator will assume that all "memberships" are equivalent; that is, one organization member equals a single person. This treatment reflects the legal presumption of corporate personhood. Indeed, many trade associations confer equal voting members status upon every organization. The consequence is that American national trade associations are the smallest collective action organizations, averaging only 1216 members, less than one quarter of the professional associations (mean of 5575 members) and many times smaller than recreational clubs (143,095 members) or labor unions (152,658 members).

Although the range of sample organization size is impressive (two recreational groups claimed 10 and 24 million members), the distributions are highly skewed. Because Figure 4.2 groups the membership sizes by powers of ten (e.g., 1 to 99 members, 100 to 999 members, and so on), the visual effect of the skewness is reduced. Even so, the clustering of sizes at the lower end of range for each subpopulation is still apparent. For all organizations combined, the median size is only 750 members, but the mean size is 27,575. This large gap between median and mean reflects the presence of a small number of very large organizations in the right tail of the distribution.

A similar wide disparity both within and across types of organizations appears on another standard indicator of size—annual revenues from all sources. The labor unions are the wealthiest, with a mean income of $14.4 million, followed by the recreational (mean $1.30 million) and trade associations (mean $1.26 million), and professional societies a distant fourth at $716,000. These mean revenues mask an even more pronounced skew than that for membership size, as shown in Figure 4.3. Although the large majorities of trade, professional, and recreational organizations have revenues under $1 million per year, small percentages of each group exceed $10 million. The great aggregate wealth of labor unions derives from their large total memberships. When per-member revenues are calculated, the largest contributors are found in trade associations ($1,036 per member), who ranked far ahead of professional society ($128) and union members ($94). Joining a recreational group is especially cheap, averaging only nine dollars per member. Of course, sources other than members are involved in generating total revenues, as discussed in Chapter 5.

The apparent large differences in membership and revenue sizes between types of collective action organizations should not obscure the existence of

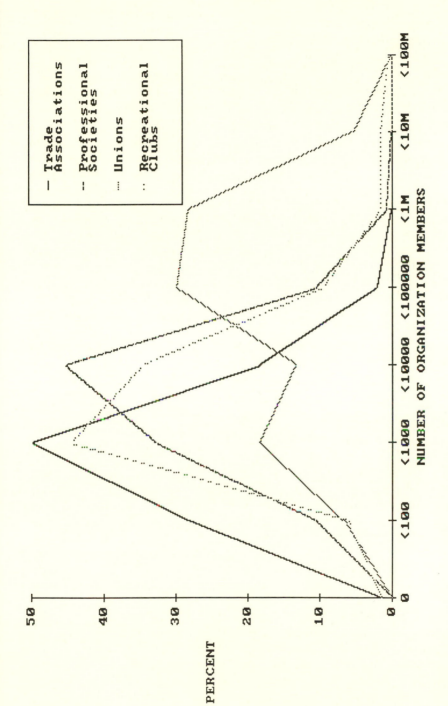

Figure 4.2. Distribution of Membership Size by Type of Organization

substantial within-type variation. The close overlap in distributions shown in Figures 4.2 and 4.3 suggests that size variance cannot readily be explained by the four subpopulation categories. In fact, very little variation can be explained in a statistical sense by type of organization. Chapter 5 examines some of the more important factors affecting revenue and expenditure patterns.

Administrative Structure

Bureaucracy is a perennial theme in the organization research literature. Organization theorists variously view bureaucracy as a rational structure or as a symbolic form, but the implications for resource management are similar. Under the rational model, bureaucracy is a purposeful design to maximize collective efforts toward explicit objectives (Scott 1987, pp. 20–22). The Weberian image of bureaucracies—comprising circumscribable authority, specified roles, procedures, and rules—is alleged to be technically superior to other forms of imperative coordination and control (Weber 1947). An elaborated vertical and horizontal division of labor permits more effective cultivation of both internal and external resource exchanges, since specialists are assigned to deal with members, constituents, and organizational sponsors. Similarly, bureaucratization enlarges associations' capacities to handle many resource expenditures, because specialized units again deal with the diverse internal and external objectives.

Under the natural systems approach, organizational structures reflect unplanned and spontaneous processes that enhance organizational success and survival. Many associations do not face the technical efficiency constraints or the market mechanisms of control encountered by production organizations. They are freer to adopt shared, institutionalized structures that reflect prevailing social norms about what organizations should look like and how they should operate (Pfeffer 1981, pp. 94–95). Often a bureaucratic facade may be displayed in order to satisfy dominant cultural values and expectations—a ceremonial conformity to symbols that obscures the real decoupling between formal structure and actual activities (Meyer and Rowan 1977). Associations conforming to bureaucratic principles should be more successful in acquiring funds from external constituents and sponsors, who have come to take such elements for granted as signs of fiscal competence, accountability, and effectiveness. Thus, both the rational and the institutional approaches converge, for different reasons, to an expectation that bureaucratically organized associations will enjoy improved resource management capabilities.

For collective action organizations, a bureaucratic administration involves an elaborate internal role structure, consisting of paid professional staff, de-

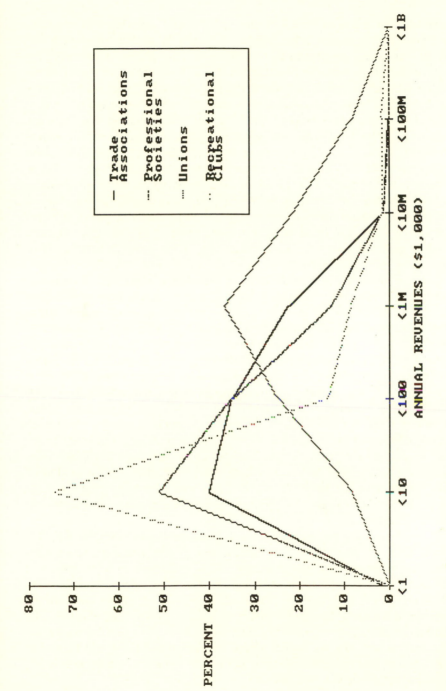

Figure 4.3. Distribution of Annual Revenues by Type of Organization

partmentalized functions, and a hierarchical chain of authority. Alternatively, the administrative tasks may be carried out largely by member volunteers, using the "amateur" form described by Weber (1978). Based on informant reports, a three-level scale was created for the national organizations: (3) three or more hierarchical levels or horizontal departments; (2) fewer internal layers but a full-time chief staff officer, or at least three other managerial or professional staffers; (1) a lack of both internal differentiation and full-time managerial-professional staff. For all associations combined, roughly equal numbers of organizations fall into these three classifications (37% highly, 29% moderately, and 34% nonbureaucratized). But considerable contrasts occur across types of organizations. Three quarters of the unions are highly bureaucratized, compared to less that one third of the recreational groups. Almost two thirds of the recreational organizations operate under the amateur form of administration. The trade associations and professional societies are more evenly distributed across the three categories, with slightly higher levels of bureaucracy among the former.

Level of bureaucratization strongly covaries with a number of organizational characteristics, as shown in Table 4.2. Highly bureaucratic associations are significantly older on average than the nonbureaucratized organizations. They are also substantially larger, by a ratio of almost 50 to 1. Consequently, these large bureaucracies have more formalized structures, making greater use of local branches and chapters and establishing more permanent committees within the national body. The large bureaucracies employ substantially more full-time-equivalent support staff (nonmanagerial and nonprofessionals, such as technicians, secretaries, and clerks), who are twice as likely to be guided by written rules in the conduct of their jobs (formalization). The number of volunteers working for the national office (excluding officers and board members) is the only characteristic that does not differ. Although the means seem to increase with greater bureaucratization, the effect arises from a handful of labor unions that use hundreds of volunteer workers during election campaigns. In all three categories, two out of every three associations claimed no volunteer workers.

In conclusion, the bureaucratic features of national associations strongly resemble those of other types of organizations: greater longevity, large size, complex division of labor, specialization and formalization in work roles. For at least one third of American associations, however, bureaucratic elements are absent, whether from choice or sheer inability to maintain the scale of operation that makes the bureaucratic mode both necessary and feasible. The result is an enormous range of variation, equivalent to the gulf between multinational corporations and neighborhood small businesses. As will be shown in the next chapter, bureaucratic structure has an important effect on how associations acquire and use resources.

Table 4.2. Characteristics of Associations by Level of Bureaucratization

Association Characteristics	Level of Bureaucratization			
	High	Medium	Low	*p*
Organizational age (years)	37.5	32.5	29.6	.02
Members (mean)	67,118	11,068	1,489	.01
Local chapters (mean)	62.9	13.7	6.6	.001
Standing committees (mean)	9.9	5.2	3.9	.05
FTE Support staff (mean)	14.6	1.4	0.2	.001
Written rules for staff (%)	79.4	61.1	40.5	.001
Volunteers (mean)	17.3	5.4	2.7	N.S.
(*N*)	(163)	(128)	(150)	

Organization Goals

As discussed in Chapter 3, associations support diverse mixtures of member-servicing, legitimating, and policy-influencing goals. Some organizations focus on a narrow agenda, while others maintain a broad spectrum of concerns. Where an association finds its funds, and how it subsequently uses them, is very much a function of its commitments to different types of objectives. For example, recreational clubs, such as the Antique Airplane Association and the Rotary International, have no conceivable interest in affecting government decisions. Therefore, they do not spend money on lobbying, but devote all their resources to enhancing their members' enjoyment of the private pursuits for which they were founded: fun and fellowship, education and research, civic service work. Other associations, such as the U.S. Special Olympics, proclaim a broad but disinterested public mandate that allows them to seek donations from private sector and even government sponsors. Yet still others, with partisan goals of advancing their members' economic interests, such as the United Mine Workers and the National Dairy Council, sustain their existence through efforts to shape legislation and influence regulatory decisions. Direct member services are often secondary to urgent political combat needs. All these examples imply a link between an association's goals and both the sources of its revenues and subsequent spending patterns.

Given the limited interview time available, an extensive open-ended inquiry into organizational goals was not feasible. Even a request for a brief summary in the informants' own words often produced vague statements; for example, mentions of types of member services offered. A systematic alternative procedure for measuring goals was to present a list of eight broadly stated topics. The informant indicated whether each one was "a major goal, a moderate goal, a minor goal, or not a goal of the (organization name)." Table 4.3 dis-

Table 4.3. Organization Goals: Percentages Indicating Goal as Moderate or Major

			Type of Organization		
Organizational goals	All assns.	Labor unions	Trade assns.	Prof'l assns.	Rec'l assns.
Conduct research or member education	77	76	61	83	73
Affect the lives of nonmembers	63	59	55	66	44
Change values and beliefs in the larger society	50	59	38	57	36
Influence public-policy decisions of the government	49	86	58	53	22
Raise members' status and prestige	45	88	63	56	30
Improve members' incomes or economic conditions	36	100	57	38	10
Develop members' social or recreational lives	27	29	18	13	59
Enhance members' cultural or artistic lives	25	31	13	25	46
Mean number of goals	3.72	5.15	3.73	3.88	3.15

plays the percentages for all organizations and within the four subsamples for which the moderate or major designation was picked.

Four goals are considered major or moderate by half or more of all associations: conducting research or member education (77%); affecting nonmembers' lives (63%); changing values and beliefs in the larger society (50%); and influencing public-policy decisions of the government (49%). The other four goal statements are endorsed by fewer than half of all organizations. These goals involve a focus on some sort of selective good or benefit for the members: raising their status and prestige; improving incomes or working conditions; developing social/recreational lives; and enhancing cultural/artistic lives. Some substantial differences emerged across the subpopulations. For example, every labor union and a majority of trade associations seek to improve their members' incomes or economic conditions, but only one in ten of the recreational clubs find that objective important. The majority of unions, trade, and professional organizations try to influence government policies, but only one fifth of the recreational groups have political goals. On the other hand, a majority of the recreational groups try to develop their members' social or recreational lives, and almost half seek to enhance their members' cultural or artistic lives. These objectives are minor concerns for the other types of organizations. The differing goal profiles are, not surprisingly, consistent with common stereotypes about the purposes of these kinds of collective action organizations. But, even within categories, noticeable variation in goals remains to be accounted for.

The last line in Table 4.3 tallies the mean number of important (major or moderate) goals mentioned by the organizational informants. Unions maintain the largest number, more than five per organization, while the recreational clubs have the smallest, barely more than three. The trade associations and professional societies fall in between, naming just under four types of important goals. Inspection of the frequency distributions (not shown) shows fairly symmetrical patterns. Very few organizations claim that less than two or more than six goals have moderate or major importance. Thus, typical American associations seem to hold eclectic interests, contrary to some images of "single issue" organizations. About half the organizations consider government policy influence an important objective, the other half do not. Further differences between political and nonpolitical organizations will be highlighted in later chapters.

Environments of Associations

Theorists writing about organizational environments typically conceptualize them in multidimensional terms (Jurkovich 1974; Starbuck 1976; Pfeffer and

Salancik 1978). The range of the dimensions is diverse and potentially un-wieldy. For example, Aldrich posited six dimensions derived from population-ecology and resource-dependence principles: rich-lean; homo-heterogeneity; stability-instability; concentrated-dispersed; consensus-dissensus; and turbulent-placid (Aldrich 1979, pp. 63–70). More recently, Dess and Beard (1984) ar-gued that industrial organizations' task environments could be characterized in just three dimensions—munificence, dynamism, and complexity—by collaps-ing several of Aldrich's domains and omitting consensus as too difficult to apply to profit-making organizations. If six dichotomies are completely crossed, the resulting 64-cell typology would keep many researchers fully em-ployed for several years trying empirically to sort out their interconnections. Even three dichotomies yields eight distinct types of environments ($2^3=8$). Simplification can be achieved by concentrating on two distinct environmental dimensions of fundamental importance: resource scarcity and information flow.

Most organizations vary in regard to the level of resources available to them. From this perspective, an association responds to the amount of re-sources and to the various conditions under which resources become available for collective use (e.g., competition, sponsorship, concentration, and the like). For associations, the two most obvious indicators of resource scarcity are their financial revenues and numbers of members. When an association enjoys a large income and has many members, it can more readily satisfy a greater diversity of constituencies and goals than under scarcity conditions. Thus, total revenues are *both* an object to be explained and an index of an association's position within the resource-scarcity environment that may help to explain how the organization obtains and uses resources.

A less common approach to organizations' environments is to view them from an information-flow perspective: "a source of information used directly by decision makers as one basis for maintaining or modifying structures and activities"(Aldrich 1979, p. 122). The flow of information about external conditions across the organization's boundaries to relevant actors comprises a perceptual dimension of the environment that may be just as significant as resource scarcity in shaping organizational behaviors. The two most relevant indicators of information flow are uncertainty and complexity.

In the organizational literature, *uncertainty* has received the most attention (Duncan 1972; Leblebici and Salancik 1981; Argote 1982). Uncertainty exists "to the extent that relationships between elements are unpredictable and there is a low degree of constraint between environmental elements"(Aldrich 1979, p. 123). But a strong case can be made that *complexity* constitutes a second dimension in the information-flow environment (Child 1972; Dess and Beard 1984). Perceived complexity refers to actors' perceptions that many varied el-ements are intricately interconnected, though not necessarily in an unpredict-

Table 4.4. Items Comprising the Environmental Complexity and Environmental Uncertainty Scales

Scale Items	Percent Agreeing
Environmental complexity	
1. Without this organization to defend their interests, the members would be much worse off than they are	60.5
2. To achieve our goals, it is essential to work formally with many other organizations	60.3
3. This organization's members face strong pressures from a difficult environment	46.9
4. The techniques, skills, and information needed to conduct this organization's business are changing very rapidly	46.1
5. The political climate of the country right now is very favorable to our goals[a]	36.7
6. Our relations with other organizations are sometimes marked by conflict	32.5
7. This organization responds rapidly to new opportunities, making it a leader in several areas[a]	21.5
Environmental uncertainty	
1. This organization takes few risks, and mostly reacts to environmental pressures[a]	53.4
2. This organization is not at the forefront of new developments, but concentrates on doing the best job in a limited area	51.4
3. Making long-range plans for this organization is hindered by difficulty in predicting the nature of future events	43.5
4. It is frequently difficult to obtain adequate information about what is going on outside the organization	17.9

[a] Item reversed coded.

able fashion. Both uncertainty and complexity may independently pose serious problems for organizational decision makers because of the limited information processing capabilities of people and organizations (Wilensky 1967; Anderson 1983). An uncertain environment feeds unreliable information to decision makers, while a complex environment generates huge volumes of data that overwhelm the organization's capacity to assimilate it usefully.

Two scales were constructed to measure the perceived uncertainty and complexity aspects of each association's information-flow environment. During the interview, informants were read 22 statements about external conditions. They were asked how strongly they agreed or disagreed with each statement's applicability to their associations (strongly agree, agree, neither agree nor disagree [neutral], disagree, strong disagree, or inapplicable; this latter response was recoded under the heading neutral). Exploratory factor analysis, using principal components, uncovered two dimensions whose contents seem to tap the complexity and uncertainty dimensions discussed above. For example, the uncertainty items refer to risk taking and innovation, unpredictability, and information flow. The contents of the complexity dimension emphasize goal diversity, external pressures, interorganizational cooperation, and political conflict. Table 4.4 reports the exact wording of the items in each scale and the percentage of association informants agreeing that those conditions exist for their organizations.

Scale scores were calculated by assigning numerical values to item responses (strongly disagree=1 to strongly agree=5), then averaging the responses to the seven complexity items and the four uncertainty items, respectively. High scores mean that an association is perceived to face more complex and more unpredictable information-flow environments. The two scales each achieved respectable levels of internal-consistency reliability (Cronbach's alpha=.69 for complexity and .68 for uncertainty).

The modest positive correlation between these two information-flow scales ($r= +.20$) indicates that relatively complex environments are only a bit more likely to be seen as unpredictable, compared to less complex environments. Among the four basic types of associations, unions and recreational club leaders were somewhat more likely than professional and trade association informants to perceive uncertainty. Unions were considerably more likely than others to face complex environments.

Member Attributes

The questionnaires filled out by organization members apply only to persons belonging to professional societies, recreational clubs, and women's organizations. The social characteristics of these people can be compared to those of the 1819 respondents in the 1987 General Social Survey, an annual national sample of American adults by the National Opinion Research Center. Table 4.5 shows that organization members tend to be drawn from the upper socioeconomic strata of the population, a finding consistent with previous studies (e.g., McPherson 1977; McPherson and Lockwood 1980; Olsen 1982). However, the NAS respondents are even better off than the multiple-association members in the general population. The mean NAS education level is 17 years, in contrast to just under or over 12 years of schooling for the three categories of GSS respondents. Almost one quarter of the NAS respondents hold a doctoral or equivalent professional degree. Annual household incomes from all earners in NAS families was $45,000, more than double that of people belonging to no organizations.

Table 4.5. Mean Social Characteristics of National Association Study and General Social Survey Respondents

Characteristics	GSS respondents			NAS respondents
	No orgs.	1 org.	2+ orgs.	
Education (years)	11.1	12.3	13.6	17.0
Occupational prestige	35.7	40.4	43.9	57.1
Income ($000)	21	27	30	45
Age (years)	45.1	47.6	44.1	42.2
(N)	(575)	(475)	(755)	(8746)

Sources: 1987 General Social Survey and National Association Study.

Two thirds of all NAS respondents' occupations are in the professional category, with another one fifth in managerial positions. Only 7% work at manual occupations. Their mean occupational prestige on the NORC scale is 57, equivalent to accountant, economist, and publicity writer. More than three fourths of these respondents have prestige scores of 50 or higher, in contrast to the GSS respondents, who ranged 15 to 20 points lower. The highly skewed occupational distribution is not surprising, given the many professional societies of scientists, engineers, medical workers, and social scientists in the membership survey. Even among the recreational and women's organization members, nonmanual occupations comprise the overwhelming majorities. The NAS sample is also notably younger than the GSS groups. Most of them are middle-aged, since few are in their twenties (14%) and even fewer are 70 years or older (9%). Consequently, the larger majority are currently still employed (72%), rather than retired (14%) or going to school (5%).

The NAS members are almost evenly divided between males and females, although considerable within-organization gender homogeneity occurs (see McPherson and Smith-Lovin 1982, 1986). They are overwhelmingly white (95%), with blacks (2%) and others (3%) underrepresented relative to the total population (about 13% nonwhite). Although the majority are currently married (65%), only about one third of the households still contain children under 18 years of age. The NAS median member has belonged to his or her organization for only 6 years. Later chapters provide more detail on members' involvements in their organizations.

Conclusion

The National Association Study used a two-stage sampling design to draw representative samples of (1) 459 collective action organizations from the population of 13,000 national associations, and (2) 8746 members from 35 professional, recreational, and women's organizations. High response rates were attained for both projects. Extensive telephone interviews and mailed questionnaires collected data on diverse aspects of these organizational political economies. Measures of several important theoretical concepts—organization size, administrative structure, goals, and environments—used reports from the organizational informants. Some of the properties of these measures, as well as basic personal characteristics of members, are described above. The importance of these variables will become clearer in the following chapters, which examine the propositions in the political economy theory.

PART III

ORGANIZATIONAL ECONOMY

5

FUND-RAISING AND RESOURCE ALLOCATION

Collective action organizations cannot survive without continuous infusions of resources. Because few associations, apart from cooperatives and communes, actively produce revenue, almost all depend upon their members and external constituents for a steady flow of funds and other types of sustaining resources. The importance of members' psychological commitments and participatory activities are explored later. The present chapter examines the amounts and sources of revenue acquired by collective action organizations, and the allocation strategies they follow in spending these monies.

Budgetary processes comprise a central component in any association's economy, whether the organization manages hundreds or tens of millions of dollars. Resource management can never be reduced to purely administrative actions, with major decisions made by accountants in green eyeshades (or, these days, with IBM-XT personal computers). Resource acquisition and allocation ultimately affect collective policy decisions, implicit and explicit, reflecting the purposes and goals that an organization seeks to implement. The consequences of budgeting for the success or failure of collective actions eventually feeds back into future resource management opportunities or limitations. That purse strings shape the collective enterprise is well known by many political and economic entrepreneurs, who face constraints imposed by a finite budget line. When scarce dollars force hard trade-offs between competing objectives, organization politics inevitably enters into budget deliberations. Hence, to focus, as this chapter does, on budget making without explicitly involving the organizational polity is to impose an arbitrary separation on the intertwined aspects of association political economies. This expedient is resorted to only from sheer inability to analyze simultaneously the budget process and the polity. Bringing association goals into the budget analyses of this chapter at least captures one global political element in the organizational economy. A fuller treatment of the polity follows in later chapters.

The social science literature on collective action organizations has completely neglected budgetary matters. Apart from a few case studies of individual organizations, we know nothing about the basic facts of income and outgo. The National Association Study appears to be the first survey that ever collected comparative budget data, albeit using rather broad categories. Thus, even the crude description parameters reported herein make a unique contribution; this is a first step toward understanding the range of fiscal resources that American associations have at their disposal (see Knoke 1989b). However, this chapter aims to move beyond simple description to an analytic exploration of how associations obtain and use their funds.

Budgetary Compositions

At the end of the telephone interview, each association informant was asked to send the National Association Study a copy of his or her organization's most recent annual budget. Less than one third eventually mailed a copy, too few for systematic comparative analysis. Nevertheless, these documents illustrate the diversity among collective action organization budgetary configurations. Table 5.1 presents the complete budgets for two organizations at contrasting ends of the affluence spectrum. The Community Education Association (all organization names in the NAS are pseudonyms) had fewer than one thousand members, drawn from community and junior college continuing education programs. It relied solely on volunteer labor, employed no paid staff, and depended on annual $30 member dues for most of its revenue. Publications—a quarterly newsletter, semiannual working papers, and occasional research monographs—comprised its main expenditures. The CEA's annual national conference was largely self-funding. One tenth of the budget went to officials' travel to attend meetings. The bylaws prohibited "carrying on propaganda, or otherwise attempting to influence legislation" under the Internal Revenue Code's Section 501(c)(3) restriction. Thus, no overt political activity was budgeted by the CEA.

The Health Professionals Society was formed after World War II by a merger of seven specialized associations. By 1983 it numbered over 20,000 individual and 2000 organization members. Its New York headquarters employed 150 people, recently reorganized along functional lines: accreditation, consultation, continuing education, testing, research and public policy, and public relations. As Table 5.1 reveals, membership dues accounted for less than one

Table 5.1. Annual Budgets of Two National Associations

Income		Expenses	
Community Education Association 1983–1984			
Membership dues	$ 22,010	Publications	$ 14,500
Conferences	3,500	Conferences	3,900
Miscellaneous	1,600	Travel	3,500
		Membership	2,400
		Office supplies	2,000
		Miscellaneous	1,964
Total	$ 27,110		28,264
Health Professionals Society, 1981			
Fees for services	$ 5,331,910	Salaries, benefits	$3,906,942
Membership dues	2,069,915	Travel, meetings	1,026,341
Individual	(438,987)	Printing, postage	1,506,165
Agency	(1,617,830)	Rent, Phone, Electric	660,072
Other	(13,098)	Professional fees	446,785
Sales (printed material)	351,839	Bienniel convention	265,065
Grants and awards	286,254	Equipment	198,363
Interest and dividends	280,716	Depreciation	170,471
Bienniel convention	276,623	Interest expense	51,494
Net on securities sale	72,333		
Contributions	26,898		
Total	$ 8,696,488		$8,231,522

quarter of its annual revenue. The major source of income was the sale of services and publications. On the expenditure side, professional staff salaries and benefits were the largest category, followed by building rental, maintenance, and office equipment. Publications—including a dozen regular print series plus audiovisual materials—involved less than one fifth of all expenses. Although the HPS was also classified as a 501 (c)(3) organization, its Office of Public Affairs regularly monitored White House and Capitol Hill health-care legislation. It alerted HPS members to developments through a monthly newsletter and periodic mailings. Its representative testified before congressional committees on health manpower needs and regulatory issues. For 1984, HPS projected almost a quarter-million dollars for combined public policy and research activities, a decrease of nearly one third from the previous year because it had shelved a staffing information service.

The CEA and HPS budgets reflect contrasting financial patterns of acquisitions and allocations. For all 459 NAS sample organizations, rough estimates of income and outgo were provided during the telephone interviews with leaders. Informants were asked to estimate either the amount or percentage of income obtained from each of four sources: (1) membership dues and assessments; (2) contributions from corporate or individual nonmembers; (3) government grants and grants from private foundations; (4) sales of services and merchandise. On the allocation side, three expenditure categories were used: (1) direct services to members; (2) public relations and information programs; and (3) lobbying activities. All revenue and expenditure categories were transformed to percentages of total revenue, not necessarily totaling 100% of an association's annual budget. All but 20 sample associations provided these breakdowns.

Table 5.2 displays the mean sources of revenues and expenditures for all organizations, and for each of the four main types. Revenue sources exhibit relatively little variation across types: member dues and assessments account for almost two thirds of an average organization's income. However, averages conceal a great deal of variation among organizations, as revealed by Figure 5.1. Although skewed to the high end, the percentages of organizational income derived from members ranges across the full spectrum from zero to 100%, with nearly one quarter of the organizations obtaining less than one third of their revenue from members.

Table 5.2. Annual Revenues and Expenditures by Types of Associations[a]

Budgetary category	All assns.	Labor unions	Trade assns.	Prof'l assns.	Rec'l assns.
Revenue sources (%)					
Member dues	64.6	83.8	62.0	58.8	66.2
Sales	18.0	2.6	22.8	23.3	17.9
Nonmembers	5.1	1.5	1.7	4.4	5.7
Govt & Foundations	1.8	1.1	1.1	1.6	1.4
Other	10.5	11.0	12.4	11.9	8.8
Total	100.0	100.0	100.0	100.0	100.0
Expenditures (%)					
Member services	69.8	70.9	62.5	67.9	77.8
Info-public relations	7.6	4.2	10.4	6.0	5.4
Lobbying	2.9	6.5	3.7	1.7	1.5
Other	19.7	18.4	24.4	15.3	15.3
Total	100.0	100.0	100.0	100.0	100.0
Total revenues ($000)					
Mean ($)	2,695	14,412	1,255	707	1,290
Median ($)	72	2001	175	80	18
(N)	(439)	(54)	(104)	(105)	(123)

[a] Miscellaneous associations not tabulated separately.

Figure 5.1. Organizations Separated to Reflect Percentages of Annual Revenues from Member Dues

Table 5.2 discloses that unions, more than other types of associations, depend on member dues (mean of 83.8%), while professional societies depend on dues least (58.8%). Many organizations calculate dues on a sliding scale geared to members' ability to pay, sometime resulting in substantial imbalances across members. For example, the National Association of Manufacturers' minimal fee is $100, but major corporations such as General Motors and DuPont contribute $75,000 (Levitan and Cooper 1984, p. 14). Informants were asked how dependent their organizations were for annual income on a small number of large contributors. More than one quarter of the trade association informants said their organizations were "somewhat" or "heavily dependent," while only 11% of the recreation clubs and fewer than 5% of the unions and professional societies admitted to such dependency.

Almost one fifth of association revenues come from sales of services and merchandise (undoubtedly, some unknown proportion of these purchases are made by the members). Unions are considerably less likely than other types of organizations to obtain revenue this way. About 7% of revenue is generated from external sources, either from corporate and individual nonmembers (5.1%) or from government and foundation grants and contracts (1.8%). The remaining association income, about one tenth of the total, comes from various unspecified sources (including rents, endowments, investments). According to half the informants, association incomes had risen over the preceding three years (1981–1983), even after taking inflation into account. Only one out of six associations experienced declining revenues, despite America's worst postwar depression during that period. As might be expected from the antilabor campaign launched by the Reagan administration, unions were hit heavily in the pocketbook: only 36% reported increased incomes while 37% reported falling revenues.

On the expenditure side of the budget ledger, members receive largest portion of association expenditures—almost 70%. Recreational groups are the most likely to spend their money on member services (78%), trade associations the least likely (63%). Information programs and public relations aimed at external audiences account for one dollar in 13, with trade associations spending at twice the rate of unions and recreational clubs. Expenditures for lobbying comprise less than 3% of all association spending. Unions and trade associations account for the bulk of these funds. Given the large budgets of unions, their 6.5% average translates into almost $1 million spent yearly by *each* union on lobbying. Recreational clubs and professional societies are least prone to lobby. The "other" category is a residual obtained by subtracting the total of the three expenditure categories from 100. It may conceal various maintenance accounts, such as mortgages and rents and office operations. One type of expenditure for which no figures were collected is philanthropic activity on behalf of nonmembers. For example, fraternal and sororal groups often raise funds for charitable causes, such as hospitals that treat handicapped children. Although volunteer efforts are not reflected directly in the internal budgets of these associations, they are nevertheless a significant part of their economies. At least one fourth of the sample informants said that their association sponsored a charitable or philanthropic organization, with more than half of the unions doing so. Data on the magnitude of these efforts is not available. The income and outgo accounts in Table 5.2 are category averages that conceal much variation among the individual associations. The following sections seek to explain these variations in terms of organizational bureaucracy, environments, and goals.

Predictors of the Budget Process

The theoretical neglect of collective action organization budgets means that sophisticated models are not available for empirical testing. As an exploratory effort to specify some basic factors, this section examines three variables that may affect how associations acquire and spend their fiscal resources. The level of bureaucracy refers to formalized administrative arrangements in the national association office, the internal division of labor among the staff. Organizational environments comprise the information-flow dimensions that associations face in interacting with the larger social system. Association goals are the overt objectives that organizations seek to attain through collective actions, succinctly summarizing internal decisions about organizational priorities. Measures of these variables and some of their basic distributional properties were described in Chapter 4.

Bureaucracy, environments, and goals may each affect collective action organization budgets in obvious or subtle ways. An important theoretical proposition in Chapter 3 argued that organizations cope with turbulence outside their boundaries by adopting a bureaucratic internal structure:

Proposition 5:   The more complex and uncertain an organization's environment, the more bureaucratic its administrative structure.

Because the basic problem of administration is the management of unpredictability, the environments within which organizations operate exert strong pressures on leaders to create some system of control over subordinates and external exchange partners (McNeil 1978, pp. 68–69). The administrative logic of hierarchies, formalized procedures, and employee selection according to expertise gives leaders a strategic advantage in achieving calculable criteria such as profitability, growth, and market share. Additionally, as rationalized, institutional rules expand throughout an environment, formal organizations increasingly incorporate these societal norms and procedures as part of their formal structures (Meyer and Rowan 1977; DiMaggio and Powell 1983; Scott

1983). Although collective action organizations operate under different sets of performance expectations than do profit-making firms or government bureaus, they are susceptible to the same sets of historical and societal contextual factors. Hence, the expectation that environmental uncertainty and complexity will lead to internal bureaucratic structuring of an association's national administrative body.

The empirical data from the interviews with the NAS informants do not strongly support the theoretical proposition. Environmental uncertainty is uncorrelated with the three-level measure of association bureaucracy (Pearson's $r = -.09$). However, environmental complexity does correlate modestly with the level of bureaucracy ($r = +.14$). Complexity is also moderately related to the number of goals that an organization considers of moderate or major importance ($r = +.22$). The more complex the environment appears, the more likely its leader is to report that public-policy influence goals are important ($r = +.39$). Similarly, when social change goals are measured by averaging the importance of changing societal values and beliefs with the importance of affecting nonmembers' lives, environmental complexity also positively covaries with social change goals ($r = +.14$). Finally, highly bureaucratized associations are just slightly more likely to consider a larger number of goals as important than are nonbureaucratized organizations. Presumably, the former have greater capacity to handle a broader agenda. These modest relations among the independent variables are encouraging, for they suggest that their unique effects on resource acquisition and allocation decisions will not be distorted through multicollinearity.

The relationships of bureaucracy to revenues and expenditures among all organizations appear in Table 5.3. Bureaucracy's effect on total revenue is striking: moderately bureaucratized associations boast almost ten times the incomes of the nonbureaucratic groups, and heavily bureaucratized organizations enjoy more than a hundred times larger incomes. Of course, this relationship is to some extent causally reciprocal: with larger resource bases, associations can afford to hire sufficient numbers of staff that must be bureaucratically organized. Still, the trilevel measure of bureaucracy accounts for less than 4% of the total revenue variation among associations (the correlation ratio, eta-square, is only .037).

Membership dues account for a decreasing proportion and external revenue sources for an increasing percentage of association revenues as the level of bureaucracy increases. The presence of a full-time, specialized staff enables an organization to seek out and cultivate alternative income sources more effectively. Expenditures are less clearly related to bureaucracy: only information–public relations spending is concentrated at the highest bureaucratic level, although spending for member services falls off slightly. However, spending on lobbying does not vary significantly across the three levels.

Table 5.3. Relation of Bureaucracy to Association Revenues and Expenditures

	Total revenue ($000)	Member dues revenue (%)	External sources revenue (%)	Member services expend. (%)	Info-PR expend. (%)	Lobby expend. (%)
Bureaucratization						
High	2,753	50.9	16.1	62.9	12.5	3.9
Medium	202	60.1	9.8	70.3	8.1	1.7
Low	23	70.8	6.3	69.8	8.3	3.3
Average	1,075	60.5	10.9	67.4	9.8	3.1
Eta-square	.037	.071	.031	.014	.026	.009
(*p*)	(.001)	(.001)	(.001)	(.05)	(.01)	(N.S.)

Statistical Procedures

Many data analyses in this book involve multiple regression and related general linear model methods. For readers who are unfamiliar with these statistical techniques, a brief explanation is in order [see Bohrnstedt and Knoke (1987) for an extended treatment]. Because of their great flexibility in simultaneously analyzing relations among a large number of variables, multiple regression methods have proven particularly attractive to contemporary organization researchers. The widespread application of regression makes an understanding of their basic components imperative.

A multiple regression equation is used to determine whether a particular dependent variable is "explained," in the statistical sense that its variation can be predicted from knowledge of its covariation with two or more independent variables. The variables considered to be dependent and independent are specified in the research proposition under investigation. For example, assume the following substantive question: in comparing two collective action organizations that have the same goals, environments, and membership sizes but differ in their level of bureaucracy, how much would we expect their annual revenues to differ? In this specification, bureaucracy, goals, environments, and size are all treated as independent variables that are used simultaneously to predict revenues. An estimated multiple regression equation takes the typical form:

$$\hat{Y} = B_0 + B_1 X_1 + B_2 X_2 + \ldots + B_n X_n$$

The expected values of the dependent variable, $\hat{Y}$, are a linear (straight-line) additive combination of an organization's values on the n independent vari ables, X_i. Each B_i regression coefficient (slope) reveals how much two organizations are expected to differ on $\hat{Y}$ for a one-unit difference in X_i, controlling for (holding constant) all other independent variables in the equation. The numerical estimates of the regression coefficients are calculated from the observed values of the dependent and independent variables of the sample organizations. The estimation procedures use so-called least-squares methods, which minimize the sum of squared differences between the observed values of Y and the $\hat{Y}$ values estimated by the equation. The B_0(constant term) shows the value of $\hat{Y}$ expected if the values of all the predictor variables equal zero.

The equation above presents regression coefficients in ''unstandardized'' form. They show the amount a dependent variable is expected to change for a one-unit difference in an independent variable, where all variables are measured in metric units—such as dollars of revenue, years of age, or numbers of members. However, some variables are measured in arbitrary metrics, for example, derived from factor score transformations that render substantive interpretations of the B_i's problematic. Furthermore, comparisons of effects *across* different variables in the same equation are impossible when each is measured in differing units. A procedure that converts the B_i coefficients to ''standardized'' scales renders them comparable. An alternative regression equation form is:

$$\hat{y}=b_1{}^*x_1+b_2{}^*x_2+ \ . \ . \ . \ +b_n{}^*x_n$$

where y and x_i are now measured in standard deviation units of the original Y and X_i variables and the $b_i{}^*$ are ''standardized'' or beta coefficients. These are obtained by multiplying each B_i by the ratio of its X_i standard deviation to the Y standard deviation (this standardization also eliminates the need for the B_0 constant term). A $b_i{}^*$ represents how much of a standard deviation difference in y can be attributed to a one standard deviation difference in x_i. Direct comparisons of the magnitude of effects in this form are simple: the larger the $b_i{}^*$, the more important is that x_i in ''explaining'' variation in y, holding constant the other x_i effects.

Another important statistic associated with multiple regression coefficients is the significance level. Each B or b^* is based on sample data, which can be viewed as an estimate taken from a sampling distribution of possible coefficients from all other samples of the same size that could have been drawn from the organization population. Thus, a standard error for each coefficient can be calculated from the sample data. Dividing an estimated coefficient by its standard error gives a t-ratio. This ratio tests, at a given level of probability, one's confidence that the sample coefficient was not drawn from a sampling distribution whose population value is zero. For example, a t-ratio whose significance level is less than .01 means that in only one sample in a hundred would a sample statistic of this magnitude occur when the true population parameter is zero. This book does not report actual *t*-ratios, but asterisks (*) the regression estimates to indicate the probability levels for rejecting the null hypothesis.

A final multiple regression statistic is the R^2_{adj} (adjusted coefficient of determination, or multiple *R*-square). It indicates the proportion of variation in *Y* that can be attributed to ("explained by") the combined linear effects of all the independent variables in the equation. (The adjustment takes into account the number of independent variables relative to the sample size.) R^2_{adj} ranges between 0 (no predictive value to the equation) to 1.00 (perfect prediction). Thus, an R^2_{adj} of 0.10 means that one tenth of the variation in *Y* is (statistically) explained by the variation in the set of independent variables in the equation, but 90% remains unexplained. As with the *B* and *b** coefficients, a statistical test of the significance of R^2_{adj} (the *F*-test) is available to test the hypothesis that the true population value is zero. In this book, the values of R^2_{adj} are asterisked to indicate the probability levels at which the null hypothesis may be rejected.

Although the preceding overview of multiple regression features is necessarily cursory, special care will be taken in the following analyses to interpret the results in substantively meaningful ways. A little patience and effort at understanding these powerful statistical procedures will result in great theoretical benefits.

Revenue and Expenditure Effects

Table 5.4 shows a series of multiple regression equations in which the various budgetary category amounts as percentages of revenue or expenditure are the dependent variables. Because of the small numbers of organizations in each of the four main categories, separate analyses were not performed for these subtypes. To conserve space, only the standardized coefficients (*b**) are reported, thus permitting comparisons of variable effects within equations. The predictor variables in each equation are bureaucracy, two goal measures (public-policy influence and the societal change scale described above), two environmental information flow measures (uncertainty and complexity), and member size and total revenue, both values logged to reduce skewness. "External sources" of revenue refers to the sum of percentages of funds from nonmember contributors plus government and foundation grants and contracts.

In the estimated total dollar revenue equation (first column of Table 5.4), bureaucracy, member size, and policy influence goals each have highly significant coefficients. Altogether, these three independent variables account for more than half of the explained variation in total dollar (logged) revenue among the associations ($R^2_{adj} = .537$). The effect of bureaucracy on total reve-

Table 5.4. Standardized Coefficients for Multiple Regressions of Association Revenues and Expenditures on Organizational Characteristics

Independent variables	Total revenue (log)	Member dues revenue (%)	External sources revenue (%)	Member services expend. (%)	Info- PR expend. (%)	Lobby expend. (%)
Bureaucracy	.56***	−.11*	.17**	−.04	.27***	.02
Societal change goals	−.06	−.19***	.22***	−.08	.20***	−.02
Policy influence goals	.14***	.10*	.08	−.30***	.17***	.32***
Environmental complexity	.06	.11*	−.07	−.01	−.04	−.01
Environmental uncertainty	.00	−.03	.02	−.02	.04	−.01
Size (log)	.27***	−.02	.14**	.04	−.12*	.01
Revenue (log)	—	−.24***	−.11	−.04	−.19***	−.07
R^2_{adj}	.537***	.124***	.092***	.120***	.124***	.087***

*$p<.05$;
**$p<.01$;
***$p<.001$.

nue ($b^*=.56$) is twice that of logged member size ($b^*=.27$) and four times as large as policy influence goals ($b^*=.14$). Each of these coefficients are net effects; that is, they hold constant the linear additive effects of all other predictor variables in the regression equation. The standardization procedures allow interpretation predictor variable effects in terms of standard deviations, as explained in the previous section. Thus, two associations that differ by a standard deviation in bureaucratic structure are, on average, about .56 standard deviations apart in total revenue (logged dollar amounts).

The effects of a given predictor variable on the various budgetary decisions can be examined by comparing coefficients across equations. Although bureaucracy has a powerful impact on total revenues (as shown in Table 5.3), it has only modest effects on the percentages of revenues from member dues and external sources; in fact, the latter effect is found to be contingent on organizational goals. Bureaucracy substantially increases expenditures for information–public relations. Thus, many of the bivariate differences observed in Table 5.3 between the highly bureaucratic and nonbureaucratic associations diminish upon controlling for other factors. Societal change and policy influence goals both affect revenues and expenditures in generally expected directions. The more important that policy influence is to an association, the more total revenues it acquires, the larger the percentage that it spends on lobbying and information–public relations, and the less it spends on direct services to its members. In other words, organizational budgets are geared toward achieving ostensible external goals. Societal change goals, which need not involve governmental policy influence objectives (the two are correlated only .43), generally exhibit contrasting patterns. Societal-change oriented associations acquire fewer resources from member dues and more funds from external constituents, and they spend their funds on information–public relations, not on lobbying or member services.

The political economy theory in Chapter 3 hypothesized that collective action organizations' resource acquisition was related to external environments:

Proposition 1:   The richer the environment, the more discretionary resources there are available to a collective action organization's constituents and members.

Proposition 3:   Environmental uncertainty and complexity generate unstable flows of information to constituents and members.

In terms of the data and measures available in the National Association Study, the information-flow measures of environmental complexity and uncertainty and the revenue and membership measures as indicators of a resource-rich environment should each affect revenues and expenditures. However, neither the environmental complexity nor the uncertainty variable attains a significant net effect in most equations. Logged member size and total revenues produce only a few significant coefficients. More members mean greater total revenues (certainly true within organizations, but also between them as well, despite varying dues structures). The negative value for logged revenues in the dues equation suggests that associations operating in a richer environment tend to acquire a larger share of their funds from *nonmember* sources. In the external sources equation, the positive member-size effect suggests that external constituents may be more prone to contribute to larger groups, even taking into account those with societal change goals. Total revenues and member size both negatively predict information–public relations spending, suggesting that, with bureaucracy and goals held constant, the richer and larger associations are less likely to engage in such external publicizing of themselves.

The multivariate equations generally support the importance of bureaucracy and organizational goals for understanding budgetary decisions. The information-flow environments, at least as measured here, proved irrelevant. Except for the total revenue equation, the amount of variance explained in the dependent measures is disappointingly small, in the range of about one eighth of the total variation. Clearly, much room remains for specifying other factors that enter into resource management decisions. Before introducing some possibilities, the next subsection examines a conditional relationship of some interest.

Interaction Effects

The relationships examined in Table 5.4 are all additive. That is, the effects on budgetary decisions by one predictor, say policy goals, are specified as identical within every level of another predictor, such as bureaucracy. The additivity assumption may be reasonable for most instances, especially in the absence of a theoretical rationale for nonadditivity. Sometimes, though, the relationships among independent variables may be sufficiently complex that an additive equation conceals important effects that only an interaction specification can reveal. A careful examination of the combination of association goals and bureaucratic structures with external sources of revenue uncovered a significant set of conditional relations that appears to have substantive importance. Table 5.5 presents the basic finding in a cross-tabular format.

Bureaucracy, societal change goals, and policy influence goals were each dichotomized so that the high category contained a small number of cases. These three independent variables were then cross-tabulated, and the mean percentages of revenues from external sources was calculated for each of the eight cells. An analysis of variance found that bureaucracy significantly interacts with societal change goals ($F=20.5$, $df=1$, $p<.001$) and policy influence goals ($F=6.1$, $df=1$, $p<.01$) but the two goals do not interact ($F=2.1$, $df=1$, n.s.). However, all three independent variables interact to affect external revenue sources ($F=3.7$, $df=1$, $p=.05$). Although any multiway interaction is open to several alternative interpretations, a plausible one emphasizes the fol-

Table 5.5. Interaction of Bureaucracy, Societal Change Goals, and Policy Influence Goals on Percentage of Revenues from External Sources

	Societal change goals	
	Low	High
Low policy influence goals		
Bureaucratization		
High	15.4%	38.1%
(*N*)	(48)	(16)
Low	4.0%	1.6%
(*N*)	(125)	(24)
High policy influence goals		
Bureaucratization		
High	3.4%	21.5%
(*N*)	(42)	(44)
Low	7.6%	20.8%
(*N*)	(58)	(53)

lowing features in the table: among associations with slight interest in societal change goals, neither policy influence goals nor bureaucracy has much effect on the level of external revenue. Among associations with significant societal change goals, bureaucracy and policy influence goals have contrasting effects: bureaucracy increases the amount of external funding obtained by apolitical organizations (from 1.6 to 38.1%), but bureaucracy has little effect on external funding among political associations (20.8–21.5%).

These findings suggest that external funding sources may take their cues from the formal structure when deciding whether to support certain types of associations. In the presence of both strong social change and policy influence objectives, the facade of bureaucratic structure is unimportant. In the absence of both bureaucracy and policy goals, however, potential external sponsors seem unlikely to take seriously an association's proclaimed societal change agenda. Groups that do not reinforce their societal change goals with strong government influence efforts can still compensate by displaying a formal administrative structure that implies accountability and professionalism to potential funders. Money from outside sources is more readily provided to associations that present a bureaucratic face than to those that fail to back up their claims of societal change with an appropriate structure. Apparently, the "institutional myths" surrounding the bureaucratic form help to legitimate such societal change associations in external eyes (Meyer and Rowan 1977; Knoke and Wood 1981, pp. 130–31).

Member Contributions

This section reports the tests of two propositions from the political economy theory that relate the external environment to collective action organizations. The portions of Propositions 2 and 4 that refer to members can be tested with the membership data:

Proposition 2: When members and constituents control more discretionary resources, they increase their contributions to the organization.

Proposition 4: Unstable flows of information reduce member and constituent support for and contributions to the organization.

If Proposition 2 is correct, then members who have higher socioeconomic status are more likely to contribute larger amounts of money to their organizations than are the members with lower status. Similarly, if Proposition 4 is correct, then the members of organizations that operate in uncertain and complex environments are less likely to contribute money than are members of organizations with more stable environmental conditions. Both hypothesized

Table 5.6.   Multiple Regression Analysis of Member Money Contributions

Independent variables	Regression coefficients	
	B	*b**
Constant	131.9	—
Bureaucracy	49.2	.14***
Societal change goals	8.4	.01
Policy influence goals	−22.6	−.04*
Environmental complexity	−.6	.00
Environmental uncertainty	−47.1	−.08***
Years of membership	.8	.02
Family income	1.2	.10***
Occupational prestige	.6	.04**
Education	−14.0	−.09***
Gender	−22.3	−.04**
Age	−.1	−.01
R^2_{adj}	.033***	

*p<.05;
**p<.01;
***p<.001.

relationships can be tested by regressing the amount of money that members say they contributed to their organizations based upon personal and organizational characteristics. The questionnaire item asked: "During the past year, *about how much money* did you give altogether to the [Org. name] including dues and contributions?" Although this measure does not differentiate between required dues and additional voluntary donations, the sum total combines the member's willingness and ability to pay, especially as many professional associations assess larger fees according to their members' earnings.

Table 5.6 shows both the unstandardized and standardized coefficients from the regression of annual contributions on various personal and organizational independent variables. Although the total explained variance is meager (R^2_{adj} is only 3%), the individual coefficients support the two theoretical propositions. A member's annual family income has a strong positive effect on contributions: each thousand dollars of income increases giving by $1.20. This effect produces more than a fifty-dollar difference in annual giving between a member whose income is one standard deviation above the sample mean ($67,700 annual income) and one whose income falls a standard deviation below the mean ($21,500 per year). The occupational prestige effect is also positive, but less strong: the two-standard deviation difference results in only $20 difference in contributions. In contrast, holding everything constant, more highly educated persons are less prone to contribute money: persons with bachelor's degrees give nearly $36 more than persons with doctoral degrees.

The effects of the two environmental measures support Proposition 4. Although the negative coefficient for complexity is not statistically significant, that for uncertainty is highly significant. Collective action organizations whose environments are a standard deviation above the mean in uncertainty receive on average about $48 less per year from each member than those whose environments are a standard deviation below the mean uncertainty.

The strongest effect in the equation is that for bureaucracy ($b^* = .14$). In dollar terms, the most highly bureaucratic organizations receive $147.60 per year from each member, compared to only $49.20 for the least bureaucratic organizations, holding all other factors constant. Having political influence goals or female membership marginally reduces contributions. Neither personal age nor longevity of membership has any significant impact on annual giving.

Conclusion

Although these findings are based on cross-sectional data, they imply a possible sequential development in the revenue strategies of associations. In the early stages, associations are small, structurally undifferentiated, and heavily dependent upon their members for resources. Indeed, many originate as simple social movement organizations in which structural differentiation is minimal and membership control is substantial. The nascent organization may lack connections to the larger society, seeking to sustain purity by isolating itself from a larger pool of potential supporters. With growing membership size and heterogeneity and a consequent need for greater revenues, bureaucratic restructuring becomes essential. Conformism to the structure of a "responsible" formal organization may be genuine or a facade for other practices. In any event, a bureaucratic form conveys a message of professionalism and responsibility that may attract the attention of external constituents. It may predispose potential supporters to trust that association with resource contributions.

Association goals enter into the contributions process in a complex fashion. Nonpolitical associations attract substantial resources from external constituents when bureaucratic structure occurs in the presence of societal change goals. When associations combine strong interests in *both* public-policy influence and societal change goals, bureaucratic structure makes little difference to external funders. Contributions are substantial, compared to associations that lack societal change goals. Presumably, these divergent sponsor responses to association bureaucracy arise because different types of external sponsors are solicited. Unfortunately, the data do not provide enough detail on the identities of the associations' sponsors to test this proposition. This intriguing finding has an important implication for the public-policy paradigm discussed in Chapter 1. It suggests that organizations desiring to play in the policy influence game need not become bureaucratized in order to attract outside support. Rather, a convincing demonstration that the organization is committed to policy change goals seems to suffice, perhaps because savvy sponsors recognize that the new breed of lobbying depends much more on external visibility, political access, and constituency mobilization than on formal organization (Smith 1988, pp. 236–240). The main resource value of bureaucracy lies in internal integration: members are likely to give more money to a more bureaucratized association.

At the level of individual members' monetary contributions to their collective action organizations, both of the theoretical propositions involving personal resources and environmental stability were supported. The higher a member's annual family income and occupational standing, the greater his or her annual financial contribution to the association. However, men and less educated persons are more likely to give money, once their incomes are held constant. And the more uncertain the external environment within which the organization operates, the less money its members are likely to contribute. These relationships persist even when controlling for the effects of bureaucracy and goals on contributions.

These results enhance our understanding of the social integration paradigm. Persons who have more tend to give more, in line with numerous studies showing that people enjoying high status are more strongly involved in community activities. On the other hand, those with more education reduce their financial involvement, perhaps because they discern fewer merits to their organizations or because they spread their obligations among many competing activities. More information on the broader social contexts of members' lives would be helpful. The negative impact of environmental uncertainty suggests that associations are particularly vulnerable to their members' stinginess when great turbulence is perceived. Groups that create strong, dependable ties to the community reap the double benefit of strong financial support from their memberships and better conditions in which to pursue collective action goals. The trick, of course, is deciding how best to invest organizational resources to achieve these more predictable conditions.

6

ORGANIZATIONAL INCENTIVE SYSTEMS

Incentive systems are patterned transactions between members and their collective action organizations. These exchanges are supervised by the leaders acting in their roles as agents of the collectivity. The essential feature of an incentive system is an exchange of organizationally controlled values (material and symbolic) for individuals' resources, financial and participatory, that are needed by the association to pursue its collective goals. A central part of any association's internal economy is the structure through which leaders organize and coordinate the pooling of personal resources relinquished to the group by individual members. Leaders use some portion of the collective resources to provide either private- or public-good inducements of various kinds that will motivate these participants to continue supplying such resources to the organization.

Clark and Wilson (1961) classified incentives as material, purposive, or solidary in nature. Speculating in the absence of comparative data, they hypothesized that "few organizations can easily combine the three values (or three incentive systems)" (p. 240). However, associations are not inherently restricted to a single type of incentive and thus to only a single basis for inducing member participation. Several incentives may be offered simultaneously to attract new members as well as to maintain current supporters. Hence, fairly elaborate incentive systems may be constructed to appeal to a diverse range of association members and constituents. For example, the president of the Association of School Business Officials, a rapidly growing organization of 6000 members, wrote in the December 1983 issue of its *School Business Affairs* magazine that "this growth . . . tells us that ASBO membership is a high priority among school business officials due to the high quality of membership benefits and services.'' He went on to enumerate items such as an information referral service for employment opportunities, a dozen insurance plans, continuing education workshops around the country, professional certification and registries for three specialties, numerous publications, an annual meeting and exhibition featuring two graduate student scholarship awards, public relations liaisons with related national associations, peer consulting on research activities, low-cost travel, discounts for joining another management association, and recent testimony before the Internal Revenue Service that opposed pending code revisions detrimental to school districts. Every inducement probably does not appeal to each member of the ASBO.

The main purpose of this chapter is to test the theoretical propositions about organizational incentive systems presented in Chapter 3. As an analytic introduction to the empirical analyses, the next sections review individual motivations and organizational responses.

The Predisposition/Opportunity Framework

According to the individual decision-making model discussed in Chapter 2, members of associations may be motivated (predisposed to act to attain valued goals) by three general processes:

1. *Rational Choice.* Cost–benefit calculi that maximize the individual's expected utility.

2. *Affective Bonding.* Emotional attachments to the other persons and groups.

3. *Normative Conformity.* Adherence to standards of conduct grounded in socially instilled values about principled behavior.

These motivators are presumed to affect jointly basic decisions about an individual's involvement in collective action: whether to join an association, whether to remain a member, how much to participate in collective actions, and what amount of personal resources should be contributed to the collectivity. The initial assumption is that each component independently affects these behavioral decisions. The greater the magnitude of a person's predisposition toward each type of motive, the higher the probability of his or her involvement in the organization. To attract resources from members, collective action organizations offer three types of incentives based on these motives in varying combinations. Utilitarian services appeal to persons' rational choice motives, social/recreational activities elicit involvement on the basis of affective bonding, and public policy influence efforts (lobbying) attract persons with strong normative conformity predispositions. Although Clark and Wilson (1961, p. 240) asserted that "few organizations can easily combine the three values (or three incentive systems)," they offered no systematic empirical evidence that organizational incentive systems exist only as pure types. Knoke and Wright-Isak (1982, p. 234) identified seven distinct systems, ranging from single-benefit types (such as the utilitarian services provided by the American Automobile Association) to systems that provide substantial amounts of all three types (such as utopian communes; see Kanter 1972 and Zablocki 1980). In the absence of systematic comparative data, a simple classification of incentive systems according to their relative mixture of utilitarian, normative, and affective inducements should suffice to guide initial research efforts.

Collective action organizations operate their incentive systems in both prospective and reactive ways. Prospectively, associations seek to manipulate deliberately the factors that enter into members' and potential members' or donors' decisions, so as to convince them to relinquish control over personal resources for collective use in return for the benefits of various combinations of incentives (Browne 1976). Several entrepreneurial accounts of association creation stressed the alleged promotional efforts of organization founders. A leader scouts for "customers" to whom she can sell "shares" in the association's activities, from which the leader can reap a "profit" in the form of private goods, such as status and the perks of office (Salisbury 1969; Frohlich *et al.* 1971; Riker and Ordeshook 1973, pp. 75–77). The enterprising leader seeks to shape members' perceptions of the benefits they will gain through participation, thereby convincing them to make contributions they otherwise might not make. Reactively, associations also respond to changing demands by members for different mixes of incentives. Such demands may come from changing interests among current members, or through the recruitment of new participants holding different "tastes" for public and private goods. For example, a social movement organization that initially survived on promises of legislative concessions may discover that it must now offer social and recreational activities if it is to hold on to its membership once the public goods program is accomplished (see Messinger 1955).

A strong covariation is expected between organizational incentives offered and member resources contributed, as each component of the economic system reinforces the other. The greater the amount and variety of "visible, valued, and utilized" incentives (Burgess and Conway 1973, p. 36) that an organization offers to its members and constituents, the greater the total volume and per capita amounts of personally controlled resources the participants will relinquish to collective control. Systems that provide multiple types of incentives will attract and retain a wider variety of resource contributions from a broader range of participants than will systems that are built on a narrower set of incentives. These relations presume that the types of benefits offered are congruent with the potential contributors' interests in these inducements. Obviously, if an organization advertises incentives for which little demand exists, very few contributions can be expected. However, when an association's incentives are highly valued, then the greater the amounts offered, the larger will be the total amount of resources acquired by the organization.

To some degree, the relationship between member interests and organizational incentives is reciprocal: the more resources an association collectively controls, the greater the amount (or value) of incentives and the greater the variety of incentives it can offer to attract contributions from potential supporters. Thus, wealthier associations should tend to have more elaborate incentives and to extract greater contributions from a more diverse set of participants. Poorer associations must perforce provide more meager inducements, relying more heavily upon the less costly normative incentives (see Piven and Cloward's [1977] account of the demise of the National Welfare Rights Organization).

Substantial covariation should occur between an organization's incentive offerings and its membership's needs, dispositions, and resources. A mismatch between supply and demand may disrupt the association's internal economy and render it unable to achieve its collective goals. Evidence for a basic congruence between organizational incentives and member interest in benefits, at least among well-functioning associations, can be found in surveys of economic associations (Moe 1980, 208–209), social influence associations (Knoke and Wood 1981, pp. 50–69), a professional medical society (Cafferata 1979), and the American Agricultural Movement (Cigler and Hansen 1983). The congruence should also be evident in matches between members' interests in specific kinds of incentives and their contributions. Members whose interests center around utilitarian incentives (services) will contribute mainly financial resources to the organization, but avoid participation or deep psychological attachments to the group. Members with high interest in affective (social and recreational) inducements will respond with high rates of internal participation that involve interpersonal contacts, such as meetings and projects. Members with strong interests in public goods incentives (normative principles and lobbying) will engage in higher levels of external political actions, such as collective efforts to influence public-policy makers. These congruence propositions are expected to hold across all kinds of collective action associations. They are *ceteris paribus* relationships, which should persist even after controlling for individual and organizational differences on other factors.

The more complex an organization's incentive systems, the greater the proportion of its aggregated resources that must be channeled into maintaining and operating the systems. Complex systems may target different organizational functions with special incentives (for example, salaries and wages for leaders, normative inducements for activist cadres, and social benefits for ordinary members). Greater complexity in incentive systems typically requires creation of specialized positions to perform these functions, such as advertising and public relations, client and member servicing, information collation and dissemination (by means of a newsletter or magazine staff), and social affairs arrangements. Association leaders find themselves increasingly engaged in daily incentive management decisions, which may absorb the bulk of their energies. Consequently, the more complex an association's incentive systems, the smaller the share of collective resources allocated to other goal attainment activities such as legitimation and policy influence efforts. At one extreme can be found the organization whose sole rationale has become the nurture of its incentive systems to the exclusion of all other objectives.

To achieve the covariation between incentive offerings and resource acquisition at the organization level, some value-added transformations are necessary. Association leaders perform this important task as managers of the incentive systems. The dues collected from members are not simply paid out again to the members, in hopes that they will continue to make additional monetary and other contributions. Instead, leaders use some portion of the pooled dues to create enticing new forms of services or goods, such as workshops and seminars, slick-paper magazines, picnics and social mixers, a lobbyist's testimony before a congressional subcommittee. Thus, the internal economy of an organization can be viewed as a structure through which leaders organize and coordinate the acquisition of personally controlled resources from individual participants. They use some portion of these collective resources to provide either private- or public-good incentives of various types that will motivate these participants to continue supplying such resources to the association.

The three basic types of incentives are not equally efficacious in binding participants' loyalties to the organization. Normative incentives are generally inferior to comparable amounts of utilitarian or affective inducements. Normative conformity motivations tend to be factors over which an association can seldom achieve monopolistic control. The formation of values and standards held by individuals is subject to many external social forces, such as family socialization, peer influence, professional criteria, and mass media. People who are strongly motivated by basic value commitments, for example by women's equality or by pro-life principles, often see organizations only as convenient vehicles for promoting a cause. When a more attractive means for normative expression comes along, obligations to a specific organization are easily severed. Splits and splinters are common among "cause" organizations.

In contrast, utilitarian benefits and affective bonds are more contingent on members' continued involvement in a specific collective action organization. That is, utilitarian and affective incentives generally have a selective nature, thus allowing an organization to restrict their enjoyment to participants in good standing. For example, insurance plans and close friendships are "side bets"(Becker 1960) that are staked upon a person's continued involvement in the particular association that provides them, in a way that normative rewards derived from expressing global values are not. Therefore, utilitarian and affective incentive programs should more strongly bind participants to an organization and will call forth larger amounts of resource contributions for collective use. As managers of the incentive systems, leaders will prefer where possible to use utilitarian and affective inducements rather than normative incentives, because the latter generate smaller returns. For national associations, then, the creation of local chapters that provide settings for face-to-face interaction among members may be an essential step in creating affective inducements. Over any organization's lifetime, incentive systems tend to move from a pure- to a mixed-incentive type, resulting in a corresponding increase in the heterogeneity of member motivations to contribute (Cigler and Hansen 1983). Mixed-incentive systems probably have greater longevity and survival value for an association (Knoke and Wright-Isak 1982, p. 245; Knoke and Adams 1987).

Incentive Systems and Organization Goals

Considerable congruence is anticipated between the predominant organization goals and the character of its incentive systems. When goals are primarily oriented around direct services to members, the incentive systems will emphasize utilitarian and affective inducements. When goals concentrate on public legitimation and policy influence, the incentive systems will rely more heavily on normative inducements. Such tendencies do not preclude the emergence of hybrid structures; for example, an organization that offers utilitarian or affective incentives to members in order to obtain collective resources that will then be applied to public-policy influence goals in which the members have little interest. Some trade unions do this. A notable example is the United Automobile Workers under the Reuthers, which held social amelioration goals for nonmembers (the poor and minorities) that had little appeal to the rank-and-file, who were interested in personal benefits through collective bargaining. Even in such cases, however, a collective action organization must satisfy the direct service demands of its members before it can allocate some surplus portion of the collective resources to goals that have limited appeal to its contributors.

Etzioni's (1975) treatise on organizational compliance posited that social order is most feasible when the power used by superiors and the orientation of subordinates to that power are compatible. His concept of compliance is very similar to incentive systems, as it combines both social structural and motivational elements (Etzioni 1975, p. xv). He argued that "organizations that have similar goals tend to have similar compliance structures," because "certain combinations of compliance and goals are more effective than others"(p. 103). In Etzioni's compliance typology, order goals are most congruent with coercive structures (prisons, armies), economic goals with utilitarian structures (production corporations), and cultural goals with normative structures (universities, voluntary associations). Other goal/structure combinations are unstable and tend to change toward one of the three congruent combinations. Etzioni's hypothesis embraces all kinds of organizations, whereas the National Association Study was restricted to collective action organizations, which Etzioni had entirely subsumed under the "normative compliance structure" classification (pp. 41–44). However, considerable variation in both goals and incentive systems remains within the American national association population.

By extending Etzioni's concepts, the types of incentives offered to induce member involvement will systematically differ according to the types of goals sought by the organization. Goals and incentives will covary in a direct fashion. For example, when the goals are predominantly oriented around members' social lives, social incentives will be emphasized. Associations with goals of helping nonmembers will tend to induce participation by stressing normative or altruistic incentives. When an association tries to improve the material wellbeing of its members—such as by boosting their incomes—a utilitarian-based incentive system is more likely to develop.

The theoretical literature is unclear about the emergence of heterogeneous incentive systems. Organizations may offer their members a variety of additional incentives, such as those listed above for the ASBO, which may be unrelated to and hence not congruent with their primary purposes and goals. For example, an association may offer utilitarian incentives to members in order to obtain collective resources, which it then uses to pursue public-policy influence goals about which members have little concern. Or, a fraternal group whose avowed purpose is to serve the affective needs of its members may also encourage participation by offering low-cost insurance packages. In these examples, utilitarian incentives are compatible with a wide variety of other formal goals. The possibility of heterogeneous incentive systems should not obscure the fundamental tendency: organizations will organize their incentives in ways that are congruent with their basic goals.

The preceding considerations set the stage for empirical analyses of collective action incentive systems in this chapter and the next. Tests of the relevant theoretical propositions from Chapter 3 require measures at both the organizational and individual member levels. The NAS, with data on incentives from collective action organization informants and from association members, offers the best opportunity to date for such assessments.

The Structure of Incentives

Toward the middle of the interview, each association leader was read a list of 16 kinds of incentives available to members and was asked "how important you believe [each] item is as an inducement to your members." The informant was instructed to respond "extremely important, very important, somewhat important, or not important, or your organization does not offer this type of incentive." These response choices were scored from 4 to 0, respectively. Table 6.1 shows the results of a principal components factor analysis performed on this set of incentives and also the percentage of organizations that rated each item as extremely or very important.

Briefly, the purpose of factor analysis is to reduce a set of items to a smaller number of underlying, latent variables (factors) that account for the total pattern of observed correlations among these sixteen indicators of incentive offerings. The factor solution tells how many dimensions are necessary to reproduce the correlation matrix; whether there is a single "general incentive" dimension or multiple specialized dimensions; the relative importance of each factor in contributing to total variation in the measures; and, through use of factor scales, what items to include in constructing multi-item measures for use in substantive analyses. The factoring method used in this book transforms a large set of observed measures into a smaller set of factors that are obliquely related (allowed to be correlated with one another). The solution is then rotated to a new set of axes (varimax rotation), which offers the clearest substantive interpretation of the latent factors. For more information about factor analysis, see Kim and Mueller (1979a, 1979b).

Using the sixteen items about incentives offered by the organizations, five significant factors emerged. Every incentive item loaded highly on only one factor (except for social/recreational activities). The larger the magnitude of the coefficients for items on a particular factor, the more that factor is defined by the substantive contents of those measures (see Marradi 1981). For example, the four items with high loadings on the first factor (.30 or greater) suggest that that factor taps associations' provision of selective utilitarian benefits to members. Although an oblique solution was used, none of the factors were highly intercorrelated (the largest $r = -.24$).

The first factor is clearly a utilitarian incentive dimension composed of private-goods benefits for members, such as group insurance, travel plans, purchasing or marketing opportunities, and certification or licensing programs run by the association. The second factor reflects primarily information and data produced by the organization for its members. The third factor taps a normative incentive construct that combines purposes, goals, prestige, and altruism with tax deductible contributions as inducements for member involvement. The fourth factor is the political dimension, consisting of lobbying

Table 6.1. Pattern Loadings From Principal Components Factor Analysis (oblique rotation) of Incentives for 459 Associations

Factors	I	II	III	IV	V	Important (%)
Utilitarian incentives scale						
Offering group travel plans	.69	−.15	.11	.06	−.10	4.2
Offering group insurance plans	.59	.10	.06	−.05	−.08	6.5
Offering group purchasing or marketing opportunities	.43	.07	−.11	−.08	.10	5.5
Running certification or licensing programs	.41	.02	.09	−.11	.06	17.6
Information incentives scale						
Sponsoring research activities	.00	−.81	.01	−.14	−.19	47.2
Providing information or data services	.11	−.53	−.03	−.08	.06	42.5
Publishing newsletters, magazines, journals	−.11	−.49	.01	.11	.15	77.9
Normative incentives scale						
Emphasizing main principles and goals of the org.	−.05	−.08	.55	−.01	−.01	88.5
Trying to change the lives of non-members	.02	−.01	.52	−.06	−.16	37.6
Stressing the general prestige of the organization	−.01	.03	.51	−.08	.19	82.8
Contributions to the organization are tax-deductible	−.10	.06	.41	.09	.04	35.9
Lobbying incentives scale						
Lobbying governments to influence legislation	.01	.01	.01	−.50	.08	18.7
Representing members in organization negotiations	.15	−.16	−.04	−.61	.03	27.0
Occupational incentives scale						
Providing professional or business contact opportunities	.01	.00	.08	−.20	.55	50.8
Running seminars, conferences, and workshops	.01	−.21	.25	−.01	.37	69.4
Social incentives scale						
Offering social or recreational activities	.19	−.07	−.12	.10	.15	19.7
Eigenvalues	2.76	1.76	1.71	1.18	1.09	
Variance (%)	17.3	11.0	10.7	7.4	6.8	

governments and representing members in contract negotiations. The fifth factor combines business-professional contacts with various face-to-face organizational activities, possibly another form of utilitarian incentive. The only incentive indicator that did not load highly on any factor was the ''social and recreational activities'' item, intended as a measure of affective inducement. It comprises a single-item sixth dimension. Six incentive scales were constructed based on the factor analysis, by averaging an organization's values on those items that loaded highly on each factor (with the social/recreational item as a singleton scale).

The expected consistency between organizational incentive systems and goals can be examined with the NAS organization-level measures:

Proposition 7:   Organizational incentive systems are constrained to be congruent with organizational goals.

That is, goals and incentives cannot deviate greatly from one another without producing untenable strains on the organization, as discussed in Chapter 3. If this proposition is correct, specific types of goals will significantly predict corresponding types of incentives used by associations to attract members. Each of the six incentive scales was regressed upon a set of explanatory variables, whose resulting standardized coefficients are shown in Table 6.2. The independent variables include: eight organization goals (discussed in Chapter 4); five dichotomous or ''dummy'' variables representing type of organization (only four are entered into the regressions, to avoid linear dependency); and various indicators of organizational structure that might be presumed to affect the provision of incentives—membership size, total revenue (both logged to reduce skewness), age, bureaucracy, and environmental uncertainty and complexity (See Chapter 4).

Some support for the congruence proposition appears in every equation, with different types of association goals having significant regression coefficients, even after controlling for the effects of other association characteristics. For example, in the first equation of Table 6.2, the significant .36 coefficient for research and education goals means that associations which espouse these objectives are more likely to offer informational inducements to their members than are groups which do not stress such goals. Trade associations are less likely (−.15) and recreational organizations are more likely (.15) than professional, labor union, and other organizations to offer information inducements. (In each equation, the regression coefficients for the four included dummy variables are net effects from the omitted category, ''other organizations.'') Organizations that rely upon informational incentives are more likely to be younger (−.18), to have more total revenue (.17), be more bureaucratized (.13), and to have fewer members (−.16).

Table 6.2. Standardized Coefficients from Multiple Regression Analyses of Association Incentive Scales

Independent variables	Dependent variable scales					
	Info.	Lobby	Business	Utilit.	Normat.	Social
Organization goals						
Member income	.09	.17**	−.03	.09*	−.07	−.01
Research and education	.36***	−.02	.21***	−.07	−.12*	.10*
Member status	.01	−.04	.16*	−.01	.04	−.03
Member social lives	.03	.10*	.02	.20**	−.08	.43**
Member cultural lives	−.04	−.13**	−.02	−.05	−.11	.01
Lives of Nonmembers	−.04	−.01	.06	.02	.25***	.01
Change values of society	.00	−.03	.01	.02	.13*	−.07
Influence public policies	.11	.47***	.10	.12	.07	.12*
Organization type:						
Trade association	−.15*	.08	.17*	.16*	−.06	.16*
Professional society	.02	.12*	.16**	.22***	−.01	.03
Labor unions	−.01	.13**	−.04	.06	.00	−.04
Recreational associations	.15**	.09*	−.07	.14*	−.07	.10
Other associations	—	—	—	—	—	—
Membership size (log)	−.16*	−.05	−.09	−.06	.06	.09
Total revenues (log)	.17*	.02	.11	.21**	.06	−.09
Organization age	−.18***	−.04	−.03	.06	.13*	−.05
Bureaucracy	.13*	.02	.06	−.07	−.06	.19**
Environmental uncertainty	−.04	−.15***	−.14**	.01	−.08	−.04
Environmental complexity	−.09	.19***	.03	−.04	−.04	.05
Multiple R^2_{adj}	.239***	.435***	.232***	.129***	.156***	.201***

*$p<.05$;
**$p<.01$;
***$p<.001$.

Similar congruent relations occur in the other five equations of Table 6.2. Use of lobbying incentives is most prevalent in associations whose goals include efforts to influence public policies (.47), to improve members' incomes and economic conditions (.17), and to develop their social or recreational lives (.10), but not their cultural/artistic lives (−.13). Business contacts are major inducements in organizations that have research/education (.21) and raising members' status and prestige (.16) as important objectives. Utilitarian incentives are used mainly by associations that stress income (.09) and social goals (.20). The normative inducements are most common among groups that hold altruistic goals of helping nonmembers (.25) and changing societal values (.13), but eschew research/education goals (−.12). Finally, the use of social-recreational inducements is clearly a mainstay among associations that maintain social and recreational objectives (.43), but also, to a much lesser degree, among groups with research/education (.10) and public-policy influence goals (.12).

The overall pattern suggests that several types of goals are compatible with diverse incentive offerings. This finding indicates a more complex relationship than the theoretical literature had anticipated. The covariances between societal and policy influence measures are the most striking instances of such cross-modalities: social groups lobby and lobbying groups socialize. Still, the predominant result is the fundamental congruence between goals and inducements. These congruent relationships are robust in the presence of various controls for association attributes.

An Empirical Incentive Typology

The preceding regression analysis separately examined each of the six types of incentives offered by organizations. But organizations may offer inducements in various combinations, despite Clark and Wilson's (1961) assertion that such multiplex systems are rare. To test their hypothesis, three of the factor analytic dimensions were used to construct an empirical classification system, based on the theoretical importance of utilitarian, normative, and affective motives and incentives discussed above and in Chapters 2 and 3. Each association was classified into three dichotomies, according to whether it used or did not use social, utilitarian, or normative incentives. An association was categorized as using social incentives if it reported that social/recreational incentives are important inducements to its members (i.e., somewhat, very, or extremely important). Because of the extreme skewness of some items comprising the utilitarian and normative scales (see Table 6.1), different criteria were used to dichotomize these scales. A utilitarian incentive system requires that at least one of the four inducements be considered important, while a normative incentive system requires that all four normative inducements be important.

By completely crossing these social, utilitarian, and normative dichotomies, an eightfold classification was created, with the distributions among NAS sample organizations shown in Table 6.3. These systems are arranged from simple to complex. Only 6.9% of all associations fail to use any incentives, while 29.9% offer only a single kind of inducement. Thus, a majority of associations use combinations, with 27.6% offering all three kinds of incentives. These results refute Clark and Wilson's contention that most organizations cannot readily offer more than one type of incentive. Distinct profiles emerge across the four major types of organizations. For example, unions and recreational clubs are more likely to combine all three types of incentives, while professional societies and trade associations are twice as likely to provide only normative inducements. Clearly, the substantive type of association has some bearing on the selection of an incentive system, but a more thorough analysis requires the inclusion of additional explanatory variables. [See Knoke and Adams (1987) for a discriminant analysis of these data that relates incentive system types to specific goals.]

Four theoretical propositions in Chapter 3 assert that various factors create a more diverse incentive system:

Proposition 8: The more heterogeneous an organization's goals, the more diverse its incentive system.

Table 6.3. Percentage Distributions of Organizational Incentive Systems by Type of Association

Incentive systems	Frequency distributions (%)				
	All assns.	Labor unions	Trade assns.	Prof'l assns.	Rec'l assns.
None	6.9	5.3	6.0	6.7	7.3
Utilitarian only	5.5	10.5	5.0	5.8	4.9
Normative only	18.4	10.5	20.0	24.0	11.4
Social only	6.0	0.0	6.0	4.8	8.9
Normative and utilitarian	16.1	29.8	16.0	25.0	4.9
Social and utilitarian	4.6	1.8	5.0	1.0	10.6
Normative and social	14.9	8.8	18.0	3.8	20.3
All three incentives	27.6	33.3	24.0	28.8	31.7
Total	100.0	100.0	100.0	100.0	100.0
(*N*)	(435)	(57)	(100)	(104)	(121)

Proposition 9:   The greater the environmental complexity and uncertainty, the
                   more diverse an organization's incentive system.

Proposition 10:   A more bureaucratic administrative structure operates a more
                   diverse incentive system.

Proposition 11:   The more resources an organization controls, the more diverse
                   its incentive system.

If these expectations are correct, then a multiple regression analysis that includes measures for each of these concepts would result in significant positive
coefficients for each variable in the equation. The environmental uncertainty
and complexity measures and the bureaucracy variable are the same as used
previously. Goal diversity is measured by the number of organizational goals,
from zero to 8, that are considered of "moderate" or "major" importance
(see Chapter 4). Two resource measures are the annual organization revenues
and the number of members, both logged to reduce skewness. Finally, incentive system diversity counts the number of social, utilitarian, and normative
dichotomies (from 0 to 3) in which the organization was in the high category.

Table 6.4 displays two regression equations, the first using the goal diversity measure and the second replacing it with measures of three specific goals.
Although neither measure of environmental conditions has a significant net
relationship with incentive system diversity, the results support the other three
propositions. Both bureaucratic administration and larger membership size increase incentive system diversity by small amounts. By far the most important
effect is goal diversity: the larger the number of important goals pursued by an
association, the more diverse is the incentive system it operates. Using the
unstandardized regression coefficients, we can calculate that two collective action organizations that are one standard deviation above and below the sample
mean on goal diversity will differ on average by one level in their incentive
systems (i.e., one association will offer only a single type of incentive and the
other will offer two. In the second equation in Table 6.4, the societal change
goal (an average of changing public values and affecting nonmembers' lives),
the government policy influence goal, and especially the social-recreational
goal are all significantly related to increased incentive system diversity. Indeed, organizations that differ by two standard deviations in their social-
recreational goals would differ by almost one and one half levels of incentive
system diversity.

Conclusion

Almost every collective action organization offers its members some kinds
of inducements. Contrary to Clark and Wilson's speculations, a majority of

Table 6.4.   Multiple Regression Analysis of Incentive System
Diversity

Independent Variables	Regression Coefficients			
	B	b*	B	b*
Constant	.25	—	.07	—
Bureaucracy	.30	.10*	.26	.09
Annual revenues (log)	−.04	−.04	.04	.03
Membership size (log)	.15	.13**	.10	.09*
Environmental complexity	.20	.05	.28	.06
Environmental uncertainty	.05	.01	−.05	−.01
Goal diversity	.25	.20***	–	–
Societal change goals	—	—	.20	.08*
Policy influence goals	—	—	.19	.10*
Social-recreational goals	—	—	.74	.31***
R^2_{adj}		.066***		.154***

$*p<.05$;
$**p<.01$;
$***p<.001$.

associations combine two or more distinct sets of utilitarian, normative, or social incentives. Specific kinds of incentives covary with corresponding organizational goals. Organizations with social/recreational goals not only rely on social and recreational inducements, but also offer utilitarian and lobbying incentives. Groups with research/education objectives provide not only information to attract members, but also business contacts and social/recreational benefits. Even groups in which lobbying governments to change public policies is a main goal make use of some social activities to induce member support. Clearly, the patterns of goal-incentive relationships are more complex than the simple one-to-one correspondence implied by Etzioni and by Clark and Wilson. The most important implication of these results are for the social integration paradigm. Humans are complex social beings whose interests and needs span wide ranges of motivation. To compete successfully with family and jobs for a share of potential members' attention and resources, collective action organizations have had to offer diverse incentives. Reliance on one type of inducement would condemn an organization to attracting only weakly attached individuals. By offering numerous benefits, an organization can proliferate members' points of involvement to the extent that disengagement becomes materially costly, emotionally disruptive, and normatively unsettling. The more multi-stranded the web of inducements an organization spins, the more tightly it can bind its members to the collective enterprise.

A central proposition—that incentive systems tend to be congruent with the official goals of an association—was generally supported by the regression analyses. A set of propositions that relate incentive system diversity to various environmental and organizational factors were only partially upheld. The most important factor in the diversity of incentive offerings seems to be the diversity of goals sought by an organization. Social/recreational objectives are especially strong predictors of diverse incentive systems. The results reported in this chapter all refer to the organization level of analysis. The corresponding relationship of members' interest in and responsiveness to these incentives are the subject of the next chapter.

7

MEMBER INTEREST IN INCENTIVES

In *The Functions of the Executive,* Chester Barnard, then president of the New Jersey Bell Telephone Company, presented one of the earliest and still most useful theories of the motivational bases for employee acceptance of organizational goals. He described a complex "economy of incentives" consisting of both objective and subjective inducements specific to individuals (material rewards and nonmaterial benefits, such as prestige), and general incentives primarily of an interpersonal nature. Barnard recognized that different people are motivated by different types of incentives or combinations, and that their interests vary over time due to changing environments. He argued that organizations "are probably never able to offer *all* the incentives that move men to cooperative effort, and are usually unable to offer adequate incentives" (1947, p. 149). Hence, an organization must try to change people's desires through "persuasion" (including coercion, rationalization, and socialization), so that the incentives it *can* offer are sufficient to obtain employees' efforts and contributions.

> It will be evident . . . that in every type of organization, for whatever purpose, several incentives are necessary, and some degree of persuasion likewise, in order to secure and maintain the contributions to organization that are required. It will also be clear that, excepting in rare instances, the difficulties of securing the means of offering incentives, of avoiding conflict of incentives, and of making effective persuasive efforts, are inherently great; and that the determination of the precise combination of incentives and of persuasion that will be both effective and feasible is a matter of great delicacy (Barnard 1947, p. 158).

The key proposition in Barnard's incentive theory is that, in the long run, organizational inducements must equal participants' contributions if the collectivity is to survive (p. 160). Failure to achieve a "workable balance" of income and outgo for more than short periods ultimately generates inefficiencies that destroy the organization. March and Simon succinctly summarized Barnard's principle:

> Each participant will continue his participation in the organization only so long as the inducements offered to him are as great or greater (measured in terms of his values and in terms of the alternatives open to him) than the contributions he is asked to make (1958, p. 84).

An organization's incentive economy thus involves exchanges of valued goods, services, and symbolic values between individuals and the collectivity. The diversity of incentives offered by the organization must correspond to individuals' interests in these benefits if the organization is to secure collective control over adequate amounts of resources. The research implication of Barnard's theory is that a collective action organization member's contributions to the group are a function of the member's receptivity to the available organizational incentives. The precise configurations that match inducements to interests should vary greatly, both between and within collective action organizations.

The system of incentives at the organization level of analysis, examined in Chapter 6, reveal great heterogeneity in the National Association Study sample. The present chapter investigates individual members' interests in these inducements, expanding on analyses first presented in Knoke (1988). Because people's motives for joining an organization may differ from their motives for remaining and participating, an effort is made to distinguish between these processes despite the obvious limits of cross-sectional data. The central focus of the analysis is the relationship between organizational inducements and member interests, and their effects on member contributions to the collectivity.

Motives for Joining and Contributing

Members express many motives for joining a collective action organization. Once involved, they may discover other reasons for continuing to contribute their time, money, and effort. The ideal study of these shifting bases of affiliation would track a sample of participants across time, including people who dropped out of the organization. Unfortunately use of a cross-sectional sample of members restricts analyses of motivational stability to retrospective reports by current members. Due to space limitations on the questionnaire, members were asked about only six reasons for joining, using three response categories: unimportant, minor reason, major reason. Respondents were free to choose all applicable reasons. For the entire sample, the motive most frequently cited was "joined for job-related reasons"(45% major reason), followed by "direct services offered to members by the organization"(35%), "lobbying or political activities of the organization"(21%), "social or recreational activities among the members"(19%), "expected to join by other people"(9%), and "membership was a gift from a relative or friend"(2%).

Members' motivations for joining are not distributed randomly across types of collective action organizations. An association's purposes may shape its members' motivations for involvement, both through the constituency it attracts and through subsequent persuasion effects, as Barnard described. A crucial distinction is made in this book between associations that have explicit policy influence goals and those for whom such objectives are less important. In the NAS membership study, 15 organizations' informants considered that attempts to influence public-policy decisions were a major organizational goal. Among the 15 highly political organizations, 14 "sometimes" or "frequently" made their positions on policy issues known to the federal government, but only four of the 20 less political groups did so. Further, the leaders of 13 of these 15 highly political associations felt that "lobbying to influence government legislation and regulation" was a "somewhat important" to an "extremely important" incentive for their members, while only 3 of the 20 leaders of the less political association considered lobbying incentives that important.

Are the informants' perceptions of the differential importance of lobbying incentives reflected in their members' interests? Among the 4399 NAS sample members of the 15 highly political organizations, lobbying or political activity was cited as a major reason to join by 35%, compared to only 6% among the 4347 sample members of the 20 less political organizations. By contrast, a majority of members (53%) in the less political organizations gave job-related motives as their major reason for joining, compared to only 37% of the persons belonging to the 15 highly political associations. Social activities and direct services were about equally important reasons for members joining both types of organizations.

With time and experience, members may discover reasons for contributing resources to their organizations other than those that motivated their original affiliations. In a later section of the questionnaire, members indicated the current importance of various considerations "in your decision about how much to contribute personally to the [org. name]." They checked a four-point scale, ranging from "not important" to "major importance," for each of six items. For the entire sample, the three most frequently chosen reasons were normative or altruistic responses: "My contributions help to advance the knowledge available to all members of the profession/organization''(63% indicated major or moderate importance); ''contributing one's share to the organization is the fair and equitable thing to do''(58%); and ''my contributions help to shape future directions of the profession/organization''(53%). Receiving the lowest endorsements were: ''my contributions provide me with personal benefits, in the form of services offered by the organization''(44%); ''my contributions help the organization to influence government decisions''(43%); and ''contributing is a good way to improve my professional career''(31%). Apparently, members view their current contributions of time, money, and effort as a means of furthering primarily broad collective ends, rather than as a way to derive direct personal gains. Benefits in the form of direct services or career advancement may not appear sufficiently legitimate reasons for many members to justify their involvement in a collective action organization.

Association political goals also affect membership contributions. Members of the highly political organizations were more than twice as likely to cite governmental influence activities as important, compared to members of the less political organizations (60 to 27%, respectively). However, as in reasons for joining, the less political association members were somewhat more likely to cite direct services and career benefits among their important reasons for deciding to contribute.

How stable are members' motives for joining and contributing resources? Although continuity may be elevated by reliance on fallible recall measures, the covariations in Table 7.1 between three pairs of comparable items suggest substantial persistence. Each row summarizes a bivariate relationship, showing the percentage of persons citing a current reason for contributing, within a given level of importance for joining. The stability of political motivations is especially remarkable. Among members who did not join because of the orga-

Table 7.1. Reasons Members Joined and Reasons for Continuing to Contribute (Percentage Indicating Major or Moderate Importance)[a]

	Reason for joining			
	Unimportant (%)	Minor (%)	Major (%)	r
Joined for job-related reasons and contributions help career	8	32	49	.47
Joined for direct services and contributions provide personal benefits	22	41	67	.42
Joined for lobbying activity and contributions help influence government	23	53	84	.54

[a] Cell frequencies vary; total N = 8746.

nization's lobbying activities, only 23% now feel that influencing government policy is important to them; but among those for whom lobbying was a major reason to join, 84% currently cite that as an important reason to contribute. Direct services and job benefits also exhibit large covariations between original and current reasons for organizational involvement. However, these robust patterns are not definitive evidence that members' motivations remain substantially stable over time. Only a longitudinal study will reveal whether people's original impulses for affiliation undergo changes during their involvement in collective action organizations. Until such time as a panel study is conducted, the present results remain suggestive at best.

Measuring Member Interest in Incentives

Although a few prior theoretical speculations can be found, no one has attempted to measure the structure of members' incentive evaluations across a large number of collective action organizations. Chapter 6 analyzed informants' reports about 16 types of inducements offered to members of their 459 associations. The NAS membership survey of 35 professional, recreational, and women's organizations included most of those incentive items and added a dozen others, to fill in details about the underlying incentive dimensions. Members were told the following:

> Organizations offer their members various kinds of incentives. *How important are each of the* following organizational activities to you personally as a member of [org. name]? If an activity is not performed at present by the [org. name], just leave it unanswered and go on to the next item.

The response categories ranged from "extremely important" to "not important" and were scored from 4 to 1, with 0 indicating that the item was not checked.

The members' responses to 23 incentive items were factor analyzed using the principal components method and oblique rotation. The 6-factor result is reported in Table 7.2 (no pair of factors correlated higher than $+.31$). Despite the additional items, the members' factor structure is remarkably similar to the leaders' structure (compare with Table 6.1). Of the 14 items common to both data sets, only three loaded highly on different factors. "Seminars, conferences, and workshops" appeared with three information incentives items in the members' analysis, but was an Occupational Incentives factor in the organizations' analysis. "Trying to change the lives of nonmembers" and "Representing members' interests in negotiations with other organizations" switched locations: in the members' analysis they loaded highly on the Lobbying and

Table 7.2. Pattern Loadings from Principal Components Factor Analysis (Oblique Rotation) of Incentives for 8746 Members of 35 Associations

Factors	I	II	III	IV	V	VI	% Important
Normative incentives scale							
Enhancing the public status of profession/org.[a]	.73	−.02	−.27	−.01	.03	.03	21
Educating general public about profession/org.[a]	.61	.07	.08	.22	.25	.06	59
Stressing the general prestige of the org.	.65	.30	−.03	.06	−.10	−.06	33
Representing members in organization negotiations	.49	−.06	−.23	.09	−.03	−.29	18
Emphasizing main principles and goals of the org.	.40	.23	.17	.30	.26	.10	54
Social incentives scale							
Offering social or recreational activities	.01	.83	.15	−.06	.02	−.14	22
Giving opportunities to form friendships[a]	.12	.80	−.07	−.07	.06	.13	37
Enhancing members' cultural or artistic lives[a]	−.03	.63	−.11	.03	−.04	−.14	11
Occupational incentives scale							
Helping members with job searches[a]	−.08	.04	−.82	.06	.12	−.01	34
Providing professional or business contact opportunities	.20	−.00	−.77	−.12	.09	.06	37
Trying to improve members' incomes, economic conditions[a]	.04	.01	−.62	.22	−.01	−.18	29

						h^2
Lobbying incentives scale						
Lobbying governments to influence legislation	.11	-.22	.06	.76	.14	-.08	48
Trying to change the lives of nonmembers	-.07	.18	-.16	.67	-.15	.15	15
Trying to change values and beliefs of the public[a]	.22	-.04	.03	.65	.17	.07	54
Endorsing candidates for public office[a]	-.02	-.03	-.09	.70	-.14	-.23	16
Conducting public relations or information programs[a]	.40	.07	.13	.43	.23	.01	47
Information incentives scale						
Publishing newsletters, magazines, journals	.09	-.08	-.03	-.22	.78	.02	68
Providing information or data services	-.07	.09	-.05	.05	.67	-.24	56
Sponsoring research activities	-.14	.07	-.18	.29	.55	-.03	46
Running seminars, conferences, and workshops	.22	.10	-.30	.01	.47	.19	59
Utilitarian incentives scale						
Offering group insurance plans	-.01	.05	.06	.05	.11	-.79	12
Offering group purchasing or marketing opportunities	-.05	.27	-.11	.01	.05	-.66	15
Running certification or licensing programs	.46	-.02	-.17	-.11	-.07	-.52	22
Eigenvalues	6.4	2.11	1.67	1.76	1.13	1.05	
Variance (%)	28.0	9.2	7.2	7.2	4.9	4.6	
Scale reliability (Cronbach's alpha)	.79	.67	.75	.77	.65	.63	

[a] Items not included in leader's data set (see Table 6.1).

Normative Incentives dimensions, in contrast to their high loadings in the organizations' analysis on the Normative and Lobbying dimensions. Several differences in the two data sets could readily account for the divergent factor patterns: the organizations sample involved a broader range of organization types (notably, including trade associations and labor unions); only one informant per organization was queried in each leader interview, but hundreds of members responded to each organization's questionnaire; and, while leaders were asked for the perceptions of how much interest *other persons* have in organizational inducements, members were asked to report their *own* interests in those inducements. Given these operational differences, the great similarities in factor results are indeed striking.

The six factors emerging in the member incentives analysis exemplify the public/private good distinction (see Chapter 2 for an extended discussion). Four dimensions tap primarily selective goods or services available only to persons within the organization's boundaries: (1) Utilitarian incentives consist of material commodities such as insurance plans, marketing and purchasing opportunities, and certification or licensing programs. (2) Information incentives take the form of publications, data services, and research. (3) Occupational incentives, particularly relevant for professional societies and unions, involve help with job searches, business-professional networking, and efforts to improve job conditions and incomes. (4) Social incentives involve social or recreational activities, including friendship opportunities and cultural or artistic endeavors.

The other two factors measure incentives that are more broadly focused on public or collective goods whose benefits may be shared by nonmembers: (5) Lobbying incentives most notably include efforts to influence government policy decisions, as well as to affect nonmembers and the general public. (6) Normative incentives combine "emphasizing the main principles and goals of the organization" with improving the prestige and status of the profession or the organization, as well as its image held by the public at large. As noted above, two items shifted loadings across the data sets between the normative and lobbying incentives factors, perhaps because of their substantive similarities to both of these public-goods dimensions.

The degree of congruence, or consistency, between leaders' and members' evaluations of organizational incentives can be examined further by correlating the 14 importance ratings across the 35 associations common to both data sets. The higher the correlation, the greater the agreement of the leaders' and members' evaluations. Table 7.3 shows the bivariate correlations between the mean importance in an organization's membership sample and the importance attributed by its leader to the same incentive. Only about half the items produced substantial covariation: affecting nonmembers, certification-licensing, lobby-

Table 7.3. Correlations Between Leaders' and Members' Evaluations
of the Importance of 14 Incentives (*N* = 35 Organizations)

Trying to change the lives of nonmembers	.68***
Running certification and licensing programs	.67***
Lobbying governments to influence legislation	.66***
Offering group insurance plans	.66***
Providing professional or business contacts	.53**
Publishing newsletters, magazines, or journals	.49**
Running seminars, conferences, and workshops	.47**
Offering group purchasing or marketing	.37*
Offering social or recreational opportunities	.33*
Stressing the general prestige of the org.	.13
Providing information or data services	.12
Sponsoring research activities	.06
Representing members in negotiations	.05
Emphasizing main org'l principles and goals	−.10

***$p<.001$;
**$p<.01$;
*$p<.05$.

ing, group insurance plans, professional-business contacts, publications, and seminars-workshops. Five incentives did not covary significantly, suggesting that the leaders incorrectly perceived their importance for their memberships: research, information and data services, organizational negotiations, organizational general prestige, and the main goals and purposes of the group. Neither public- nor private-good incentive items seemed especially prone to higher or lower congruence.

Some of the mismatches may arise because leaders were expressing wishes that members would appreciate these values more highly than they actually do. A substantial part of the slippage between leaders' and members' evaluations may stem from such differences between intentions and impacts. Although leaders may set up a system of inducements designed to attract lower-level participants, the members may discover other, unintended benefits that bind their interest more tightly. A good example is social and recreational activity. Many leaders may not fully appreciate the extent to which interpersonal relations reinforce the formal purposes of an organization, whether these goals are occupational or public goods in nature. The low agreement of leaders and members about several types of incentives underscores the necessity to distinguish between the sources of evaluation in organizational research. Many projects follow the less costly route of relying upon a single person or a handful of key informants for data about important organizational characteristics. If the present findings can be credited, the reliability of leaders' reports about members' interests may be frightfully low. If the purpose of a research project is to understand collective behavior, there may be no good substitute for the costly and time-consuming collection of data directly from large numbers of participants.

Interests in Multiple Incentives

Chapter 6 examined Clark and Wilson's (1961) hypothesis that organizations specialize in a single type of inducement. The evidence from the informants' sample indicates that the majority of collective action organizations offer two or more types of incentives. This section examines the incentive specialization hypothesis from the individual members' viewpoints. If Clark and Wilson are correct, members of a collective action organization should confine their interest to only one type of incentive, rather than express high levels of interest in several kinds. From the political economy theory in Chapter 3 comes a cross-level proposition that links complexity in organizational incentive systems to diversity of member incentive interests, in contradiction to the Clark-Wilson hypothesis:

> *Proposition 12:*   Organizations that operate more complex incentive systems attract members with heterogeneous interests in incentives.

As discussed in Chapter 2, the multivariate model of individual motivation assumes that many members bring a variety of concerns with them. An association that offers diverse selective and public goods is likely to appeal simultaneously to the various rational, normative, and affective bases of individual decision making. Hence, a parallel between organizational complexity and individual complexity can be anticipated. Specifically, if Proposition 12 is correct, then associations that offer many inducements will have memberships with higher levels of expressed interests in many types of incentives.

To test this proposition, the 35 NAS organizations were classified according to the complexity of their incentive systems, using the scheme shown in Table 6.3: the association offers none, one, two, or all three types of utilitarian, normative, and social inducements. To measure member incentive interest heterogeneity, a simple count was made of the number of incentives out of 28 kinds in which the respondent expressed either an "extremely important" or "very important" level of interest. The mean for all members was 10.01 incentives, with a standard deviation of 5.76. These values reveal a wide range of incentive preferences among members, and strongly refute Clark and Wilson's notion of narrow incentive attraction.

Table 7.4 exhibits the results of an analysis of covariance of member incentive heterogeneity, using organizational incentive system complexity as the categoric (treatment) variable and organizational political, social change, and social-recreational goals as the covariates (see Namboodiri *et al.* 1975, pp. 339–343). As expected, those organizations with the least complex incentive systems attract members having interests in fewer incentives. However, the most heterogeneous members belong to associations that offer two rather than three kinds of benefits. Post hoc comparisons of means disclosed that a significant difference in member heterogeneity was located between the two least and the two most complex incentive systems, thus supporting the theoretical expectations. This pattern persists in Table 7.4 even after controlling for the three goal covariates. Organizations that pursue societal change or public policy influence goals attract with heterogeneous incentive interests, but social-recreational goals lure persons with much narrower interests. However, the small R^2 implies that most of the variation in member incentive interests is unaccounted for by these four independent variables.

The Lobbying-Services Trade-Off

In the preceding analyses, the sample of collective action organizations was treated as homogeneous. That is, the relationships among variables were assumed to be identical among members of all types of organizations, thus per-

Table 7.4. Analysis of Covariance for Member Incentive Interest Heterogeneity ($N = 8746$)

Independent Variables	Unadjusted	Adjusted
Mean	10.01	10.01
Incentive system complexity		
None offered	−1.40***	−0.89***
One offered	−0.30	−0.48
Two offered	0.67***	0.74***
Three offered	0.30	0.20
Organizational goals		
Societal change	—	0.54***
Public policy influence	—	0.27**
Social-recreational	—	−0.16*
R^2_{adj}	0.013***	0.028***

***$p<.001$;
**$p<.01$;
*$p<.05$.

mitting their aggregation into a single data set for analysis. This section considers whether members of different types of organizations behave differently in regard to incentives. In particular, the 15 collective action organizations in which public-policy influence goals are a major objective are compared to the 20 associations where such goals are not central.

Following Moe (1980), the membership questionnaires posed two hypothetical questions about the trade-off between lobbying and services:

1. Suppose the (org. name) were to stop offering services to its members and only engage in lobbying the government on public policies? What would be your likely reaction?

2. Now suppose that the (org. name) only offered services to its members and did not attempt to lobby the government on public policies. What would be your likely reaction?

Two choices were offered: "I would probably drop out" and "I would probably remain a member." (Fewer than 5% of the respondents did not answer both items, and they are excluded from this analysis.) The joint distribution of these two items, shown in Table 7.5, permits a classification into four types of respondents, revealing the relative salience of services and lobbying in members' calculi of loyalty to the organization. The organizations' degree of politicization is strongly related to the members' responses. Services predominate among the less political associations (70% would stay if only services were offered, compared to only 34% for the highly political groups). Lobbying is substantially more important among the highly political members, 21% of whom would stay if only lobbying were available, compared to only 2% of the less political respondents. The highly political organizations also seem to attract persons with greater intrinsic loyalty, to judge by the one third who claimed they would remain even if *neither* type of incentive were continued, while just 5% of the less political members avowed such commitment.

Table 7.5. Responses to Hypothetical Choice Between Services and Lobbying

Respondent would	Highly political organizations	Less political organizations	All orgs.
Stay if only services offered (%)	34	70	52
Stay if only lobbying offered (%)	21	2	12
Stay only if both offered (%)	10	23	7
Stay even if neither offered (%)	35	5	29
Total	100	100	100
(*N*)	(4190)	(4153)	(8343)

If the frequencies underlying the percentages in Table 7.5 are treated as a 2×2 cross tabulation, odds ratios can be calculated that reveal the extent to which members are willing to trade off services and lobbying efforts. Among the highly political organizations, this odds ratio is 2.13, while for the less political associations it is 1.65. Thus, although the members of both types of groups threaten to drop out over the loss of one type of incentive but promise to stay despite the loss of another kind, the effect is more than 25% greater (the ratio of odds ratio =1.29) for the highly political members (A log-linear model testing whether the lobbying-services relationship is identical within both types of organizations produced a likelihood ratio chi-square of 1398.6 for $df=3$, leading to clear rejection.) This interaction effect implies that members of highly political collective action organizations hold a distinctly different structure of attitudes than less political organization members about the importance of direct services and lobbying.

Incentives and Contributions

The final analysis concerns the impact of organizational incentives on members' willingness to contribute personal resources to the collectivity. The political economy theory contains three propositions asserting that individual interests and organizational incentives are related to giving:

Proposition 13: The more intensely a person values an incentive offered by a collective action organization, the greater the contribution that person will make to the organization in order to receive the incentive.

Proposition 14: Organizations that operate diverse incentive systems acquire larger contributions and stronger support from their members than those who do not offer diverse incentives.

Proposition 15: The stronger the congruence between member incentive interests and organization incentive offerings, the higher the membership support and resource contributions.

The two measures of member resource contributions are the amount of money given to the organization during the past year (logged to reduce skewness), and the average number of hours that the member devotes to the association each month. For the sample as a whole, the average amount of money given in a year was $82; the mean monthly time given was 3.25 hours. However, the variation across types of organizations was enormous. Members of recreational organizations with major political goals annually gave $166 (about 5% claimed to have given $3,000 or more), while less political recreational groups averaged only $50 per member. Similarly, the greatest amount of time was given by members of politically oriented women's and recreational groups (4.3 hours per month), and the least was given by members of professional societies, both those with high political goals (2.05 hours) and those with less political objectives (2.3 hours).

A test of Proposition 13 requires measures of member incentive interests. Six scales were computed based on the factor analyses of Table 7.2. Average responses to a factor's items were calculated, using response codes 0 if not checked, 1 if "not important," 2 if "somewhat important," 3 if "very important," and 4 if "extremely important." Scale items were not weighted according to their factor loadings, as equal weights make no substantial difference in the measures (Alwin 1973). If Proposition 13 is correct, a member who attaches greater importance to any of the six types of incentives will give more time or money to the group. No expectations are stated about which of these six inducements is likely to produce greater effects.

To test Proposition 14, the four-level measure described above was used. If the proposition is correct, the members of organizations that offer a wider variety of inducements will contribute more of their time and money to the association. Using a business analogy, organizations that provide more goods and services are able to charge their "customers" a higher price for the value received.

Proposition 15 requires a comparison of organizational incentives and individual interests. An incongruence index was created by (a) subtracting a member's interest in a specific incentive from the organizational informant's report for the same item; (b) squaring this difference to remove the signed value; and (c) averaging the discrepancies across five basic types of incentives (purposes; prestige; social-recreational; nonmember lives; and lobbying incentives). Thus, a high score indicates a greater average divergence (either above or below) between the member and his or her organization, while a low score shows greater congruence. If Proposition 15 is correct, an inverse relationship occurs between the incentive incongruence index and the amount of time or money given to the organization. That is, persons whose interests in incentives depart considerably from the incentive level reported by the informant will be less likely to contribute resources than persons whose interests more closely match the association's emphasis on those incentives.

The three propositions were tested simultaneously in multiple regression analyses, performed separately for the members of highly political and less political organizations. Tables 7.6 and 7.7 display relevant portions of the estimated equations, which included membership size to test Olson's hypothesis that people in small groups are more likely to pay for collective goods (Olson 1965, pp. 34–35). Although no equation explains a large proportion of the variance, those for the highly political organizations fare better than those for the less political. Of the six types of member incentive interests, the social and normative incentives consistently support the theoretical expectation: the more importance a member attaches to these two types of inducements, the greater his or her money and time contributions. The unstandardized coefficients (B) indicate that normative incentives have stronger effects in the highly political than in the less political organizations. Social-recreational incentive interests have roughly the same impact in both types of associations.

Most of the other incentives have mostly either nonsignificant or inverse relations. That is, the greater a member's interests in occupational, informational, or lobbying inducements, the *less* her or his money or temporal contribution. Material incentives exhibit a consistent interaction across the two types of organizations: they increase the resource contributions of members in less political associations but decrease money or time spent by the members of highly political organizations. Thus, Proposition 12 should be modified to assert that higher member interest in normative and social incentives (and to a lesser degree, material incentives) generates larger resource contributions to the collectivity.

Contrary to expectations, incentive system diversity is inversely related to member contributions in all four equations (although significantly in only two equations). That is, organizations that provide more utilitarian, normative,

Table 7.6. Multiple Regression Analysis of Logged Money Contributions on Member Incentive Interests and Other Variables[a]

Independent variables	Regression coefficients			
	Highly political		Less political	
	B	$b*$	B	$b*$
Member incentive interests				
Normative	0.13	0.05*	0.08	0.03
Social-recreational	0.21	0.08***	0.18	0.07***
Lobbying	−0.14	−0.05***	0.14	0.04*
Material	−0.14	−0.01	0.14	0.05**
Occupational	−0.22	−0.10**	−0.12	−0.05*
Informational	0.17	0.06**	−0.10	−0.04*
Incentive system diversity	−0.04	−0.02	−0.13	−0.07***
Member-org. incongruence	−0.11	−0.08***	−0.13	−0.09***
Member size (000's)	0.0002	−0.33***	−0.005	−0.07*
R^2_{adj}	0.166***		0.092***	
(N)	(4399)		(4347)	

[a] Other variables in equation are gender, education, income, age, years of membership, environmental uncertainty and complexity, bureaucracy, political goals, social change goals, social-recreational goals, diversity of member incentive interests.

*$p<.05$;
**$p<.01$;
***$p<.001$.

and social inducements actually received *less* money and time from their members. Associations that specialize in fewer types of benefits are more successful in extracting contributions, once members' incentive interests and other variables are taken into account. Members of recreational associations, which tend to offer only social inducements, give more of their time and money to their groups than do members of professional societies and women's organizations, which tend to have more diverse incentive systems. As the equations in Tables 7.6 and 7.7 divulge, controlling for a variety of personal and organizational factors does not eliminate this fundamentally negative relationship. Hence, Proposition 13 must be rejected in favor of the conclusion that associations which specialize in their incentive offerings generate greater amounts of members' time and money for their collective use.

The regression coefficients for member-organization incongruence support Proposition 15 for financial donations but not for time contributions. In both highly and less political associations, the greater the average discrepancy between members' interest and organizational importance of incentives, the smaller the amount of money given. The effects are about the same among the highly and the less political associations. Finally, the effects of membership

Table 7.7. Multiple Regression Analysis of Hours of Work Contributed on Member Incentive Interests and Other Variables[a]

Independent variables	Regression coefficients			
	Highly political		Less political	
	B	b*	B	b*
Member incentive interests				
Normative	2.40	0.13***	1.11	.05*
Social-recreational	1.58	0.09***	1.40	.06**
Lobbying	−1.46	−0.08***	−0.20	−.01
Material	−1.09	−0.05**	1.00	.04*
Occupational	−0.67	−0.05*	−0.52	−.03
Informational	0.35	0.02	−1.25	−.05*
Incentive system diversity	−0.98	−0.07***	−0.40	−.03
Member-org. incongruence	−0.04	0.00	−0.11	−.01
Member size (000's)	−0.0004	−0.09**	0.0003	.00
R^2_{adj}	0.066***		0.011***	
(N)	(4339)		(4347)	

[a] Other variables in equation are gender, education, income, age, years of membership, environmental uncertainty and complexity, bureaucracy, political goals, social change goals, social-recreational goals, diversity of member incentive interests.
   *$p<.05$;
   **$p<.01$;
   ***$p<.001$.

size support Olson's hypothesis: members of large organizations are less likely to contribute financial resources, and members of highly political associations are less likely to contribute their time.

Conclusion

The results of these analyses, coupled with those from Chapter 6, leave little doubt that organizational incentives are central to association members' interests in their collective action organizations. Both leaders and members converge on six distinct dimensions underlying incentive systems, and these different aspects are specifically related to member contributions. Members' reasons for joining and continuing to contribute to their associations remain fairly constant over time, if their retrospective reports are to be believed. Both occupational and altruistic motivations carry considerable weight in members' affiliation decisions, while social and public-policy influence considerations are less prevalent (although the latter are more so among members of highly political organizations). Interests in multiple incentives are widespread among members, paralleling organizational systems that offer a variety of inducements. A modest tendency occurs for complex incentive systems to attract members with more heterogeneous incentive interests.

In terms of incentives' effects on member contributions, complex incentive systems actually generate smaller time and money contributions than more specialized systems, contrary to expectations. However, support was found for two propositions asserting that larger contributions occur when members' interests are congruent with organizational incentive offerings, and when members attach high levels of importance to specific types of incentives. Normative and social inducements are especially potent in garnering resources from members of all kinds of organizations. However, material incentives raised contributions only within less political organizations, and reduced contributions by members of highly political associations.

These results qualify the "by-product" or selective incentive explanation of collective action, as formulated more than two decades ago by Mancur Olson (1965). His theoretical model, premised on microeconomic assumptions about rational cost–benefit calculations, requires substantial private-good incentives to overcome the tendency of public goods to induce free-ride taking. The NAS results, on the other hand, reveal that several selective benefits (occupational, informational, and material) tend to attract apathetic members. Public goods, in the form of normative inducements, are among the strongest factors motivating member contributions. These patterns are consistent with evidence from several case studies and experiments (see Chapter 2) suggesting that equity concerns, fairness principles, and altruistic norms regarding the well-being of others (including nonmembers) are exceptionally powerful social forces shaping the collective action decisions of individuals. The only Olsonian hypothesis receiving strong support is his prediction that members of small organizations are more likely to contribute resources to the group.

Members' decision making can be characterized as a wholly rational choice process only by stretching that concept to the point where it accommodates everything—and therefore explains nothing. Some analysts wish to integrate public-good inducements into the economic self-interest model by arguing that "purposive benefits can also serve as selective incentives"(Moe 1980, p. 118). This transformation allegedly occurs when people derive personal satisfaction from expressing their support for a group by the very act of contributing [see a similar *ad hoc* effort by Riker and Ordeshook (1973, pp. 62–69) to explain observe high voting rates by adding a civic-duty or "voting per se" term to an equation that otherwise predicts nonvoting as the rational actor's decision]. By torturing the logic of rational choice enough, one can dilute the concept beyond any possibility of constructing empirical tests capable of falsifying its predictions. Thus, normative inducements could be redefined as selective incentives equivalent to magazines, insurance plans, picnics, and other private goods. This effort to rescue the by-product explanation of collective action by interpreting all types of incentives as "ultimately" selective in nature is indefensible. Either social behaviors are entirely self-interestedly rational by fiat, or some actions must be acknowledged as a product of member motivations that simply cannot be reduced to cost–benefit calculi of personal advantage. From the evidence of 35 collective action organizations, at least some significant proportions of their memberships respond strongly to inducements that have few, if any, private-good components. While much remains to be investigated about the conditions under which members' decisions are reached, the centrality of noneconomic, public-good incentives cannot be denied.

These results bear most heavily on the paradigm of social integration. The cross-level effects reveal that organizations are most effective in persuading their members to support the group financially when they match incentive offerings with the members' incentive demands. Incongruence between supply and demand provokes the withdrawal of contributions from members of all kinds of associations. Normative and social-recreational benefits in particular, are the most potent inducements for involving members in the collectivity. Least important, even counterproductive, are public-goods inducements of lobbying and selective incentives such as occupational and informational benefits, although material incentives seem to be positively beneficial for members of less political organizations. A complete picture of organizations' political economies requires examination of aspects of association governance, the subject of the next chapter.

PART IV

ORGANIZATIONAL POLITY

8

ASSOCIATION GOVERNANCE

Collective action organizations continually engage in policy-making activities—setting salient goals, choosing among alternative priorities, allocating collective resources to various purposes, mobilizing group participation in strategic and tactical actions. How they make these choices, who is involved in them, and their implications for the organizations all reveal significant aspects of associations' polities. The characteristic set of arrangements for making collectively binding decisions about fundamental policies comprises an organizational polity's governance structure. The question of governance—the unequal distribution of power and its consequences—is important in shaping what organizations do and who benefits from the choices they make (Pfeffer 1978, p. 4). This chapter examines two basic dimensions of power that shape organizational governance. The first is constitutional authority, the formal relationships and procedures that stipulate the decision-making responsibilities held by various organizational participants. The second component is influence, which concerns the actual distributions of internal organizational control that emerge from the ongoing decision-making processes.

Although constitutional authority and influence are analytically distinct dimensions of governance, they may covary to some degree in actuality. Their common underlying element is the degree of involvement of association members in policy-making activities. Two ideal-typical governance structures indicate the extreme fusions of authority and influence. In an autocratic governance structure, all influence and authority resides with a single person or very small subgroup. The oligarchs run the organization in complete disregard to the interests and preferences of the majority (Benson 1986, p. 324). Neither the memberships' indifference nor its opposition to the elite's control carries any weight. Its only choice is to remain loyal or to exit (Hirschman 1970). At the other extreme lies the radical democratic governance structure. Both constitutional authority and actual influence over policy-making rest in the unanimous involvement of the entire rank and file. Democratic association leaders serve as agents for the collectivity, carrying out actions decided directly by the membership (Knoke 1981b, pp. 277–81). The relative control of leaders and members contrasts starkly between these two types of organizations:

> Autocracy and totalitarianism are similar and emphasize procedural due process because power is centralized and used to control members. Such governance designs use technical rationality as the primary criterion for participation and have externally oriented control systems. Governance systems using democracy and federalism are more decentralized, use participation to achieve substantive due process, and require more self-control from members (Jennergren 1981, p. 148).

To identify autocracy and democracy as polar ideal-typical governance structures implies that most empirical organizations fall somewhere in between. Constitutional structures designate greater formal authority to some positions than to others. However, the actual distribution of influence may or may not conform to the constitutional authority design. Diverse interest groups within the membership contend for control over the outcomes of collective decisions. Dominant coalitions manage temporarily to mobilize sufficient resources to prevail and to impose their policy preferences on the entire organization. The coincidence of authority and influence is necessarily partial and subject to continuous change. At any time, governance structures reflect the ongoing struggles among organization participants to shape collective decisions.

Governance structures are also shaped by the constraints and opportunities posed by external environments within which organizations and their subunits operate. Open systems theories in the organizational and managerial sciences assert strong connections between environments and internal structures. The structural and strategic contingency approaches argue that organization structures, including governance, tend toward congruence with environmental contexts (Lawrence and Lorsch 1967; Child 1972; Galbraith 1977; Zey-Ferrell 1981; Hsu *et al.* 1983). Ecosystems that offer organizations rich, diverse resources permit more elaborate internal division of labor, vertical hierarchy, and coordination of functions (Bidwell and Kasarda 1985). Factors such as technology, uncertainty, complexity, interorganizational dependency, and resource fields define ecological niches that favor the selection of specific internal structures, including influence and authority configurations (McKelvey and Aldrich 1983). Because external conditions vary so greatly among organizations, a wide range of governance structures results.

An alternative cultural institutionalization perspective suggests a much looser coupling between formal structure and technical activities, arising from an organization's conformity to ritually defined meanings and categories supplied by its environment (Meyer and Rowan 1977; DiMaggio and Powell 1983; Zucker 1983). Environments include widespread belief systems about rules for conduct and action that organizations are rewarded for adopting. To the extent that organizations become isomorphic with their cultural environments, they gain the requisite legitimacy and resources for their survival. The rationalization of modern society, so compellingly noted in Weber's analysis of bureaucracy, increasingly imposes a homogeneous structural design among organizations in an institutional environment, regardless of their actual efficiencies. Thus, the prevalence of particular authority and influence arrangements within organizations discloses the effects of a dominant institutional thought structure in the larger culture. In contrast to the structural contingency hypothesis, which asserts that varied governance structures are imposed by diverse external environments, the cultural institutional perspective implies that homogeneous governance structures result from a pervasive cultural context.

This chapter examines governance designs in American collective action organizations and explores the relationship between governance and other organizational and environmental forces. The next section offers an analytic discussion of the key conceptual components of organizational governance.

Power: Authority and Influence

Organizational governance structures consist of two basic forms of patterned social relations among participants: authority and influence. These components involve analytically distinct dimensions of social power. Following Bertrand Russell, Wrong defined power as "the capacity of some persons to produce intended and foreseen effects on others" (Wrong 1979, p. 2). Notably absent here is Weber's notion that power operates mainly in oppositional situations:

> In general we understand by 'power' the chance of a man or a number of men to realize their own will even against the resistance of others who are participating in the action (Weber 1968, vol. 2, p. 926).

The broader Russell-Wrong definition acknowledges that in many circumstances, intended effects arise not by coercive domination but through the willing assent and cooperation of people whose actions are directed and coordinated by others. That concept is especially useful in studying collective action organizations, because they require primarily cooperative voluntary participation and lack coercive means to compel members' compliance. Thus, the Russell-Wrong concept of power captures the potential for social reciprocity that is obscured in Weber's implicitly asymmetrical notion of power as primarily domination. Although domination of one social actor over another is useful for many types of analysis, the concept of influence as the ability of one actor to alter the perceptions of another is more appropriate for present purposes (see Knoke 1990 for an extended discussion of differences between influence and domination).

Constitutional Authority

Authority is a form of power that involves explicit recognition by all participants of the propriety of the arrangement. Authority is premised on participants' mutuality and consent, unlike other forms of power, such as force and manipulation.

> Legitimate authority is a power relation in which the power holder possesses an acknowledged right to command and the power subject an acknowledged obligation to obey (Wrong 1979, p. 49).

Legitimacy depends on a consensus about norms and beliefs held by association members that the distribution of power and its exercise by designated power wielders are acceptable and appropriate (Pfeffer 1981, p. 5; Scott 1987, p. 286). Legitimated power *is* authority. Authority in social relationships presupposes shared norms that prescribe obedience to instructions within limits irrespective of the content of the commands. Thus, a subordinate's compliance with an authority-holder's commands may be regarded as a special case of normative conformity. As discussed in Chapter 2, motivations based on conformity to normative standards require neither a cost–benefit calculus nor an emotional bonding between social actors.

In an organizational governance structure, the authority component is created through constitutionally stipulated systems of roles and the rules for their enactment. Once established, a constitutional order specifies sanctions for violations of its provisions, but the primary basis of participant compliance is belief in its legitimacy, not the threat of sanctions. The authority structure specifies the positions that possess legitimate powers and the procedures that allow the exercise of their authority. It specifies processes for selecting incumbents to fill these positions and for regulating their behaviors in these roles. Without a stable authority structure, an organization remains vulnerable to continual power struggles among its participants for control over collective resources and policy decisions. Leaders become unable to lead effectively and members are unwilling to provide political support for the regime. A stable authority structure provides explicit due process mechanisms, both substantive and procedural, by which consensus may be achieved and consequent binding decisions reached and implemented (Scott *et al.* 1981).

Influence Distribution

The second component of a governance structure is the actual distribution of influence among organization participants. Apart from incumbency in formal authority positions, association leaders and members differ in the extent to which they try to shape the outcome of collective decisions. Although a constitution might stipulate that rank-and-file members must ultimately sanction collective policies, the actual practice may diverge markedly. In one organization an inner circle of leaders conducts its affairs without outside consultations. In another leaders take great pains to ensure that its members' wishes become known and respected in policy affairs. Thus, an influence structure exposes power in action. An association has a decentralized influence structure to the extent that decision making is delegated or dispersed among its members, rather than concentrated in relatively few hands. In others words, centralized associations exhibit greater intraorganizational inequalities in policy influence, while decentralized associations practice greater equality in decision making.

For work organizations, the centralized-decentralized distinction refers to the hierarchical levels of authority within which decisions are concentrated (Jennergren 1981, p. 39). Because the employment contract imposes clear superior-subordinate relationships among managers and employees, this vertical dimension of decision-making influence is relatively easy to identify. However, the prevailing democratic ideology minimizes vertical authority distinctions in associations. Members are neither employees nor subordinates of the leaders. Indeed, at least formally, leaders received their authority to act as agents of the organization from those being governed. To speak of influence as concentrated at higher or lower levels of an associations's authority hierarchy is misleading. Instead, decentralization refers to the dispersal of influence over decisions throughout the entire organization, without regard to vertical distinctions among organizational roles. This equilibration of decentralization with extensive decision making is consistent with definitions provided by Price and Mueller (1986), Hage (1965), and Pennings (1976).

What is the expected relationship between these two basic components of organizational governance structure, the authority structure and the influence distribution? In corporations and government bureaus, an isomorphism generally prevails: the amount of influence increases the higher the position in the formal authority hierarchy. In several studies of work organizations, using a "control graph" technique discussed below, Tannenbaum (1968) repeatedly found that the higher authority positions in various types of organizations were imputed to have greater influence over policies. Boards of directors and managers were substantially more likely to affect the corporation's decisions than production line workers, although the magnitude of the influence differences was not constant across different firms (see also Tannenbaum *et al.* 1974, pp. 58–62). In contrast, a study of 112 branches of the League of Women Voters of the United States disclosed that members were rated more influential than leaders in one eighth of the leagues. These branches obtained more loyalty and activity from their members (Tannenbaum 1968, pp. 199–211). The League puts into practice an exceptionally democratic ideology. Through elaborate constitutional safeguards, the League begins formulating national policy positions and priorities within its local branches. State and national leaders are strongly constrained by prevailing norms to adhere to policy preferences forwarded by the rank-and-file members (McFarland 1976).

Differences of influence between authority positions may be less important for organizational performance than is the cumulative amount of influence over internal decisions among all organizational participants. The participative systems of management identified by the human relations school (Likert 1967) pointed to mutual dependence between higher and lower authority positions. When leaders interact and communicate often with members, welcome opinions and suggestions, and encourage influence efforts, an association forms a highly integrated, tightly knit social system. All participants are more receptive to mutual influence, with their total influence exercised on behalf of the organization's collective objectives.

> The effective, participative organization is likely to be characterized by influential leaders *and* members, by a high *total amount* of control, contrary to stereotypes that assume participation to be a vaguely permissive or laissez-faire system (Tannenbaum *et al.* 1974, p. 195).

Total influence was found to be more important than influence differentials in explaining association members' satisfactions and commitments in Protestant churches (Hougland and Wood 1979, 1980) and social influence associations (Knoke and Wood 1981, pp. 84–90).

The remainder of this chapter describes measures of the authority and influence concepts and their empirical relationships in the National Association Study sample of national collective action organizations. Figure 8.1 summarizes the relationships among the two basic components of governance structures and their indicators.

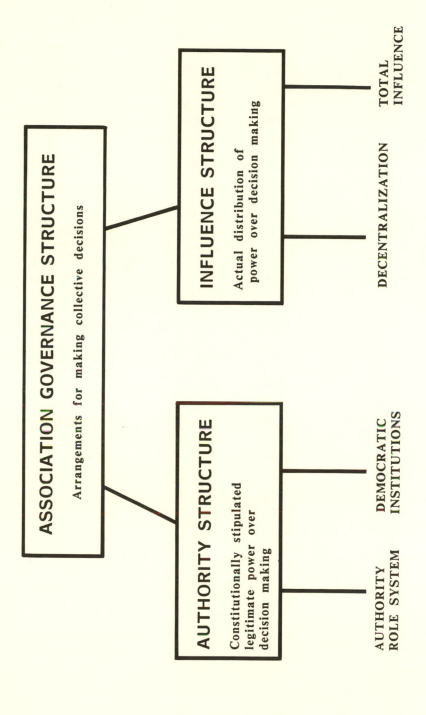

Figure 8.1. Relationships among Governance Structure Concepts and Measures

Authority Structures

Every organization designates certain roles and formal procedures for the legitimate exercise of power by its participants. Together these roles and rules constitute the authority structure of a collective action organization. This section examines the empirical distributions of authority role systems and democratic institutional arrangements created by American national associations.

Authority Role Systems

Written constitutions typically spell out the number of authority roles, their unique rights and duties, and the procedures for selecting and removing the role incumbents. American national associations display a remarkable uniformity of authority role systems. Almost all elect a president, a chairperson, or similar chief officer, as well as additional officials such as treasurer and secretary. More than 95% have a board of directors, trustees, or similarly named group. And more than four fifths maintain standing (permanent) committees for conducting special portions of the association's business, such as running elections or editing newsletters. This virtual unanimity of formal role positions suggests that the authority component of association governance is strongly institutionalized in the American political culture.

Given this structural uniformity, the main source of variation among associations occurs in the relative sizes of these three types of governing bodies. Roughly equal numbers of organizations with large and small role structures can be identified by dichotomizing the units as follows: small boards have 12 or fewer members; small officer cadres have 4 or fewer incumbents; and small committee systems have 5 or fewer standing committees. Table 8.1 shows the

Table 8.1. Authority Role Systems by Types of Associations

Authority role systems	All assns.	Labor unions	Trade assns.	Prof'l assns.	Rec'l assns.
No or small boards, few officers, few committees (%)	35	32	21	26	42
Only one large authority unit (%)	21	28	31	19	26
Two large authority units (%)	26	20	29	33	27
Large board, many officers, many standing committees (%)	18	19	19	23	15
Total	100	100	100	100	100
(*N*)	(459)	(60)	(109)	(109)	(127)

distributions for all organizations and for each of the four main types of associations when the three dichotomous measures are jointly considered as authority role systems.

More than one third of all associations are governed by small-scale authority role systems. Labor unions and recreational clubs are especially likely to have such governance. At the other extreme, fewer than one fifth of all organizations maintain large boards, many officers, and many committees. Professional societies are just slightly more likely to possess this large authority role combination.

Formal authority role systems affect the procedures that associations use to govern themselves. For example, an association's officers may be either elected by the mass membership or chosen by the board of directors. Among organizations that have only a few officer positions, the board makes the selection in about half the cases (47%). This is more than twice the rate (22%) at which the board chooses officers when the association has a large number of officer slots to be filled. That is, the membership retains the right to vote directly for its leaders when the officer cadre is large.

The size of the board of directors also affects governance procedures. When a large board of directors exists, it is more likely to conduct some of its important business through a smaller executive committee (63%) than if the association's board is small (only 46% of these organizations use an executive committee). Presumably, a smaller board can act as its own executive committee, while a large board may prove too unwieldy to act efficiently in all matters. The authority role system is also implicated in the frequency of board meetings. Associations with large authority systems are twice as likely to convene their boards three or more times each year (64%) than are associations whose authority units are all small (only 31% have frequent board meetings). When associations must process a substantial volume of important policy work, they presumably require both numerous authority roles and frequent face-to-face interaction among their incumbents to handle the decisions effectively.

The people occupying an association's authority role positions are typically charged with formulating the overall policy directions for the organization, not with supervising its detailed daily activities. One solution for groups facing complex task environments, providing they have sufficient resources, is to hire administrative personnel to manage the daily business. As Table 8.2 shows, a significant covariation exists between authority structures and bureaucracy (chi-square=42.0, $df=4$, $p<.001$). As noted in Chapter 4, highly bureaucratic associations are internally differentiated into three or more vertical or horizontal divisions, and employ full-time chief staff officers and other professional or managerial staff. These associations are more likely to be governed by large authority role systems, presumably because their scope of operations requires

Table 8.2.   Authority Role Systems by Bureaucratic Administration

| Authority role | Bureaucratization | | |
systems	None	Less	Highly
No or small boards, few officers, few committees (%)	48	28	32
One or two large authority units (%)	38	63	38
Large board, many officers, many standing committees (%)	14	9	30
Total	100	100	100
(*N*)	(150)	(128)	(163)

more policy directives. By contrast, almost half of the nonbureaucratic associations get by with only small authority structures. The less bureaucratized organizations (with paid staff but lacking internal divisions) fall into an intermediate pattern. The congruence between political and administrative forms is only partial, however, as seen by the large percentage of highly bureaucratic associations that use small authority bodies. Because the National Association Study measured organizations at one point in time, some of these groups may be caught in the midst of a transition toward more congruent patterns.

Democratic Structures

Apart from the formal authority role systems, associations authorize various procedural rules and practices that enhance members' access to the decision making process. Collectively, these arrangements comprise an association's democratic structure, which enables the members to exercise legitimate power over collective actions. Members may be facilitated or constrained in voicing policy preferences, selecting among alternatives, reviewing leader decisions, choosing incumbent officers, or consulting with national leaders. These structures limit leaders' discretion and autonomy by assuring members of routine opportunities to interact with the leadership and to register their concerns about governance issues. If an association fails to establish such structures, its membership enjoys fewer safeguards against the usurpation of power by leaders, however well-intentioned such seizures might be. The existence of many democratic structures does not insure that members can exercise their authority in actual decision making. Union conventions, for example, are "normally a politically manipulated body easily controlled by the national officeholders" (Benson 1986, p. 339; also Edelstein and Warner 1976, pp. 28–53). Still, the absence of democratic processes weakens members' potential authority.

The National Association Study collected five indicators of the presence of democratic structures. These procedures allow members to have greater involvement in collective decision making. The indicators, with the percentage of all associations that use them in parentheses, are:

1. The organization has an annual general membership meeting, or convention, at which some or many major policy decisions are made (56%).

2. Organizational elections usually involve two or more candidates running for the same office (49%).

3. The board of directors meets three or more times a year (42%).

4. The association has used a referendum at least once during the past three years for members to vote on important policy issues (37%).

5. Important decisions are made by national leaders in consultation with lower unit officials and the membership (30%).

A simple index of democratic structures counts the number of these practices present in each association. The mean for all organizations is 2.13, ranging from 2.03 among trade associations to 3.29 by labor unions. Highly bureaucratized associations are significantly more likely to maintain democratic structures (mean of 2.49), compared to the less and nonbureaucratized organizations (both with means of 1.85). This positive relationship is somewhat surprising, given popular perceptions that bureaucratic organizations tend to be remote and unresponsive. Apparently, American national associations create formal safeguards for their members' involvement when bureaucratic administration is a reality.

The importance of democratic structures to organizational governance is revealed in an examination of association elections. The membership's rate of voting in elections (turnout) seems to be stimulated by the existence of larger numbers of democratic practices. Recall that one of the five structures is regularly contested races, which is likely to boost interest in voting because a real outcome is at stake. Table 8.3 shows that member voting turnout is more than twice as high in associations that have all five indicators of democratic structure, compared to associations that have none. Although only a small proportion of all associations are represented by these extremes, the linear relationship across the full index is highly significant. The pattern suggests that associations which provide their members with opportunities for legitimate power are likely to see it exercised.

Table 8.3.   Percentage of Members Voting in National Association
                 Elections by Number of Democratic Structures

Number of democratic structures	Voting turnout (%)	(N)
None	29	(22)
One	39	(101)
Two	46	(108)
Three	45	(102)
Four	55	(54)
Five	72	(8)
Mean	45	(395)

Influence Distributions

The second basic component of association governance is the distribution of influence over collective policy-making among participants, particularly the relative influence of organization leaders and ordinary members. Two indicators of influence were developed from the informants' reports about decision making in their associations: decentralization and total control. The following subsections describe their measurements and distributions across the NAS sample organizations.

Decentralization

As discussed above, decentralization in voluntary associations is best conceptualized as decision making dispersal among organization participants. The association informants were presented with a series of statements "about how the [organization name] makes decisions about major policies, such as goals or programs." They were instructed to respond on a five-category scale ranging from strongly agree to strongly disagree, depending on how well they felt each statement described their organization's decision-making process. A factor analysis found that five statements, shown in Table 8.4, tap a single dimension. One item, referring to formal voice options available to dissidents, had a marginal loading on the factor but was included because of its robust loading on an identical scale for individual members (see Chapter 9).

The common theme running through these items is the discretion and autonomy leaders have to make decisions without taking members' interests into account. By recoding responses to signify informants' perceptions that leaders must attend to the policy concerns of members, we can see that a majority of

Table 8.4. Pattern Loadings from Principal Components Factor Analysis of Decentralization Scale Items

Scale items	Factor loading	Percent agree
Leaders of this organization sometimes make decisions that have little support from the rank-and-file members	.72	82[a]
Leaders' decisions more often reflect their personal interests than the wishes of the members	.67	79[a]
Major policy decisions are made only after wide consultations at all levels of the organization	.65	64
Power over major policy decisions is concentrated in the hands of a few people	.62	35[a]
If people disagree about policy decisions, there are formal ways for them to voice their opposition	.36	85

[a] Recoded to show percentage disagreeing.

the informants believed that members have a substantial say in policy matters. The one exception to this pattern is the item, "Power over major policy decisions is concentrated in the hands of a few people." Only 35% disagreed. Apparently most informants felt that decision making is not equally distributed, but that leaders nevertheless experience considerable constraints on their capacity to act unilaterally. Scores on the decentralization scale were computed by recoding three of the items so that high codes consistently indicate greater membership policy-making power, then averaging informants' responses across all five items. About two thirds of the organizations' scores fell on the agree side of the scale (higher than 3.0), while only one fifth of the scores were on the disagree side (lower than 3.0). Thus, the large majority of informants considered their associations to have more or less decentralized decision-making procedures.

Total Influence

The total influence measure of influence follows the Tannenbaum "control graph" technique for assessing positional influence in hierarchical organizations. Informants were instructed as follows: "Taking all areas of decision making into account, we would now like you to estimate how much influence each of the following groups or persons actually has in the (organization name)." For each position, the five categories ranged from "little or no influence" to "a very great deal of influence." Ideally, many participants should provide ratings for each organization, which are then averaged to smooth out random errors in evaluation. Although such multiple reports were collected in the questionnaires mailed to members of the 35 associations analyzed in the next chapter, here only the control graph judgments of a single informant are available for each of the 459 associations.

Because of the flaw in the computerized telephone interview schedule, informants rated the president or chairperson in fewer than half the organizations. Hence, the only two positions on which complete data are available are the board of directors and the general membership. For the entire sample, the mean board influence was 4.16, between "a great deal" and "a very great deal." The mean membership score was 2.68, between "some" and "quite a bit" of influence. The two ratings are unrelated across the sample, with a nonsignificant correlation coefficient of .02. The informants consider their memberships to have equal or greater policy influence than the board in only one quarter of the associations. In the other three quarters, the board influence exceeded the membership by one or more points on the five-point influence scale. As discussed above, the theoretically preferred combination of control graph evaluations is a sum of positional ratings, which indicates the total amount of influence in the organization. For the NAS sample, the mean total influence from summing the board and membership scores is 6.85, with only one seventh scoring below six and one twelfth above eight. Thus, for about three quarters of all associations, the total amount of control ranges between "quite a bit" and "a great deal."

Relationships among Governance Indicators

The four measures of governance structure described above are all moderately interrelated. The two authority indicators, authority role systems and democratic structures, correlate $+.26$. The decentralization and total influence indicators of positional influence correlate $+.23$. Similarly modest covariations occur between the authority-influence pairs. Thus, these analytically distinct components of organizational power also appear to tap empirically distinct aspects of the associations' polities.

An association's total influence increases linearly with the number of democratic structures ($r = +.23$). The source of this covariation is apparent in Figure 8.2, which plots the mean influence ratings for both boards of directors and members across the six levels of democratic institutions. The trend for the board is flat, but members' influence rises steadily until no significant difference occurs in the organizations having all five structures. Democratic processes perform exactly as expected: by providing members with more points of access to organizational policy-making, they empower the members relative to leaders and thus raise the total influence over internal policy-making.

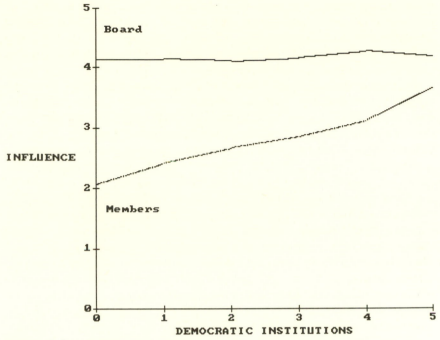

Figure 8.2. Relationship of Board and Member Influence to Number of Democratic Structures

Determinants of Governance Structures

This section considers the relationships between association governance structure and the conditions, both internal and external, under which American collective action organizations operate. Various writings on organization science speculate about formal structure, although the vast majority of theory and data pertain to work organizations' centralization, spans of control, complexity, technology and the like (see Scott 1987 for a review). These perspectives identify a set of factors that may affect each of the four governance indicators. For some variables, a priori expectations are unclear or contradictory. Large organizations may lead to centralized decision making through reliance on bureaucratic administration and "rule by experts" (Hage 1965). The structural complexities of large, highly differentiated organizations may render widespread decision-making participation less feasible than in small organizations. On the other hand, large size may induce decentralization out of sheer necessity, forcing leaders to delegate some decisions that they cannot handle themselves due to the huge volume of work (Jennergren 1981, p. 42). Several studies discovered inverse relationships between size and centralization (Pugh *et al.* 1969; Blau and Schoenherr 1971; Hickson *et al.* 1971). The unclear implications of size and bureaucracy argue for including separate measures of both variables in the governance analysis.

External environments may shape internal governance structures in a variety of ways: through legal mandates, technical imperatives, market pressures, constituency pressures, political regulation, cultural expectations, and so on (Mintzberg 1983). For example, the Labor-Management Reporting (Landrum-Griffin) Act of 1959 requires public disclosure of union finances and regular union elections. Thus, unions are required to adopt formal democratic structures. Any conditions that increase uncertainty and decrease predictability are likely to foster complex organizational structures (Powell 1985, p. 201; also Scott and Meyer 1983, p. 142). Environmental turbulence is incompatible with autocratic governance designs, as the rigidities of leader domination are antithetical to rapid adaptations. In placid and simple environments, more authoritarian structures have a better chance of survival, while complex and uncertain environments are conducive to decentralization and power-sharing within an organization (Scott *et al.* 1981, p. 148).

Other factors that may be expected to affect governance designs include: incentive system complexity (heterogeneous associations are more likely to use democratic decision making); organization age (older associations are likely to be more oligarchic); revenues (richer groups are able to support more elaborate, and hence more democratic, structures); and formal organizational goal diversity (associations that pursue external objectives of political influence and social change may need to conform their governance to the dominant cultural ideology of democracy). These expectations are summarized in a single proposition from the political economy theory:

Proposition 16:   Collective action organizations develop democratic governance structures under conditions of large size, complex incentive systems, nonbureaucratic administrative structures, multiple organizational goals, and greater environmental complexity and uncertainty.

Measures of all these variables are available, at least in the contemporary period, for use in multivariate analyses of association governance. Table 8.5 contains the estimates from four regression equations.

The effects of independent variables tend to be consistent across all equations, although they are not always statistically significant. Bureaucratic administration generally reduces democratic governance. The more bureaucratized an association, the smaller the size of its authority role system, the less decentralized its policy-making, and the lower the total control exercised by the organization as a whole. Only in the democratic institutions equation is the bureaucracy coefficient positive, revealing that a more elaborate administrative apparatus coexists with formal means of member access to policy-making. Apparently, a larger administrative staff substitutes to some degree for a small lay leadership, but is consistent with greater safeguards for democratic procedures. Larger organizations, as measured by the logged value of membership size, create fewer institutional safeguards and rely upon more centralized decision making. The total revenue effect is the opposite, encouraging more numerous authority roles, decentralization, and higher total influence.

As in earlier analyses, environmental conditions exert modest effects on internal organization matters. Greater uncertainty is associated with smaller authority systems and more centralized decision making, while complexity increases total influence. One important limitation on these relationships is the cross-sectional measurements of both governance and environment. Organizational designs laid down early in an organization's life cycle tend to persist relatively unaltered during subsequent periods where environments may change markedly (Stinchcombe 1965). The absence of environmental measures taken at earlier times undoubtedly reduces the impact of these factors on governance structures. The modest effects of organizational age—older associations providing larger authority role systems and more democratic structures— may capture part of this historical process. But the signs of these coefficients also contradict the hypothesis that organizations become more oligarchic over their life cycles. Neither complex incentive systems nor multiple formal goals

Table 8.5. Standardized Coefficients from Regression of Governance Measures on Organizational Variables

Independent variables	Dependent variables			
	Authority roles	Democratic structures	Decentral- ization	Total influence
Bureaucracy	−.20***	.16**	−.16**	−.14*
Member size (log)	.05	−.07	−.24***	−.04
Total revenue (log)	.47***	.00	.23***	.11
Environ. uncertainty	−.16***	.05	−.07	.01
Environ. complexity	.10*	.09*	.02	.15**
Organization age	.11**	.16***	.04	.00
Incentive complexity	.09*	.19***	.06	−.12**
Multiple goals	.04	.09*	.08	.03
R^2_{adj}	.250***	.125***	.052***	.027**

*$p<.05$;
**$p<.01$;
***$p<.001$.

exert consistent pressures toward expansion of democratic governance. Incentive diversity raises the number of democratic institutions, but it is inversely related to total influence. Most of the goal multiplexity coefficients fail to reach significance.

None of the equation specifications accounts for much variance in the governance design dimensions. The multiple R^2 reaches almost one quarter in the authority systems equation, where the main source is the logged revenue variable. Total influence is especially poorly explained. Although the analysis in Table 8.5 offers a beginning toward understanding the origins of association governance designs, much more work remains to be done, particularly in accounting for the developmental process over the organizational life cycle. For present purposes, the four measures of governance structures are used in the next two chapters in analyses of the participation of individual association members.

Conclusion

The governance of collective action organizations is conducted through both constitutionally stipulated authority structures and the actual struggle for influence over decisions by participants. For all 459 NAS organizations, empirical indicators of authority (democratic structures and authority role systems) and influence (decentralization and total influence distributions) disclosed only modest positive covariation among these variables. Similarly, efforts to relate governance to environmental and organizational factors found only small degrees of predictability. Most associations exhibit both democratic constitutional authority structures and decentralized influence patterns.

These results dispute the organizational governance problem of pervasive oligarchy advanced by Michels and others. Numerous democratic structures exist that rein in tendencies toward power usurpation by leaders. Members are perceived to affect collective decision making in ways comparable to leaders. The threat of minority control in American associations seems to be severely constrained by pervasive cultural expectations that the membership will retain ultimate authority and influence over collective actions. Egalitarian norms not only integrate members into these institutions, but innoculate the organizations against antidemocratic inclinations.

The empirical evidence that four dimensions of association governance structure are weakly predicted by organizational variables implies that governance may be less a matter of structural or strategic contingency and more a consequence of cultural institutionalization. American national associations' formal authority structures almost universally include boards of directors, officers, and standing committees; only the size differences among these components distinguish them from one another. Although other dimensions of governance show wider variation, they appear unpatterned by conventional organization attributes. Instead, governance structures may reflect pervasive cultural standards about proper organizational forms and procedures. The larger American society expects democratic principles to be expressed, regardless of their technical efficiency or their fit with organizational goals and environments. Thus, the observed differences in governance structures are relatively random and not systematically related to external or internal conditions. Whether governance has an impact on organizations' and members' participation in collective actions is a subject for the following two chapters.

9

MEMBER INVOLVEMENT*

Members are involved in their collective action organizations in many ways beyond monetary contributions; these include participatory actions such as working on group projects and psychological orientations such as commitment to the association. These "in-kind contributions are the functional equivalent of surplus capital" in work corporations (Bidwell and Kasarda 1985, p. 89). By making their efforts and moral engagement available for collective use, members provide invaluable sustenance to organizations, enabling them to pursue their goals. This chapter examines how association structures and individual orientations affect variations in the intensity of members' involvements.

Although participation and attitudes are expected to covary positively, they are not expected to correlate perfectly. Some members may be strongly committed to their organizations although they are unable to participate frequently in collective actions because of job and family obligations, or financial and health incapacities. Some members may make generous financial donations, but hold back on other forms of participation, maintaining an aloof, dispassionate attitude toward the group. Others may compartmentalize their participation, engaging in public-policy lobbying efforts while eschewing the social activities that go on inside the organization. Given the complex patterns of member involvement that can occur, the distinct behavioral and attitudinal dimensions must be analyzed separately.

The key assumption of this chapter is that member involvements are primarily functions of both individual dispositions and conditions created by organizations. This assumption underlies the construction of the theoretical propositions below. Organization governance structures, analyzed in the pre-

*Written with Denise Floe.

ceding chapter, are important in the explanation of member involvements.
(This approach parallel's Halaby's 1986 "authority cost" conception of worker
attachments to their employers.) People bring into the association perceptions
about democratic norms of organizational governance that specify their proper
relationship to the collectivity. Stemming from the larger culture of democratic
pluralism in the American voluntary tradition, these expectations establish a
prescriptive baseline that members use to judge their association's exercise of
authority and thus to determine their level of involvement. To the extent that
organization structures and leaders' behaviors satisfy the members' perceptions
of legitimate democratic governance, members become involved in association
activities and form strong psychological attachments. But, if organizations and
their agents fall short of these democratic standards, the long-term consequences are detachment, apathy, and withdrawal, especially if exit is a freely
available alternative. In effect, members who perceive that governance con-
forms to principles of egalitarian democracy will assign lower costs to their
member roles and thus will exhibit high involvement levels. Conversely, when
governance appears to express arbitrary member exclusion and satisfaction of
leaders' interests, members will perceive that the cost of membership is high.
Their involvement will weaken, regardless of other benefits they may receive
from the association's political economy (Knoke and Wood 1981; Knoke
1981a, 1988). In addition to governance, the incentive system and other organizational structures and processes affect member involvements. As discussed
in Chapters 6 and 7, the internal association economy revolves around exchanges of association inducements for member resources. Besides the generic
money and time contributions analyzed earlier, members' participation and
psychological attachments also respond to the greater amounts of utilitarian,
affective, and normative benefits in which they hold strong interest. Structural
arrangements such as bureaucracy and size, and external environmental conditions may constrain or facilitate the expression of member attachments. Finally, personal characteristics and interests must also be taken into account in
analyzing the impact of organizational forces on members' involvements.

Theoretical Expectations

The political economy theory outlined in Chapter 3 contains four propositions relevant to member involvement. The first relates members' interests to
communication:

Proposition 17:   The more intense members' interests in organizational policy
                    issues, the greater their communication interaction.

Policy issues are matters about which the association is engaged in collective decision making. These issues range from the trivial (such as changing the name of the newsletter) to the fundamental (whether to become active in national policy influence efforts). Members may be indifferent to many issues, intensely concerned about only a few, or heavily interested in the entire spectrum. The political economy theory is silent about the sources of members' interests. Their orientations may originate outside the association, constituting part of their reason for joining. Or, interests may be formed through experiences and socialization processes within the organization. Regardless of the origins of interests, the proposition argues that it is important to stimulate members' discussion of these matters. The broader the range and the greater the intensity of concern about issues, the more extensive the rate of interpersonal communication.

Communication is "any process whereby decisional premises are transmitted from one member of an organization to another" (Simon 1965, p. 154). This exchange can assume many forms: formal conferences, informal discussions, memos, newsletters, public address announcements, and so forth. The total pattern of information exchange among participants comprises an organization's communication structure. As a social network, its linkages can be characterized by several dimensions: intensity, frequency, density, reachability, degree of centralization, and so on (Lincoln 1982; Rogers and Kincaid 1981). Similarly, individuals and organizational subunits occupy social positions within communication structures that vary in their degrees of prominence and centrality (Knoke and Burt 1982). A communication structure is the primary mechanism for relating an organization to its task environments, both internal and external, and for changing its operations when necessary. Indeed, the management process in work organizations consists largely of talk as a means of control over subordinates' behaviors (Gronn 1983; Kanter 1977, pp. 55–59). Barnard (1947, p. 90) went so far as to assert that communication technique shapes the form and internal economy of an organization. The coordination of complex activities is accomplished entirely through authoritative communication (p. 163; see also Brewer 1971).

The formal patterns of communication flow in work organizations are related to but distinct from hierarchical distributions of status and power. Experimental studies suggest that centralized networks result in superior efficiency of information processing and problem solving, at least for routine tasks (Vroom 1969; Arrow 1974, pp. 68–69). Katz and Kahn (1966, p. 223) likewise observed that information exchanges are concentrated more heavily in centers of organizational control and decision making. However, hierarchies may inhibit interactions about nonroutine or ambiguous tasks by undermining social supports necessary to engage all participants fully in the search for solutions (Blau and Scott 1962, pp. 116–28). Decentralized communication structures are more likely to emerge under conditions of task complexity, uncertainty, nonroutine technology, and people- or idea-oriented objectives (Hall 1987, pp. 176–96).

The second theoretical proposition relates organizational governance structures (authority and influence arrangements, discussed in Chapter 8) to communication:

> *Proposition 18:*   Organizations with more democratic governance structures generate higher rates of policy communication.

Democratic governance promotes more extensive communication (recall Michels' famous observation that oligarchies perpetuate themselves largely through control over the means of intraorganizational communication). Structures that allow members and leaders to exercise more direct and continuous control over one another encourage the high volumes of communication required to make their varied policy interests known (Smith and Brown 1964; Brewer 1971).

Other structural factors tend to inhibit the flow of internal information in associations. Formal bureaucracy and large size tend to shift responsibility for collective affairs from typical members to specialists, thus reducing people's sense of their importance in the scheme of things (Wicker 1969). It is also true that external environments which generate pressures of complexity and uncertainty can stimulate much upward communication that transmits demands to the leadership (Simpson and Gulley 1962). The implications of members' incentive system interests for communication flows are parallel to the effects of incentives on member involvements discussed at the beginning of this chapter. Thus, the discussion of communication must take into account factors other than member issue interests and democratic governance structures:

> *Proposition 19:*   Smaller size, absence of bureaucracy, environmental complexity and uncertainty, and stronger member interests in incentives stimulate a greater rate of communication on policy issues.

In collective action organizations, communication is used less to coordinate participants through information exchange and more for normative social integration purposes. A substantial portion of communication content is expressive and emotional, aimed at generating the high levels of member trust, consensus, and cohesion essential for effective performance in voluntary associations (Etzioni 1975, pp. 244, 395–417). Interpersonal interactions among leaders and members socialize both role incumbents to collective goals, procedures, and practices of the organization. Extensive communication between leaders and members and among the members reinforces a common belief system or ideology. This preponderance of socialization over instrumental information content creates a robust relation between the volume of communication and high levels of member loyalty and commitment to the group (Knoke and Wood

1981, p. 85). Thus, a fundamental consequence of member issue interests, democratic governance structures, and policy communication is to increase member involvement:

> *Proposition 20:* Higher levels of policy communication, stronger member interests in policy issues, and more democratic association governance structures produce more member commitment to and participation in organizational affairs.

Commitments comprise a set of subjective attachments that members form to the group and the individuals in it. In general, commitment depends on "the willingness of social actors to give their energy and loyalty to social systems, the attachment of personality systems to social relations which are self-expressive" (Kanter 1968). Commitment concerns the degree of organizational "introjection" into the member's personality (Gouldner 1960). Association values become subsumed into one's personal values and goals, often by an intensely emotional identification process:

> [T]hrough his subjection to organizationally determined goals, and through the gradual absorption of those goals into his own attitudes, the participant in an organization acquires an "organization personality" rather distinct from his personality as an individual (Simon 1965, p. 154).

Following Knoke and Wood (1981) and Knoke (1988), we view organizational commitment as a multidimensional relationship, in which diverse aspects of the person-group connection form distinct foci of psychological involvement. Among the possible dimensions are the centrality of the organization in the person's life, the intensity of member support for the organization's purposes and goals, the salience of the member identity in the larger social self, and perceptions of others' commitments to the association.

A related but distinct aspect of psychological involvement is detachment, which resembles the classical concept of organizational alienation: "an expectancy construct regarding personal control, *not* an omnibus synonym for feelings of despair, maladjustment, unhappiness, or generalized negativism" (Neal and Seeman 1964). Detachment from a collective action organization expresses feelings of personal distance from the group and inability to affect association actions and policies. It is the organizational analog to powerlessness and efficacy in the political system. Detachment can occur with high levels of commitment, as Knoke (1981a) found in an analysis of 32 local Indianapolis chapters of social influence associations. Thus, rather than polar ends of a single continuum, commitment and detachment constitute distinct dimensions of membership psychological engagement.

Participation, the second basic type of member involvement, is the behavioral aspect of attachment to collective action organizations. Participation may range from attendance at regularly scheduled meetings to occupation of major leadership positions. Paralleling Verba and Nie's (1972) discovery that political activity occurred along several distinct dimensions, Knoke and Wood's (1981) exploratory factor analysis found that participation in local social influence associations also was differentiated into several forms, including internal activities (such as providing transportation; trying to recruit new members), external activities (contacting government officials; writing to newspapers), and occupation of formal leadership positions. Analyzing the same data with a confirmatory measurement model, Parker (1983) uncovered only a simple split between official (past and current office holding) and unofficial (all other types of activity) participation. The nature of members' participation in national collective action organizations is a matter for empirical solution in the present chapter.

The two general types of member involvements, commitment and participation, are expected to be strongly related to one another, but neither equivalent to nor identical in their response to the antecedent communication, interest, and governance variables. The following section describes the measures used in testing the theoretical propositions.

Measurements

The next subsections describe details of the measurement procedures for variables being introduced for the first time.

Exogenous Factors

Two external environment measures are the familiar complexity and uncertainty scales based on the association informants' reports. Other macro-organizational measures include the logs of total annual revenues and association size (number of members), bureaucracy, political goals, societal change goals, democratic structures, and authority role systems. The measurements of these variables for the 35 sample organizations, derived from the telephone interviews with leaders, are described in preceding chapters.

Two governance structure measures used in the following analyses are based on the members' reports: perceptions of total influence and decentralization. The membership questionnaires contained items identical to those used in the informant interviews, thus allowing construction of scales that duplicate the measures used in Chapter 8. The two referents for computing the total influence scores were the national president or chairperson and the general membership. Each association's total influence score simply sums the sample respondents' perceptions of the influence of these two positions. For the members of all 35 samples associations, the mean influence imputed to the president/chair was 3.96 (almost "a great deal") and the mean influence attributed to the membership was 2.84 (almost "some"), yielding a total influence mean score of 6.80. The perceived decentralization scale was computed using members' responses to the same five items presented to the informant sample (see Table 8.4 for item wordings). The internal reliability of this scale is high (Cronbach's alpha =.81). In the member sample as a whole, the mean decentralization score was 3.11, slightly to the "agree" side of the "undecided" midpoint category. For both total influence and decentralization variables, organization means and individual scores permit contextual effects analyses to be performed, as described below. The six incentive interest scales (normative, social, material, informational, occupational, and lobbying) were included at both the individual and the organizational levels of analysis to examine their contextual effects on individual involvements. (Details of their construction are described in Chapter 7.) Other personal attributes include the respondent's age in years, gender (1=female, 0=male), education (number of years of schooling completed), occupational prestige scores on the NORC scale, and current total income of the family in thousands of dollars (using midpoints for 12 brackets). An organization-related attribute is the number of years that the respondent has been a member of his/her association.

Members' interests in organizational issues were computed from their responses to a set of questionnaire items provided to the NAS by leaders from each association. From two to six current or recent "issues facing the organization" were stated in short phrases or sentences. For example, the Professional Women's Association's set included "raising funds for a building project" and "editorial policies and operations of PWA." The Health Sciences Organization listed "creation of a smoke-free society by the year 2000" and "inadequacies of the Medicare and Medicaid programs" among its six issues.

The 186 issues provided to the NAS by the 35 association leaders were classified independently by two coders using the 24-category coding scheme presented in Table 9.1. A 75% agreement rate on issue placement was achieved, and all disagreements were resolved by discussion. The table expresses the issue distributions in two ways: the percentage of all 35 organizations that have one or more issues in each category, and the percentage of all 186 issues falling into each category. The 24 broad categories were further aggregated into internal and external content domains, a classification central to the analyses below. Large majorities of the organizations designated at least one external (80%) or one internal issue (77%). A majority (57%) had both types of issues. Among internal matters, the most frequent issues concerned acquiring resources, conducting meetings and programs, producing publications, and increasing or broadening the membership. Heading the list of external issues were lobbying governments and conducting publicity campaigns about general or specific public policy issues, and raising the organization's public status and prestige.

Table 9.1. Classification of Organizational Issues

Issue category	% of orgs.[a]	% of issues[b]
Internal Issues		
Increasing resources available to the organization	37.1	9.1
Planning and operating conventions, meetings, programs	34.3	7.0
Publishing newsletters, magazines, journals	28.6	9.0
Increasing or broadening membership base	20.0	3.8
Member participation in organization governance	17.1	3.8
Social-recreational opportunities, celebrations	11.4	2.7
Relations among sections of association, affiliates	11.4	2.2
Provision of information services	11.4	2.2
Offering wider variety of member benefits	8.6	1.6
Location of association headquarters	8.6	1.6
Communication with and among members	5.7	1.7
Member participation in nongovernance activities	5.7	1.1
Organization by-law changes	2.9	0.5
Group insurance, purchasing, marketing opportunities	2.9	0.5
Total	77.1	46.8
External issues		
Lobbying or publicity campaigns on general issues	42.9	17.7
Lobbying governments about specific public policies	37.1	13.4
General level of org. involvement in political matters	28.6	5.4
Enhancing org's status and prestige in community	20.0	4.8
Proposing changes in the larger profession	14.3	3.8
Running certification, licensing programs for profession	14.3	3.8
Relations with other organizations	11.4	3.2
Endorsing candidates for public office	2.9	0.5
Public information program unrelated to lobbying issues	2.9	0.5
Total	80.0	53.2
Total (%) all issues	100.0	100.0
(N)	(35)	(186)

[a] Percentage of all organizations with at least one issue in category.
[b] Percentage of all issues provided by all organizations in category

The questionnaires instructed respondents to check one of four categories, from "none" to "major," that "best describes the *level of interest or concern that you had or have about each issue*" (emphasis on original). (Subsequently, they were asked about their level of activity on each of the issues; as described below, these latter responses were used as one measure of involvement.) A member's scores on her internal issue interest and external issue interest scales were constructed by coding 0 if the organization did not have issues of this type; 1 if the respondent had no interest in the issues; 2 for minor interest; 3 for moderate interest; and 4 for major interest. To create comparable values between associations, a member's responses for internal or external issues were averaged over the number of internal or external issues for that type offered on each questionnaire. For example, if the survey for a particular association presented three external and two internal issues, a respondent's scores for external and internal issue interest were computed as averages for three external items and two internal items, respectively. For all associations, the mean level of member interest in internal issues was 1.9, just below "minor interest." For external issues, the mean was 2.6, halfway between "minor" and "moderate interest." As with several other exogenous factors, both individual and group scores were computed to allow contextual effects analyses.

Communication

Members were asked, "During the past year, *about how many times* did you communicate—in person, by phone, and by letter—with the following people or groups about [org. name] matters of all kinds?" Seven response categories were offered, from "none" to "40+" times per year. These were transformed to the midpoint values of each category, using "40" for the upper level. On most questionnaires, five targets of communication appeared: the national president or chairperson; the executive director; other officers; committees; and the general membership. An overall index of communication frequency was calculated in two steps. First, communication was averaged across the three leader categories (or two, where no executive director existed), and across the two nonleader categories (committees and general membership). Second, both leader and nonleader communication rates were added together. The resulting total measure weighs communication with leaders more heavily than their relative frequency in the association, consistent with the greater importance of officers as nodes in the internal communication networks. Among the members of all associations, the mean level of communication was 3.18 times per year, the sum of mean rates of 1.35 with leaders and 1.83 with nonleaders.

Commitments

Three multi-item measures of psychological commitments were identified through a factor analysis of a large pool of candidate items on feelings about the organization. The panels of Table 9.2 give the item wordings and the sample means for five-point scales ranging from "strongly disagree" (1) to "undecided" (3) to "strongly agree" (5). The reliabilities of the organizational commitment scale (alpha =.89), central life interest scale (alpha =.79), and detachment scale (alpha =.70) are all in the acceptable range. The sample means for each of the nine items on the organizational commitment scale fall into the "agree" end of the scale, with one exception. The ninth item, degree of personal commitment to the organization, used a different response format,

Table 9.2.   Items and Means for Scales of Psychological Commitment in Collective Action Organizations

Scale items	Means
Organizational commitment scale	
To be perfectly honest, I don't care what the (org. name) says or does[a]	4.30
What the (org. name) stands for is very important to me	4.18
I feel this organization would deserve my support even if if were unable to participate	3.99
I feel a sense of pride in being a member of the (org. name)	3.88
It is important to me to maintain the values of the (org. name)	3.82
I am indifferent about being a member of the organization[a]	3.76
I feel a strong sense of belonging to this organization	3.48
Without contributions like mine, the (org. name) would be unable to carry out its programs	3.21
Personally, how committed do you feel to the (org. name)?	2.80
Organizational commitment scale mean	3.72
Central life interests scale	
I feel there are very few things more important in my life than the (org. name)[a]	2.57
I have put so much time and effort into this organization that it would be difficult for me to leave	1.97
My membership in the (org. name) influences most aspects of my life[a]	1.90
Central life interest scale mean	1.90
Detachment scale	
I don't have much say about what the organization does	3.38
Since other members are active, it doesn't matter whether I participate	2.47
As a member, I play an important part in the organization[a]	2.91
Detachment scale mean	2.99

[a] Item coding reversed in scale construction.

ranging from "not committed at all" to "very strongly committed." That item's 2.80 mean falls between the "slightly committed" and "moderately committed" categories. The overall scale mean of 3.72 lies well above the neutral "undecided" point, but still below the "agree" category.

For the central life interest scale, member responses clearly fall into the "disagree" end: for most members, their associations simply do not count very heavily in the overall scheme of their lives. The detachment scale has a sample mean that falls almost at the "undecided" point (3.00). Not surprisingly, the typical individuals attracted to American associations evince only lukewarm passions for their groups. Although we lack comparative data on members' other social formations, such as family, church, and occupation, we suspect that collective action organizations would rank much lower in intensity of psychological support by the participants.

Participation

Two multiple indicator scales of members' participation in internal activities of their organizations were constructed. For the first scale, members were asked how often during the past year they had participated in a series of association level activities, including those at the national, state, or local level. A factor analysis disclosed that all 10 items formed a single scale of activities taking place within the organization's boundaries. These internal participation items and the sample means are shown in Table 9.3. The scale was constructed by averaging members' frequencies of performing these ten activities on a four-point scale ranging from "never" (1) to "regularly" (4). The scale reliability (Cronbach's alpha) is .84. As an inspection of the individual items

Table 9.3. Items and Means for Scale of Member Internal Participation in Collective Action Organizations

Scale items	Means
Voted in organizational elections	2.22
Phoned or contacted other members	2.07
Tried to recruit new members	2.00
Attended conferences or workshops	1.86
Worked on special projects	1.76
Ever held office in the (org. name)	1.59
Represented organization to other groups	1.54
Provided transportation to members	1.47
Gave or loaned equipment and supplies	1.45
Solicited donations for the organization	1.34
Internal participation scale mean	1.71

reveals, the most frequently performed activities are relatively low cost ones, such as voting in organization elections and contacting other members. More time-consuming actions, such as representing the association to other organizations, or providing transportation to other members, were less frequently performed. (The item on holding office is inflated due to the "ever held" time frame.) On the whole, internal participation averaged closer to "rarely" than to "never," although approximately 45 to 75% of the sample members said they had never engaged in particular activities.

A second participation scale, the internal issue activity index, was based on the same set of policy decision items that comprised the issue interest variables described among the exogenous factors. (Chapter 10 examines the activity index for external issues.) For internal issues about which members had expressed some interest, they were asked to "check the category that best describes *how active you are or were* in [org. name] on that issue." Their responses were scored from 1 for "not active" to 4 for "highly active," with 0 indicating that their association's questionnaire did not include internal issues. To create comparable scores across associations, responses were averaged across the number of issues presented to each organization's members. The sample mean of 1.06 indicates that most association members were not active on the set of internal issues nominated by their leaders. (Even after excluding the 23% of sample organizations with no internal issues, the mean activity level increases to only 1.36.)

Contextual Analysis Methods

The availability of identical data from large samples of members from each of many associations gives us a rare chance to combine both individual preferences and organizational conditions in analyzing member involvement. We approached this problem as a contextual effects analysis. The basic premise of the procedure used is that individuals' behaviors tend to move in the direction of their groups' social compositions, even after taking into account the individuals' personal characteristics. The hypothesis that a person behaves in an organizational context implies that he interacts with and perceives characteristics of others in that situation, and these situations influence his own actions. Typically, in assessing an association's context, the basic measure is the proportion or density of group members exhibiting a particular attribute. For example, a person belonging to an association in which many members value lobbying incentives should be more likely to participate in external activity than would a person belonging to a group that is largely indifferent to such inducements.

A contextual effect process assumes that peoples' attitudes and behaviors are influenced through their social relations, and that social relations are structured by the social composition of their relevant environments. Unlike many ecological contexts, such as local neighborhoods and communities (Sprague 1982, Huckfeldt 1983), collective action organizations constitute nonarbitrarily circumscribed social settings that are meaningful units of interpersonal interaction and social comparison for their participants. Hence, the basic assumptions and propositions of contextual analysis lead us to expect significant attitudinal and behavioral consequences that are a complex result of individual dispositions operating within the constraints and opportunities of a collectivity.

The contextual analysis employed here uses the single equation additive model (Blalock 1984; see also Boyd and Iversen 1979). The basic equation may be written:

$$Y_{ik} = a + b_1 X_{ik} + b_2 \bar{X}_k + b_3 Z_{ik} + b_4 W_k + e_{ik}$$

where the subscripts i and k refer to the ith member of the kth association; Y is the response (score on a measure of member involvement); X_{ik} is the member's personal score on a contextual variable; X_k is the mean level for the kth group on the same variable, created by aggregating over the sample members in the association; Z_{ik} is the member's score on an individual noncontextual variable (i.e., an individual-level measure with no corresponding organizational-level aggregate); W_k is the kth association's score on an organizational noncontextual variable (e.g., a global measure that has no corresponding individual-level value); and e_{ik} is the error term in predicting the member's involvement as linear function of the independent variables. The a and b parameters, to be estimated from the data, represent the intercept and net effects of the independent contextual and noncontextual variables, respectively. Although the equation designates only one variable of each type, in actual analyses, many contextual and noncontextual individual and organization measures are specified in equations that seek to explain member involvement.

Equation estimates are obtained by ordinary least-square regression, which also produces standard errors used to assess the statistical significance of the parameters and a coefficient of determination (multiple R^2, adjusted for degrees of freedom), which shows the overall fit of the model to the data. Significant effects of the contextual variables measured at the individual level (the X_{ik}) indicate the presence of effects on member involvement that operates at the individual level. If the coefficient for the aggregated contextual variable (the $\bar{X}_k$) is significant, an organization effect on individual behavior is operating independently of the impact of the individual-level effect. Both effects are additive; that is, they operate identically for all persons and organizations.

Finally, other individual-level (Z_{ik}) and association-level (W_k) variables are included, both for intrinsic theoretical importance and to control for factors confounded with the contextual variables whose omission from the model might lead to erroneous estimates of effects.

The specification assumes additive effects on individuals' behaviors at both the micro (individual) and macro (organizational) levels of analysis. That is, the microlevel variable (X_{ik}) is independent of the macrolevel effect $(\bar{X}_k)$, although the pair are probably correlated. In general, we expect that both the individual effect coefficient (b_1) and the contextual effect coefficient (b_2) will have the same sign (both positive or negative), consistent with the basic contextual hypothesis stated above. Where the signs are opposite (one positive and one negative), the effect of the organizational context is to move members' behaviors in an opposite direction from the effect of their personal attributes. Though rare, such inverse effects have been known to occur.

Nonadditive contextual models, in which the b_1 coefficient is a function of the $\bar{X}_k$ [i.e., a product term $(X_{ik}\bar{X}_k)$ is included in the equation] can be specified (Boyd and Iversen 1979, p. 19). These more complex models assert that individual effects vary across contexts, or, equivalently, that group effects are not homogeneous. In practice, however, such models often prove difficult to estimate empirically, due to the high degree of collinearity among independent variables and the resulting estimate instabilities [see Knoke (1981a) for an example]. Consequently, the analyses in this chapter are restricted to the additive form of the basic contextual effects model, although in Chapter 10 more elaborate specifications are undertaken. In substantive areas where well-developed theories are absent, such as the study of collective action organizations, even initial findings can have intrinsic interest and can suggest directions that future work should take to clarify the process through which the observed contextual effects operate.

Results

A series of contextual equations was estimated for each dependent variable, using various combinations of independent variables. Table 9.4 summarizes these equations by presenting the coefficients of determination (multiple R^2 's) for three specifications: (1) inclusion of the global organizational and individual-level variables; (2) inclusion of only aggregated (mean) organization-level variables; and (3) inclusion of both levels. By comparing the differences in R^2 between pairs of equations, the unique and joint contributions of these sets of explanatory variables for each of the dependent variables can be determined. Because the predictor variables in nonexperimental

Table 9.4. Coefficients of Determination (R^2_{adj}) from Contextual Analyses

Independent variables included	Dependent variables					
	Total commun.	Org'l. commit.	Central life	Detachment	Internal partic.	Internal activity
1. Individual and global	.203	.439	.307	.397	.590	.683
2. Aggregated (means)	.127	.098	.116	.132	.301	.635
3. All levels	.240	.453	.317	.413	.616	.752

research are intercorrelated, some portion of the explained variance cannot be uniquely allocated but must be considered a product of their joint effects.

Table 9.4 shows that the full contextual equations explain between one quarter (for total communication) and three quarters (for internal issue activity) of the total variance. When the variance explained by Equation 1 is subtracted from that of Equation 3, the aggregated organization means appear to add little to the explained variance above that already accounted for by the individual-level and global organizational measures. For example, the unique effect in the total communication equation is $(.240 - .203 = .037)$, or just 3.7% of the variance. For central life interest, the means account for only a .010 increment. In most equations, the unique variance attributable to the first equation is much larger. However, the jointly held share (the variance remaining after subtracting the unique variances of the means and the individual plus global variables) is also substantial in four equations (between .084 for organizational commitment and .116 for detachment). For the two behavioral measures of participation, the joint effects are enormous: internal participation is .275 and internal issue activity is .566. (This large between-associations effect arises mainly from the measurement of internal issue activity that assigns 0 to members of the seven associations which had no internal issues.) Clearly, significant contextual effects are operating on the various indicators of member involvements. An inspection of the estimated coefficients from each of the third equations divulges the nature of these cross-level relations.

Because the various independent variables are scaled in arbitrary units, only the standardized coefficients from the contextual equations are reported in Tables 9.5 and 9.6. Given the huge NAS sample size (8746 respondents from 35 national associations), even very small coefficient estimates are statistically significant. Values smaller than ± .05 in magnitude probably should not be interpreted as having much substantive importance. In specifying the equations, three of the incentive measures (for occupational, informational, and material inducements at both the individual and group levels) had to be removed from the analyses because they created multicollinearity problems, resulting in unstable coefficient estimates. Similarly, the global organization

Table 9.5. Standardized Coefficients from Contextual Analysis of
Total Communication

Independent variables	Total communication
Personal attributes	
Age	−.10***
Length of membership	.09***
Occupational prestige	.00
Education	.03*
Income	.00
Gender (female)	.03
Organizational attributes	
Size (log members)	.03
Bureaucracy	−.03
Democratic structures	.06***
Authority role system	.13***
Political goal	−.03*
Environmental uncertainty	−.25***
Individual-level effects	
Normative incentives	.11***
Lobbying incentives	−.03
Social incentives	.13***
Internal issue interests	.25***
External issue interests	.02
Decentralization	.04***
Total influence	.04***
Organization-level effects	
Normative incentives	.04*
Lobbying incentives	.04
Social incentives	.16***
Internal issue interests	−.22***
External issue interests	−.07**
Decentralization	−.12***
Total influence	.22***
Multiple R^2_{adj}	.240***

***$p<.001$;
**$p<.01$;
*$p<.05$.

Table 9.6. Standardized Coefficients from Contextual Analyses of Psychological Commitments and Internal Participation

Independent variables	Dependent variables				
	Org'l commit.	Central interest	Detachment	Internal partic.	Internal issue act.
Personal attributes					
Age	.18***	.08***	−.01	.04***	.00
Length of membership	.08***	.11***	−.03**	.07***	.10***
Occupational prestige	.02*	−.01	.02	.00	.02
Education	−.05***	−.15***	.02	.00	.00
Income	.00	−.02*	.00	−.02**	.00
Gender (female)	−.05***	−.02	.03**	.02*	−.02*
Organizational attributes					
Size (log members)	−.13***	.04**	.01	−.04***	.05***
Bureaucracy	.08***	.08**	.07**	−.03	−.40***
Democratic structures	.03**	.06***	−.06***	.09***	.04***
Authority role system	−.01	.01	.11***	−.08***	−.17***
Political goal	.04**	−.05***	.00	.01	−.01
Environmental uncertainty	−.05**	−.14***	.06***	−.08***	−.23***
Individual-level effects					
Normative incentives	.29***	.16***	−.14***	.12***	.04***
Lobbying incentives	.07***	.01	−.02	−.01	.00
Social incentives	.02	.11***	−.04***	.08***	.00
Internal issue interests	.20***	.14***	−.14***	.14***	.33***
External issue interests	.14***	−.03	−.06***	[a]	[a]
Decentralization	.20***	.12***	−.29***	−.01	.00
Total influence	.11***	.02	−.11***	.04***	.01*
Total communication	.17***	.20***	−.28***	.52***	.19***
Organization-level effects					
Normative incentives	−.05**	−.04	−.01	.08***	.16***
Lobbying incentives	.05	.07*	−.15***	.09***	.47***
Social incentives	.04	.10*	−.17***	.14***	.46***
Internal issue interests	−.20***	−.16*	.26***	−.26***	.16***
External issue interests	−.12***	.00	.04*	[a]	[a]
Decentralization	−.09***	−.11***	.04	.00	−.10***
Total influence	.12***	.14***	.03	−.11***	−.16***
Total communication	−.04	−.04	−.06**	.21***	−.16***
Multiple R^2_{adj}	.453***	.317***	.413***	.616***	.752***

[a] Variable not included in equation.

***$p<.001$;

**$p<.01$;

*$p<.05$.

attributes of environmental complexity, social change goals, and logged annual revenues also were removed to permit proper estimation of effects of the remaining independent variables.

Total Communication

The equation for total communication in Table 9.5 simultaneously tests theoretical Propositions 17, 18, and 19, while controlling for personal attributes. The six personal attributes are only modestly related to a member's communication with leaders and nonleaders. A person's age and length of membership have inverse effects: long-time members are likely to talk more, but chronologically older individuals have lower frequencies of interaction. Members' occupations, educations, incomes, and genders are unrelated to communication frequency.

At the individual level, member interests in internal issues are strongly related to communication, as predicted in Proposition 17, but external issue interest is not significant. However, the aggregate-level effects of both variables are both negative, implying a contrasting contextual effect. That is, while individual interest in internal policy issues promotes communication, an organization in which many members express such interest actually dampens individual communication. Conceivably, such highly activist associations lessen the felt necessity for individuals to make their concerns known.

Both global indicators of organization governance, democratic structures and authority role system, are positively related to communication, as expected based on Proposition 18. Similarly, at the individual level, modest positive effects of perceived decentralization and total influence also support Proposition 18. However, the corresponding contextual effects are contradictory: the mean total influence coefficient is positive (supporting Proposition 18), but the mean decentralization effect is negative, contrary to expectations. Substantively, these results suggest that organizations in which total member and leader influence is high generate greater rates of communication, in line with findings by Tannenbaum's control graph research (1968).

Decentralization resembles member issue interests, in that greater aggregate dispersion of influence appears to reduce pressures for members to interact on policy matters. Before concluding that this unexpected sign reversal is a statistical fluke (it also appears in other equations; see Table 9.6), consider the substantive interpretation: at the organization level, the more that decision making is concentrated in leaders' hands, the larger the volume of internal communication. In contrast, within groups where ordinary members have relatively greater influence, the rate of communication is lower. This relationship makes sense once we pinpoint more precisely the patterns of communication flows. Recall that the total communication measure sums the frequencies of interaction with leaders and nonleaders. When these two components are separately analyzed (results not shown), the decentralization contextual effect becomes even more strongly negative for communication with leaders. However, for communication with nonleaders, the association mean effect does not differ significantly from zero. Hence, decentralization of decision making decreases only the rate of members' contacts with leaders, not their interactions with other members. The relationship is now clear: when an association decentralizes its decision making, less communication is necessary between leaders and nonleaders, because thc latter are already extensively involved in collective decision making. In contrast, in groups where leaders retain more power over organizational affairs, more frequent communication is essential for leaders and members to keep one another informed about what is going on.

The various relations specified in Proposition 19 yield a mixed set of results in Table 9.5. Neither size nor bureaucracy is statistically significant, while both political goals and environmental uncertainty actually reduce total communication. High uncertainty apparently overwhelms group members and renders them unable to communicate purposefully and effectively. This interpretation is also supported by the small negative coefficient for organizations with highly political goals. These organizations must interact with their external environments, yet their members are less likely than the members of less politicized organizations to communicate frequently with one another.

Two of the three incentive interest variables performed as expected based on Proposition 19. Although lobbying incentives were not significant at either level, both normative and social inducements produced significant positive coefficients at both levels. The social incentives were especially robust. High rates of total communication occur among members who have high personal interest in social and recreational benefits as well as other members who belong to groups which place a high value on these rewards. Normative incentives operate in the same fashion, although the contextual effect is not as large as for social incentives. Clearly, both public- and private-good inducements promote internal group interactions.

Psychological Commitments

The first three columns of Table 9.6 exhibit the results of the contextual analyses of the psychological commitment measures. The organizational commitment and central life interest scales are both scored so that high values show strong attachment to the association, while the detachment scale's high values reveal low member involvement with the group. Therefore, the effect coefficients are generally expected to reverse signs between the first two and the third equations.

The central interest in these analyses are the effects of higher communication frequency, democratic governance structures, and member policy interests on raising psychological involvement, as specified in Proposition 20. The equations in Table 9.6 offer strong support for all of these expectations. In the commitment equation, total communication has a positive effect at the individual level but no significant contextual effect. Democratic structures positively though weakly increase commitment, but authority role systems are insignificant. The individual-level effects of decentralization and total influence are both strongly positive, but their aggregate effects are contrasting. As in the communication analysis, higher mean total influence increases commitment, but higher mean decentralization decreases it. Both coefficients for individual interests in internal and external issues increase member commitments. However, their organization-level contextual effects are negative, again paralleling the results from the communication analysis. Similar effects of all these variables occur in the equations for central life interests and detachment (taking into account the contrasting meaning of high scores on these scales).

Other variables not specified in Proposition 20 also have significant effects on member commitments. Older people and long-term members are more attached, while highly educated people are less involved. More bureaucratized associations actually generate greater member support. Environmental uncertainty reduces commitment and central life interest, and produces more detachment. Normative incentive interests strongly increase involvement at the individual level, but the contextual effects of incentives are weak and inconsistent.

All three equations account for large proportions of the variation in members' psychological orientations toward their associations.

Participation

The contextual analyses of the two dependent measures of participation in internal association activities appear in the last columns of Table 9.6. These results strongly support Proposition 20. Total communication has large positive effects on internal participation at both the individual and organizational levels. Higher individual communication also boosts internal issue activity, but the contextual effect is inverse. In the internal participation equation, the .52 coefficient for individual communication means that people differing by one standard deviation in their levels of communication will also differ by more than a half standard deviation in their participation in internal activities. This effect is reinforced by a sizeable contextual effect (.21). However, in the internal issue activity equation, the cross-level effects are offsetting: the more a member communicates, the higher her internal issue activity; being a member of high-volume organization actually reduces participation in issue activities. We do not have a good explanation for this sign reversal, which is all the more puzzling when contrasted to the sign consistency in the internal participation equation.

In both equations, only the internal issue interest index is included, because of its exact correspondence with the items in the internal issue activity scale. (Chapter 10 reverses this procedure in its analysis of the external issue measures.) At the individual level, issue interest is an especially strong positive predictor of issue activity, but it also boosts the broader internal participation scale. However, at the aggregate level, mean internal issue interest created contrasting effects: the more issue interest within the organization, the higher the individual's issue activity, but the *lower* the general internal participation. This latter effect is consistent with the pattern in the three psychological involvement equations, and strengthens the interpretation that collective organization apathy may generate a compensatory involvement among individual members when related to specific issues, not to general participation.

Governance effects on participation are mixed. Democratic structures increase both kinds of internal involvement, as expected from Proposition 20. In organizations with larger authority role systems, however, members engage in fewer internal affairs. Turning to the two contextual measures of governance, the effects of decentralization and total influence are found to be minor at the individual level, but substantially negative for three of the four organization-level coefficients. While the negative effect of mean decentralization on the internal issue activity is consistent with previous findings in this chapter, the negative total influence effect contrasts with its positive impacts in the communication and psychological involvement equations. The provisional conclusion is that associations with lower total influence must be encouraging compensating member activity. That is, in associations with high aggregate communication, this greater volume of discussion about specific issues may convince members that a given situation is being dealt with by other people. Hence, they do not need to become personally involved. When an association's mean communication level on specific issues is low, however, persons who are plugged into the communication network are privy to information that persuades them that they must be active if anything is to be done about the matter. This interpretation must remain speculative until more detailed measures of the communication content are made.

For internal participation, all three incentive interest effects are positive at the organization level, and only lobbying incentives are not significantly positive at the individual level. In contrast, for internal issue activity, none of the individual-level incentives are substantial, while group-level lobbying and social incentives both yield the largest standardized effects (.47 and .46, respectively). Together, these results indicate that associations whose incentive systems particularly emphasize social and lobbying benefits generate substantial levels of member activity on behalf of the collectivity. Finally, long-time members participate more, environmental uncertainty decreases involvement, and bureaucracy substantially discourages internal issue activity, in sharp contrast to its positive effects on psychological attachments.

Interpretation

A critical problem for analysts who uncover evidence of contextual effects in the simple additive model is to explicate the underlying processes that produce both the individual and aggregate-level effects. The necessity is all the more urgent in the present case, where theoretical propositions stating strong expectations did not predict the results. Below are suggested some future directions for explaining the observed contextual effects on member involvements.

Conventionally, interpretations of group effects in contextual models fall into four broad types: (1) interpersonal influence processes; (2) comparisons; (3) climates; and (4) selection processes. Interpersonal influences conceptualize contextual effects as involving direct interactions with other participants who socialize, persuade, or otherwise motivate social actors to adopt the group's norms of opinion or behavior. For example, communication with association leaders is especially critical in conveying a group's standards to newcomers or more peripheral members. Comparison mechanisms (sometimes colorfully referred to as "frog pond" effects) do not require direct interpersonal contacts, but operate via an individual's perceptions of salient features of the group and one's own relative standing. The classic example is the way that high school graduates entering college adjust their academic performances according to their perceived abilities relative to their new classmates. In collective action organizations, comparison effects may operate where members lack local branches and chapters for direct interpersonal contacts and must rely on impersonal media (association newsletters and magazines) to convey perceptions of group standards.

Climate explanations typically combine both diffuse perception-mediated comparisons with the normative conformity pressures of personal contacts. The "global tenor" of an organizational context affects a participant's conformity to or deviance from the group's standards. For example, a sports club may allocate prestige among its members according to their athletic abilities as they are channeled toward team success, rather than for personal "star" performance. The recent concern among management researchers with "organizational culture" (Price and Mueller 1986) exemplifies this version of the climate mechanism. Finally, self-selection processes complicate the difficulty of attributing a causal change of individuals' original attitudes and behaviors to the group context. Potential association members may know something about an association prior to joining, especially about its goals and incentive offerings. To the extent that certain people are attracted to an organization because of these contextual features, the causal direction among independent and dependent variables becomes more problematic.

Sorting out the relative contributions of these diverse contextual mechanisms on the basis of simple empirical contextual effects is a difficult project. Some useful data are simply unavailable; for example, information about respondents' perceptions of governance at the time of joining. Other data yield ambiguous interpretations, such as the relevance of communication rates for both climate and interpersonal influence processes. What the analyses in this chapter have shown is the existence of significant contextual effects persisting across several indicators of member psychological and participatory involvements. The next step toward unraveling the contextual processes should involve more direct measures of interpersonal networks among organization members and leaders. The actual dynamics of interpersonal influence, socialization, and perception will have to be analyzed in far greater detail than our simple questionnaire could provide.

Conclusion

Collective action organization members provide psychological sustenance and participation to their associations. Policy-oriented communication is a key factor for translating member issue interests, democratic governance structures, and other organizational components into member involvements. Theoretical propositions were generally supported by the data, although simple contextual models uncovered fairly complex patterns relating individual- to group-level phenomena.

The analyses in this chapter clarify important points in the paradigms of social integration and organizational governance. Members' involvements in their collective action organizations are enhanced by extensive communication networks that plug them into the thick of policy discussions, apart from whatever degree of interest they may have in particular policy issues. These interpersonal ties are complemented at the personal level by normative and social incentive interests, and at the organizational level by democratic governance structures. Together, these social factors create compelling grounds for members to develop attachments to the collectivity and a willingness to believe and behave in ways that further their organizations' well-being. Contributions to collective action that span association boundaries are the subject of the following chapter.

10

MOBILIZATION FOR INFLUENCE

Collective action organizations enjoy a privileged position in the American national polity, along with federalism and geographic decentralization, as guarantors of civic order and stability:

> In the United States, at least, private associations have also contributed to order and stability through a pattern of relationships with government to a degree which is seldom acknowledged. In a multitude of ways, the distinction between what is private and what is public has been blurred so that it is often extraordinarily difficult to determine what is the character of a particular form of action or rule (McConnell 1969, p. 155).

This interlacing of public and private sectors has not gone as far in America as in some Western European nations characterized by corporatist polities (Panitch 1977; Schmitter 1981). In Austria, Scandinavia, and other nations with strong labor movements and socialist parties, governmental authority has devolved to a set of intermediary (''peak'') associations of employers and workers. The state authorizes and consults with them in negotiating, regulating, and implementing policies that affect their members; for example, in setting wages and prices, production and labor conditions, occupational qualifications and training, and welfare provisions (Williamson 1985, pp. 78–79). Although for historical reasons the devolution of state power was more limited in the United States (Salisbury 1979; Wilson 1982), the blurred boundaries noted two decades ago by McConnell have grown even fuzzier. State bureaucracies' strategies vis-à-vis civil society emerged from basic organizational imperatives for coping with environmental uncertainties, resource scarcities, and socio-

legal constraints (Knoke and Burleigh 1989). In their efforts to maximize autonomy, state bureaus fostered stable networks of clientele, funding sources,
and interorganizational alliances:

> The successful agencies expand, garnering more projects and larger budgets un-
> der their control. In this process of increasing the predictability of their specific
> environment, public bureaucracies incorporate external constituencies, blurring
> the boundary line between public and private sectors, as they establish powerful
> interest groups inside and outside the state with a stake in the preservation of the
> agency (Alford and Friedland 1985, p. 436).

The historical creation of the liberal democratic state was accompanied by a
parallel transformation of social segments into organized interest groups with
claims on access to the new centers of social power (McNeil 1978). Interde-
pendency and reciprocated relations between state bureaus and private associations jointly created the modern organizational state. Neither a structure for
capitalist class rule nor a neutral umpire adjudicating claims of competing
groups, the state is "a system of governmental and nongovernmental organizations that struggle for power and legitimacy in the making of public
policies" (Laumann and Knoke 1987, p. 382). Rather than reflecting rigid
ideological stances, the policy objectives sought by these participants reflect
organizational imperatives for profits, growth, market share, jurisdiction, autonomy, and similarly narrow and pragmatic concerns.

Following Wilson (1980), McFarland (1987) formulated the governmental
process as a "power triad" involving economic producer groups, state agencies with significant autonomy, and countervailing groups normally opposed to
some of the producer interests. As a result, cleavages within policy domains
display the idiosyncratic nature of shifting organizational interests, rather than
rigid and inflexible alignments structured along class, industry, or party dimensions. Most collective policy decisions involve shifting interorganizational
coalitions and influence interactions:

> Cooperation among organizations that share a common preference for an event
> outcome raises the probability that their efforts will produce a favorable deci-
> sion. Coalitions of organizations pool resources and coordinate their common
> efforts to overcome their opponents and persuade the public authorities of the
> merits of their case. Such processes of contention among opposing interest group
> coalitions, including partisan governmental organizations, are the key dynamic
> for any understanding of collective decision making in national policy domains
> (Laumann and Knoke 1987, p. 387).

This chapter examines the political activities of American national associations in the organizational state. It investigates both the mobilization of
members to influence governmental policy-making and the tactics used by

associations to convey their policy preferences to the authorities. The result is a clearer picture of how the political economies of private associations are integrated into the modern organizational state.

Associations in the Organizational State

In the conventional view, private associations in the organizational state are seen as demand aggregators, mediating relations between officials and the citizenry:

> Each intermediate organization brings together a number of people with similar concerns and goals, provides means through which these members can acquire information about relevant public issues, enables them to pool their resources to generate greater collective influence than could be exercised by a single individual, and provides an established channel through which they can exert this influence "upward" on political decisions and policies (Olsen 1982, p. 33).

Associations provide government officials, in turn, with channels to communicate information and provide political benefits to selected constituencies. American interest group proliferation is encouraged by a federal constitutional structure and electoral systems that fragment power among hundreds of separate policy domains. Each domain comprises a subgovernment ("iron" or "cozy triangle") consisting of congressional subcommittees, government bureaus, and interest group clientele that resist the intrusion of a strong central authority (Ripley and Franklin 1976; McFarland 1983). This view led to Truman's (1971) assertion that interest groups would form almost spontaneously within any group of persons experiencing a common disturbance that might be redressed through collective action. His proposition has been effectively refuted, theoretically (Olson 1965; Lowi 1979) as well as empirically, by facts such as the difficulty oppressed groups encounter in entering the American pressure group system (Gamson 1975), the vital importance of well-heeled patrons (including foundations and the government itself) for keeping interest groups in operation (Taub *et al.* 1977; Walter 1983), and the evident system biases toward business corporations' policy interests (Schlozman 1984; Gais *et al.* 1984; Domhof 1983).

An alternative view of the interest group system, which could be called the conflict perspective, depicts it as an arena in which various groups engage in political struggles to impress their policy preferences on the authorities at the expense of other groups whose interests are either less powerful or simply were never organized in the first place (Hayes 1978; McFarland 1987). In this view, organizations do not simply articulate member interest. They create demands, instill them in their members, and participate in governmental policy-making on equal terms with political parties and public bureaucracies. Subgovernments rapidly become unable to contain the contentious regulatory and redistributive issues—environmental protection, civil rights, consumer and occupational safety—that spill over into the full Congress and the White House for collective resolution (Gais *et al.* 1984). The system may be evolving into a mass society in which interest group executives become remote from, and unresponsive to their mass memberships (Hayes 1983).

Ultimately, only efficient, resource-rich organized interests can gain access to the state's managerial elites, as poor and unorganized social groups are relegated to sporadic challenges (Gamson 1975; McAdam 1982). Even those interest groups nominally based on mass membership and support—labor unions, parties, trade associations, and professional societies—increasingly become disadvantaged relative to the dominant position of institutions such as corporations or local governments, with respect to interest representation in the central government (Salisbury 1984). Policy-making in the organizational state emerges from cooperative and antagonistic interactions among large-scale public and private sector organizations. Combining aspects of both the traditional and the conflict perspectives, this chapter analyzes how American collective action organizations attempt to influence national public policies by mobilizing their members.

An Advocacy Explosion

A collective action organization affects national policy-making primarily by mobilizing the political resources at its disposal and using them to influence government authorities whose decisions are central to the association's interests. Several salient examples of association participation in national policy-making events illustrate this resource mobilization/application process:

- In 1978 the Federal Trade Commission (FTC) proposed to remove antitrust exemptions on physician advertising and price fixing (setting minimum fees). The American Medical Association and American Dental Association called upon its extensive grass-roots network to pour more than $3 million into congressional campaigns. By 1982, 219 House members sponsored a bill to exempt "learned professions" from antitrust prosecution. However, the FTC, in conjunction with the American Association of Retired Persons and Ralph Nader's Congress Watch, launched its own grass-roots and mass media counterattack that produced more than 150 newspaper editorials favoring the anticompetition regulation. In the Senate showdown, the AMA/ADA amendment to restrict the FTC action was tabled (Pertschuk 1986, pp. 82–114).

- In 1977 Congress narrowly defeated an effort to legalize common-situs picketing in the construction industry, which would have allowed unions with a grievance against a single employer to shut down an entire building site. Favoring the bill were the AFL-CIO and 17 craft unions, while the Chamber of Commerce, National Association of Manufacturers (NAM), Business Roundtable, and Associated General Contractors, along with 40 other interest groups, opposed it. The two-year fight featured "the use of computers to generate grass-roots pressure in crucial districts; provision of 'hard facts' to members of Congress . . . face-to-face contact between members of Congress and group lobbyists; and last-minute lobbying 'blitzes' and 'fly-ins' of group representatives from the member's home district" (Ornstein and Elder 1978, pp. 152–53). Although the unions could not match the employers' massive resources, finances were not the sole factor: "The scope of employer mobilization and the degree to which different segments of the business community were able to work together and build a winning coalition were probably the most important aspects of the campaign" (Levitan and Cooper 1984, pp. 134–35). Consequently, business became an increasingly potent player in Washington during the Reagan era.

- In late 1986 the President's Commission on Americans Outdoors prepared to issue its recommendations that at least $1 billion a year be put into a new trust fund to acquire and preserve remaining open space and protected "greenways" between urban centers. Surprisingly, the report ran counter to the Reagan administration's efforts to take land out of the public domain. As information about the commission report leaked out, it provoked a letter to President Reagan from the NAM, American Farm Bureau Federation, American Mining Congress, Highway Users Federation and many other industry groups urging him to "take immediate action to change the direction of the commission report." The Mountain States Legal Foundation threatened possible legal action. On the other side, the major national conservation groups supported parts of the report but called "woefully inadequate" its failure to address mismanagement and poor conditions in existing public lands (New York Times 1/4/87). The controversy seemed likely to heat up as the issue moved into Congress.

These examples and countless others that could be offered unveil the central features of association participation in national policy-making: the mobilization of grass-roots resources and participation; the formation of action sets (coalitions) to coordinate lobbying efforts; the publicizing of positions and rationales through the media; the contacting of key government policy-makers; the partisan involvement of government agencies and politicians—all leading to the ultimate resolution of a given issue in Congress, courts, or executive agencies.

Over the past two decades, a demonstrable advocacy explosion in the nation's capital triggered a renewed academic attention to the phenomenon. Several surveys used interest groups' founding dates to estimate rapid rates of growth in lobbying organizations in Washington since the 1960's (Walker 1983; Schlozman and Tierney 1983; Berry 1984, pp. 18–26). Citizen lobbies (so-called public-interest groups, or PIGS) were especially likely to be born in this era (Berry 1977, p. 34), although the rate of increase is distorted to some unknown degree by mortality prior to the survey. Of the nearly 7000 organizations with a continuing presence in Washington (either by keeping an office or hiring legal counsel to represent them), almost half are corporations (Schlozman 1984). Probably more than 2000 associations are headquartered today in that area.

Speculations about the causes of this expanded activity abound. Congressional reorganization provided additional points of political access and leverage (Schlozman and Tierney 1986). Post-Watergate election reforms created those ubiquitous political action committees (PACS) with their overflowing coffers of political money (Malbin 1980; Conway 1983). Successive waves of regulatory and deregulatory policies stimulated citizen, labor, business, and professional countermobilizations (Gais *et al.* 1984; McFarland 1987). An unraveling two-party system left a vacuum into which interest groups flowed (Berry 1984). Vastly greater volumes and quality of information are available today, making governments and interest groups better able to form policy judgments, present their cases, and shape public opinion. And ideological polarization in the populace has promoted liberal and conservative insurgencies through single-interest social movements (Hershey and West 1983).

To date, no one has attempted the ambitious, systematic, quantitative model-building that will be necessary to winnow the anecdotal chaff from the substantive wheat. Such an undertaking must necessarily track the changing structure of the pressure group system over several decades, possibly at multiple levels of aggregation ranging from the organizational arena to the policy domain to the entire polity. Although much of the information for this project is available in secondary sources or through reconstruction from informant interviews, the costs of assembling and analyzing the vast volume of data can be prohibitive, to judge from research on just one decade of policy-making in the energy and health domains (Laumann *et al.* 1985; Laumann and Knoke 1987).

Several recent empirical efforts have concentrated upon modes of interaction between interest groups and government targets. The expanded numbers of participants accompanied an enlarged repertoire of political influence tactics and strategies. Especially noteworthy were the greater use of electronic mass media, computerized direct mail (McCarthy 1983; Godwin and Mitchell 1984), constituency-legislator linkages, and greater reliance upon conventional lobbying practices such as congressional hearing testimony and personal contacts (Schlozman and Tierney 1983). PIGS are especially likely to use grassroots mobilizations, appealing to the public through the mass media, launching letter-writing campaigns, and mobilizing local lobbying efforts (McFarland 1984; Gais *et al.* 1984). Corporations are more apt to work through law firms, consulting or public relations firms, and other institutional representation (Salisbury 1984; Laumann and Heinz 1985; but see Loomis 1983, on the Chamber of Commerce's grass-roots politicking). The relative availability of members or money as resources undoubtedly explains much of the variation in choice of interaction modes. Less attention has been paid to coalitions among interest groups to pool their scarce resources for collective action. However, some studies at both local and national levels found extensive collaborative efforts, suggesting that networks of interorganizational exchange may be a significant factor shaping the dynamics and outcomes of influence activities (Heclo 1978; Chubb 1983; McFarland 1984; Berry 1984: 202-5; Galaskiewicz 1979; Knoke and Laumann 1983; Salisbury *et al.* 1987).

Whether viewed primarily as demand aggregators or combat organizations, interest groups have clearly entrenched themselves as significant players in the political game. However, assessing their impact on public-policy decisions remains imprecise. Association activity is considerably easier to measure than the effectiveness of such activity in securing desired policy decisions. Because the American polity is so intricately convoluted, tracing input demands through to policy outcomes is a herculean task for which both theory and data are wanting. But given the concern aroused about these matters, especially over whether the proliferation of narrow interest groups is stalemating liberal democracy (Thurow 1980; Olson 1982), we can anticipate a vigorous assault on the question in the years ahead.

Mobilizing Members

Still unclear is the relationship between collective action organizations' mobilization of member resources and their impact on public policy-making. Several processes may operate simultaneously in democratic societies to translate members' nonpolitical involvements into political participation:

(1) Association membership broadens one's sphere of interests and concerns, so that public affairs and political issues become more salient to the individual. (2) It brings one into contact with many diverse people, and the resulting social relationships draw the individual into a wide range of new activities, including politics. (3) It gives one training and experience in social interaction and leadership skills that are valuable in the political sphere. (4) It provides one with multiple channels through which he or she can act to exert influence on politicians and the political system (Olsen 1982, p. 32).

Political mobilization by associations is most effective when the organization becomes the object of an individual's commitment; that is, an intense psychological bonding occurs in which the member "is willing to let the group serve as a source of identification and direction for his own beliefs and behaviors" (Wilson and Orum 1976, p. 194; also Knoke and Wood 1981, pp. 8–14). Such reference group processes are shaped by the symbolic, interpersonal, and ideological devices examined in Chapter 9.

Several empirical efforts have tried to specify further the components of the mobilization model. Rogers and Bultena (1975; Rogers *et al.* 1975) concluded that organizational involvement explained more variation in political participation in three Iowa counties than did social status and political attitudes, although the relationship was stronger for "instrumental" than for "expressive" associations. They concluded that the overall mobilization effect of voluntary group involvement serves to widen class differences in political participation. Schulman's (1978) Buffalo, N.Y. survey found little support for hypotheses that formal democratic structures or direct organizational involvement enhances external political participation, although he suggested that some instrumental task learning may take place.

Olsen's (1982) analyses of Indianapolis and Gavle, Sweden surveys supported the proposition that the political mobilization process takes place across all types of organizations, from labor unions and business associations to fraternal, recreational, and church-related groups. Political discussions, voting turnout, partisan activities, and contacting of government officials all covaried positively with the number of associations to which individuals belonged, net of age, education, income, and occupation. However, contrary to Verba and Nie (1972), mobilization did not seem to depend upon an individual's activity level within an association, at least in the American data: "Sheer number of memberships by itself may lead to political participation, even with age and socioeconomic status held constant" (Olsen 1982, p. 138). Knoke's (1982) analyses of political influence efforts by members of 32 Indianapolis social associations disclosed that mobilization may depend on both members' degree of associational involvement (measured by frequency of communication) and the organization's attempts to rouse its membership to contact government officials. That is, when the association in question attempted to mobilize its members, those persons in heavy communication with others were much more likely to contact officials. This interaction effect did not generalize to the conventional external behaviors studied by Olsen, such as voting turnout or campaigning, implying that the mobilization process may be quite specific with regard to the targets and objectives of political participation.

Association Political Capacity

A necessary condition for a collective action organization to influence national policy-making is the development of sufficient capacity to participate in political actions. An association's political capacity is determined by the number of specialized roles and programs it maintains that are responsible, implicitly or explicitly, for monitoring and intervening in important policy decisions (see Laumann *et al.* 1985, where a version of this characteristic is called "monitoring capacity"). The larger an organization's political capacity, the more quickly it can identify and take advantage of opportunities for influence that arise in the national polity. In other words, the association can better act as an agenda-setter in formulating and initiating policy actions. Of course, the development of political capacity must take into account the organization's goals. Many collective action associations do not overtly pursue objectives that require them to engage in political combat, and thus they do not need to develop substantial political capacities. The political economy theory addresses association political capacity in the following proposition:

> *Proposition 21:* The more complex an organization's structures and environments, and the more important its public-policy goals, the greater the political capacity it develops.

Political capacity of the NAS organizations was measured by a simple index of the number of distinct roles and programs relevant to political action. Some of these positions are explicitly involved in policy influence actions, while others can be drawn on for legal or technical advice during political efforts. An association was assigned one point of the political capacity index for each of the following components: (1) staff members who monitor national policy matters of interest to the organization; (2) a public relations officer; (3) legal counsel under retainer from outside the organization; (4) staff members whose principal responsibilities are to gather systematic technical data, "such as estimates of population changes or economic activity"; (5) a program "to activate members in local areas to lobby their own congressmen and senators on national issues of interest to the organization"; (6) lawyers employed to provide in-house counsel; (7) staff whose main job is to "lobby government and legislative bodies for favorable decisions"; (8) a political action committee (PAC) belonging to the organization or one to which it contributes. The index ranges between zero and eight points, with a higher score indicating greater capacity for political activation. Note that all these arrangements involve formal staff positions or programs coordinated by staff, rather than extensive involvement by ordinary members. Thus, political capacity is expected to covary only slightly with the democratic governance measures discussed in Chapter 8.

Table 10.1 shows the percentage distributions of all eight items and the index mean for all associations and the four main types. Over half of all associations assign staff people to policy monitoring and public relations activities. The six other functions are performed less often, with lobbying and political action committee contributions in a distinct minority. The mean political capacity is only 2.64 functions for all organizations. However, substantial majorities of labor unions conduct all eight activities, giving them a mean political capacity (5.70) almost twice as large as that of the trade associations (3.37) and professional societies (2.37), and more than three times that of recreational associations (1.69).

Table 10.2 tests the proposition that organizational goals, structures, and environments predict high levels of political capacity. For all associations, only political goals and income (logged annual revenues) are strongly related to greater capacity (columns 1 and 2 of Table 10.2). The standardized regression coefficients (b^*) disclosed that these two variables have about equal impact on political capacity (.43 and .37 standard deviations for goals and revenues, respectively). The unstandardized coefficients (B) express their effects in scale units of the independent variables. For political goals, measured on a four-

Table 10.1. Percentage of Organizations with Political Capacity

Political capacity	Type of association				
	All assns.	Labor unions	Trade assns.	Prof'l. assns.	Rec'l. assns.
Policy monitors	68	90	71	71	42
Public relations	54	73	65	47	51
Outside counsel	39	70	64	37	15
Technical data	36	75	45	23	32
Congress program	29	75	38	25	13
In-house counsel	15	55	23	15	9
Lobbyists	14	70	18	10	6
PAC	9	62	13	4	1
Political capacity index (mean)	2.64	5.70	3.37	2.37	1.69
(*N*)	(459)	(57)	(100)	(104)	(121)

Table 10.2.   Regression Analysis of Political Capacity

Independent variables	All org.		Highly political		Less political	
	B	*b**	*B*	*b**	*B*	*b**
Political goals	0.66	.43***	—	—	—	—
Revenue (log)	0.33	.37***	0.37	.47***	0.35	.43***
Bureaucracy	0.17	.08	0.02	.01	0.25	.13*
Democratic structures	−0.04	−.03	−0.38	−.25***	0.20	.15***
Authority roles	0.10	.06	0.30	.18*	−0.06	−.04
Env. complexity	0.21	.05	0.53	.15*	0.44	.12*
Env. uncertainty	−0.17	−.04	−0.11	−.03	−0.13	−.04
Constant	−0.34	—	1.11	—	−1.25	—
R^2_{adj}		.468***		.316***		.309***
(*N*)		(459)		(150)		(309)

*p<.05;
**p<.01;
***p<.001.

point scale ranging from "none" to "major," each unit change increases the political capacity index score by two thirds of a unit; thus, controlling for everything else, an association with major political goals is predicted to have about two more capacity units than an organization with no political goals $((3)(.66)=1.98$ units). This expected difference is somewhat smaller than the observed differences in mean capacities of associations with major and no political goals $(3.92−1.46=2.46$ units), primarily because of the larger annual revenues of the former.

Because the annual revenue variable was nonlinearly transformed to logarithmic units, its unstandardized (*B*) regression coefficient does not give an intuitive sense of its magnitude. The partial derivative of political capacity with respect to (logged) revenue reveals that, at the mean of all association revenues ($25,000), the unstandardized effect of revenue on political capacity is 1.48 political units for each additional $100,000 in annual revenue [(.37/25)(100)]. Another way to express this effect is the increase in the number of political capacity units for a 1% increase in revenue at *any* value of revenue (Stoltzenberg 1979, pp. 468–70). This rate of change in the equation is 0.037 political capacity units. Thus, doubling an association's annual revenue (i.e., increasing it 100%) would increase its political capacity by more than one third of a unit $((0.037)(100)=0.37)$.

Various formal structural and environmental variables are not related to greater political capacity in the equation for all associations. However, when the sample is split into associations with major political goals and those with less political goals, some strong interaction effects emerge (columns 3–6 in Table 10.2). Environmental complexity promotes greater political capacity for both types of associations, as do bureaucracy for the less political ones and authority role systems for the highly political ones. Interestingly, the number of democratic structures (see Chapter 8) has substantial but inverse relations: among less political organizations democratic structures are related to greater political capacity, but among highly political associations higher capacity is related to fewer democratic structures. These contrasting effects canceled one another in the equation for all associations. Substantively, among associations with the greatest interest in influencing government policies democratic structures appear to be an impediment to developing political capacity. Apparently, these associations can better develop their means to influence policy-making when fewer institutional arrangements exist to give members access to internal governance. This configuration suggests that, holding constant authority role systems, political capacity and democratic structures are substitutable. That is, highly political associations rely on either mechanisms that encourage member involvement or functions that are carried out by staff members, but not upon both arrangements. In contrast, for less political associations democratic structures and political capacity are mutually reinforcing, and both are encouraged by greater administrative bureaucratization.

Organizational Mobilization Efforts

By itself, an association's political capacity indicates only the *potential* for that organization to enter into and try to influence the policy-making process. To understand how political capacity translates into actual attempts at policy influence requires an analysis of organizational resource mobilization efforts and members' responsiveness to these efforts. Chapters 7 to 9 examined the personal and organizational factors that affect members' internal association activities, resource contributions, psychological orientations, and participation. We now examine the effects of organizational and personal variables on mobilization of member involvement in external influence actions.

The NAS informants were asked how often their organizations "call upon ordinary members to make any of the following types of contributions": (1) to contact government officials on behalf of the [org. name]; (2) to write letters to newspapers or magazines; (3) to participate in demonstrations or picketings; and (4) to work in political candidates' campaigns. Four categories were presented—"never," "rarely," "sometimes," and "regularly." Table 10.3 shows the percentage of associations that try sometimes or regularly to mobilize their members for each of the four efforts. The table also reports the mean mobilization effort of all four items, using a scale ranging form "never"=1 to "regularly"=4.

Table 10.3. Organizational Efforts to Mobilize Members: Percentage
Sometimes or Regularly

Mobilization efforts	Type of association				
	All assns.	Labor unions	Trade assns.	Prof'l. assns.	Rec'l. assns.
Contacting government officials	37	87	42	45	21
Writing to newspapers, magazines	32	63	22	35	34
Demonstrating or picketing	6	71	3	1	4
Working in election campaigns	6	54	4	3	1
Mean mobilization effort	1.81	2.86	1.68	1.73	1.57
(N)	(459)	(57)	(100)	(104)	(121)

Only a minority of all associations frequently try to involve their members in external influence activities. About a third mobilize their members to contact government officials on behalf of the organization, and to write to newspapers and magazines. Only a handful resort to picketing and demonstrating and asking their members to work in the election campaigns of political candidates. Among the basic types of associations, labor unions stand out in their frequent use of all four mobilization techniques, especially demonstrations and electoral campaigns. Unions, of course, have a long history of direct protest via economic strikes and boycotts. They also have a vigorous tradition of providing campaign workers to local and national Democratic campaigns (Galenson 1986, pp. 63–67). Among the three other types of associations, professional societies and trade associations are both more likely to stress contacting government officials than writing to the press, but recreational associations emphasize the opposite set of tactics. More than 95% of all nonunion organizations entirely avoid political protest and campaign participation. Indeed, only a few even endorse candidates for office or channel money through political action committees (see Table 10.1). Many associations would jeopardize their tax-exempt status with the Internal Revenue Service by engaging in partisan actions such as campaign endorsements.

The political economy theory asserts that member mobilization is more likely in political associations that have created extensive political capacities:

Proposition 22:   Organizations with public-policy goals and greater political capacity are more likely to mobilize their members' policy efforts.

In the regression for all associations, reported in the first two columns of Table 10.4, goals and capacity have identical standardized coefficients ($b*=$ .40). This means that a difference of one standard deviation between organizations on either variable increases mobilization efforts by four tenths of a standard deviation. Only two other factors are significant covariates of mobilization. The negative coefficient for annual revenues implies that richer associations are *less* likely to try to mobilize their members for political action, once their political capacities and goals are taken into account. The positive coefficient for environmental complexity indicates that organizations operating in more complex conditions are more likely to try mobilizing their members. Presumably, political influence is one way of coping with this complexity. In contrast, environmental uncertainty has no significant relationship to mobilization efforts in the full sample, nor do any of the other measures of association governance.

However, when the sample is divided into two subsets of organization, those with major political goals and those with less political goals, important interaction effects emerge (the last four columns of Table 10.4). Comparing unstandardized political capacity coefficients discloses that the effect of political capacity on mobilization is twice as large among the highly political groups ($B=.20$) as it is among the less political organizations ($B=.11$). Thus, a one-unit difference in political capacity results in a one-fifth unit increase in mobilization efforts by the highly political groups, but barely a one-tenth unit increase by the less political associations.

An even more startling interaction occurs with the environmental uncertainty variable. While uncertainty increases mobilization efforts among less political associations ($B=.13$), it *decreases* such efforts among the most political organizations ($B=-.25$). These contrasting relations had canceled one

Table 10.4. Regression Analyses of Organization Mobilization Efforts

Independent variables	All org.		Highly political		Less political	
	B	b*	B	b*	B	b*
Political goals	.19	.40***	—	—	—	—
Political capacity	.13	.41***	.20	.59***	.11	.43***
Revenue (logged)	−.05	−.18***	−.06	−.20	−.04	−.18*
Bureaucracy	.06	.08	−.04	−.05	.08	.16**
Democratic structures	.02	.04	.08	.14*	.03	.09
Authority roles	.00	.01	−.00	−.01	−.03	−.07
Env. complexity	.15	.12***	.19	.16*	.20	.22***
Env. uncertainty	−.02	−.02	−.25	−.20**	.13	.16**
Constant	3.50	—	1.59	—	0.12	—
R^2_{adj}		.502***		.283***		.317***
(N)		(459)		(150)		(309)

*$p<.05$;
**$p<.01$;
***$p<.001$.

another in the full sample. Apparently, highly political associations engage in mobilization efforts only when their environments permit them to acquire more reliable information that is conducive to strategic calculations. Net of the positive effect of environmental complexity, the more uncertain environment in which these associations operate seems to overwhelm them, depressing rather than expanding their mobilization activities. These differential impacts of environmental uncertainty and complexity among highly political groups underscore the theoretical point (made in Chapter 4) that these two dimensions of the information-flow environment are conceptually and empirically distinct. In contrast, among the subset of less political associations, complexity and uncertainty have positive coefficients. Because these organizations experience less turbulent external conditions, they seem to respond to modest uncertainty and complexity by engaging in greater mobilization efforts.

Member External Participation

The central finding of the preceding section must be underscored: regardless of an association's political goals, the greater its political capacity, the more often it tries to mobilize its members for external influence activity. But organizational efforts to stimulate members' involvements in external political influence activities do not automatically generate such participation. This section turns to the membership questionnaires from 35 professional, recreational, and women's associations to examine the relationship between organizational characteristics, most especially mobilization efforts, and the individual member's involvement in these external actions. Two theoretical propositions specify the individual and organizational factors that stimulate member participation in external influence activities:

Proposition 23: The members of organizations with political goals, high political capacity, and strong mobilization efforts are more likely to engage in external influence activities.

Proposition 24: When members have strong interests in policy issues and high rates of policy communication, they are more likely to engage in external influence activities.

The questionnaire asked members, "During the past year, how often did you perform the following actions on behalf of the (org. name)?" In addition to the four mobilization items used in the informant interviews, the members were asked about signing petitions for the organization (on the four-point scale from "never" to "regularly"). A factor analysis divulged that the five items form a single external participation scale. Table 10.5 exhibits the five items and scale means for all association members, as well as the percentage of respondents who said they had never performed these actions during the past year. Given the more precise time frame in the members' questionnaires, their low rates of participation are not surprising. Still, compared to the internal activities analyzed in Chapter 9, members are clearly less involved in their associations' external activities. Parallel with the organizations' actions listed in Table 10.3, members were much more likely to contact government officials, sign petitions, and write to the press than they were to protest or participate in political candidates' campaigns on behalf of the association. Two thirds of all members participated in none of the external actions during the past year. Although the mean external participation rate was significantly higher among members of the 15 highly political associations (1.40) than among members of the 20 less political organizations (1.10), fewer than half of the former engaged in any of the five actions.

To test Proposition 23, the contextual model used in Chapter 9 to explain member involvements was applied in Table 10.6 to member external participation. (Due to multicollinearity, the organization-level measure of interest in lobbying incentives could not be included.) In the equation for all associations (columns one and two), neither political goals nor political capacity are important predictors of external participation. The most important factors are the association's mobilization efforts ($b^* = .26$) and total influence ($b^* = .19$), and the individual member's interest in lobbying incentives ($b^* = .23$) and communication with other members ($b^* = .28$). Although political goals and political capacities both increase organizational mobilization efforts, their effect on

Table 10.5. Items and Means for Scale of Member External Participation in Collective Action Organizations

Scale items	All org.		Highly political Mean	Less political Mean
	Mean	Never (%)		
Wrote, phoned, or personally contacted government officials	1.40	77	1.66	1.15
Signed a petition for the organization	1.30	82	1.47	1.13
Wrote letters to newspapers, magazines	1.25	84	1.35	1.15
Worked in political candidate's campaign	1.19	90	1.35	1.06
Picketed or demonstrated	1.09	95	1.15	1.01
External participation scale mean	1.24	68	1.40	1.10
(N)	(8746)	(4348)	(4399)	

members' external participation is almost entirely mediated through that mobilization process. Thus, only part of Proposition 23 is supported by the research results.

The effect of organizational mobilization efforts is almost entirely confined to the highly political organizations, as demonstrated by comparing the pair of subsample equations (columns three to six in Table 10.6). The variance explained (R^2) by the highly political association equation is almost three times as large as that for the less political organizations. Organizational mobilization effort has more than 17 times the impact on external participation ($B=.54$ and

Table 10.6. Contextual Analyses of External Participation

Independent variables	All org.		Highly political		Less political	
	B	$b*$	B	$b*$	B	$b*$
Personal attributes						
Age	.00	.06***	−.00	−.01	.00	.08***
Length of membership	.00	.02*	.01	.15***	−.00	−.01
Occupational prestige	.00	.04***	.00	.06***	.00	.02
Education	.00	.01	.02	.07***	−.00	−.02
Income	.00	.01	.00	−.01	.00	.01
Gender (female)	.04	.04***	.10	.08***	−.01	−.02
Organizational attributes						
Political goals	−.03	−.06***	*a*	*a*	*a*	*a*
Political capacity	.00	.00	−.07	−.17***	.01	.05**
Mobilization efforts	.18	.26***	.54	.58***	.03	.05*
Environ. uncertainty	−.13	−.14***	−.84	−.51***	.00	.01
Bureaucracy	.00	.00	−.09	−.05**	−.00	−.02
Individual-level effects						
Communication	.07	.28***	.10	.31***	.04	.30***
Total influence	.00	.01	.00	.01	.00	.01
Lobbying incentives	.15	.23***	.14	.16***	.09	.22***
Organization-level effects						
Communication	−.03	−.06***	−.38	−.57***	.00	.00
Total influence	.33	.19***	.37	.18***	−.02	−.01
Lobbying incentives	*a*	*a*	*a*	*a*	*a*	*a*
Constant	−1.53	—	0.93	—	0.77	—
R^2_{adj}	.375****		.438****		.164****	
(N)	(8746)		(4348)		(4399)	

a Variables omitted from equation
*p<.05;
**p<.01;
***p<.001.

.03, respectively). A larger political capacity actually *decreases* external participation slightly among members of highly political associations, net of mobilization efforts, while barely increasing external participation in less political associations ($B= -.07$ and .01, respectively). As in the analyses of mobilization efforts (Table 10.4 above), environmental uncertainty has a substantial negative effect on member external involvement in highly political groups. Consistent with Table 10.4, greater environmental uncertainty seems to overwhelm members' desires to participate in external influence activities in highly political associations. Apparently, less turbulent conditions seem to have no effect on the external participation of less political group members.

The contextual effects observed in the equation for all organizations are also concentrated primarily among the highly political organizations. Higher mean total influence (the aggregate level of internal policy influence by members and leaders) increases members' external policy participation, but the individual-level effect is negligible. Partial support for Proposition 24 appears in the relationship between communication and external participation. The group-level and individual-level effects are reversed: people who interact more often with other members and leaders are more likely to participate in external activities, but belonging to a highly communicative association depresses external participation. This sign reversal may be an artifact of high covariation among the contextual measures. A closer look at the mobilization process reveals that communication is implicated in a nonadditive fashion.

In an analysis of political mobilization by local chapters of Indianapolis social influence associations, Knoke (1982) found that the effect of communication on member involvement in external contacting depended on an organization's mobilization efforts:

> . . . when an association does not attempt to mobilize its members, individual variation in decision making and communication networks will have little impact on political participation. But when the association does urge its members into action, the highly involved members will respond more than the peripherally involved (Knoke 1982, pp. 172–73).

The same relationship is observed in the NAS, as shown in Figure 10.1, which graphs the effects of communication on external participation within three levels of organizational mobilization. Separate regression equations were estimated for high, medium, and low levels of mobilization (8, 11, and 12 associations, respectively; data on mobilization efforts were missing for four organizations). Communication, political capacity, bureaucracy, environmental uncertainty, and five personal attributes were used as predictors of external participation. The mean values for each independent variable in the full sample were then entered into the equation to obtain adjusted intercept values,

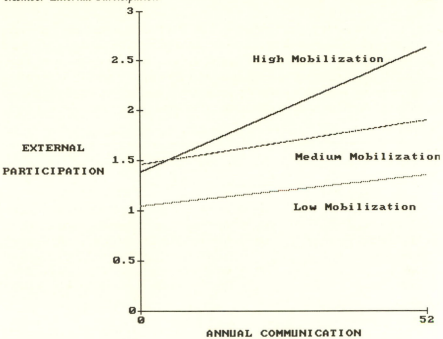

3

2.5   High Mobilization

2

EXTERNAL

PARTICIPATION   1.5
                          Medium Mobilization

1   Low Mobilization

0.5

0
0   52
ANNUAL COMMUNICATION

Figure 10.1 Relationship of External Participation to Communication within Levels of Mobilization

which are plotted in Figure 10.1 above the total sample mean communication (3.1 times per year) on the horizontal axis.

The slopes of the three adjusted regression lines show the effects of communication frequency on external participation by an average association member under a given organizational mobilization effort. The effects clearly differ according to the amount of mobilization attempted. Among organizations that tried little or no mobilization, the two nearly flat regression lines testify that greater amounts of communication produce very little increase in external participation. In stark contrast, among associations that heavily mobilize their members, external participation increases steeply with the frequency of annual communication. An average member who talks weekly with others is likely to be more than three times as involved in external influence activities as a member who communicates with other members only three times per year. The relationships represented in Figure 10.1 are compelling testimony to the joint necessity of individual and organizational factors in stimulating the political involvements of members.

The assertions of Proposition 24 concerning the effects of issue interests and communication on external activities are further examined in Table 10.7, where external issue activity is the dependent variable. As described in Chapter 9, external issue activity measures how involved members said they were on recent issues identified by the association informants, using a four-point scale ranging from "not active" to "highly active." Paralleling the results above for external participation, external issue activity was only weakly increased by larger political capacity, reduced by greater environmental uncertainty, and increased by organizational mobilization effort. The latter effect was especially

Table 10.7.   Contextual Analyses of External Issue Activity

Independent variables	All orgs.		Highly political		Less political	
	B	*b**	*B*	*b**	*B*	*b**
Personal attributes						
Age	−.00	−.03***	.00	.02	.01	.04***
Length of membership	.01	.10***	.01	.13***	.00	.00
Occupational prestige	.00	.02*	.00	.00	−.00	−.03**
Education	.02	.04***	.03	.07***	.01	.01
Income	.00	.00	.00	.00	.00	.04***
Gender (female)	−.12	−.06***	−.02	−.01	−.07	−.04***
Organizational attributes						
Political goals	*a*	*a*	*a*	*a*	*a*	*a*
Political capacity	.03	.06***	−.09	−.16***	.00	.00
Mobilization efforts	.19	.14***	.53	.40***	−.16	−.08***
Env. uncertainty	−.56	−.31***	−.77	−.32***	−.14	−.10***
Bureaucracy	.01	.01	.35	.15***	.10	.11***
Indivdual-level effects						
Ext. issue interest	.22	.31***	.26	.22***	.15	.28***
Communications	.12	.24***	.13	.28***	.08	.17***
Total influence	.03	.03***	.02	.03*	.02	.02**
Lobbying incentives	.08	.06***	.09	.07***	.05	.04***
Social incentives	.04	.03***	.10	.09***	.02	.02
Organizational-level effects						
Ext. issue interest	.24	.30***	*a*	*a*	.34	.56***
Communication	−.25	−.23***	*a*	*a*	.08	.17***
Total influence	.44	.13***	.22	.07***	.21	.05***
Lobbying incentives	.17	.08***	−.52	−.20***	−.05	−.02
Social incentives	.76	.37***	*a*	*a*	.17	.08***
Constant	−3.53	—	−0.08	—	−1.78	—
R^2_{adj}	.625***		.491***		.685***	
(N)	(8746)		(4348)		(4399)	

a Variables omitted from equation.
   p < .05;
  **p* < .01;
 ***p* < .001.

strong among the highly political associations, while actually negative for the less political organizations.

For all associations, the individual- and group-level contextual effects of external issue interests, total influence, and member interests in both lobbying and social incentives were all positive, while the communication effect was once again positive at the individual level and negative at the aggregate level. Thus, the expectations of Proposition 24 were supported. Multicollinearity problems prevented use of three of the organization-level measures in the equation for the highly political associations. For the less political organizations, external issue activity was primarily a function of personal and group communication and member interest in those issues.

In conclusion, the effect of organization mobilization on external involvement—whether measured by the external participation scale or by the external issue activity index—occurs only among the highly political associations. These groups have the greatest stake in trying to influence government authorities' decisions, and they cannot leave to chance or individual whim the generation of collective action. How these highly political associations apply their variously mobilized collective resources to attempt to influence government decision makers is the focus of the next section.

Organization Influence Tactics

American collective action organizations attain control over large amounts of monetary and human resources. For those associations that seek to influence public policy, these resources may be deployed in various ways. Schlozman and Tierney listed more than two dozen "influence techniques" that Washington interest groups could use (1986, pp. 150–51). In terms of time and resource allocations, the most frequent techniques were contacting government officials to present viewpoints, testifying at hearings, presenting research results, and mounting grass-roots lobbying efforts. Berry (1984, pp. 149–55) referred to the last as "constituency lobbying," which involves writing letters, placing telephone calls, and visiting congressmen (by rank-and-file association members). Less frequently used tactics include forming coalitions with other groups, talking with the press and media, contributing finances and manpower to electoral campaigns, litigating and running advertisements about the organization's position on a given issue (Schlozman and Tierney 1986, p. 151). Their interest group sample was restricted to organizations with offices in Washington, about a third of which were for-profit corporations (see also Salisbury 1984). In contrast, the NAS sample was drawn entirely from the collective action association population, with only 40% having Washington offices. Thus, the relevance of these influence tactics for the NAS remains to be determined.

Using the organization-level data, slightly more than half the NAS informants said that their collective action organization "makes its positions on national policy proposals known to the federal government." For these 236 associations, Table 10.8 shows the percentage that "sometimes" or "regularly" each use of nine different tactics for expressing its policy preferences. The rank-order for all associations closely follows that obtained for equivalent items in Schlozman and Tierney's survey, although the actual frequencies are not comparable. Constituency lobbying and personal contacts with federal officials and their staffs rank as the two most common influence tactics, used by two thirds of all organizations that try to influence the federal government. About half form coalitions with other groups and testify before congressional committees and federal agencies. Only a small minority resort to outside experts, mass media appeals, court litigation, or endorsements of electoral candidates. By type of association, labor unions are most frequent users of each tactic, followed by trade associations and professional societies, with recreational associations trailing behind.

Table 10.8.   Influence Tactics Used by Organizations Trying to Influence Federal Government: Percentage Sometimes or Regularly

Influence actions	Type of association				
	All assns.	Labor unions	Trade assns.	Prof'l. assns.	Rec'l. assns.
Stimulate members' letters, calls to officials	67	88	54	49	43
Personal contacts with officials and staffs	65	88	67	76	46
Coalitions with other groups	58	77	53	58	44
Testimony to congressional committees, federal agencies	49	83	44	63	32
Using outside experts to represent organization	25	32	36	22	13
Public appeals via media	15	45	13	6	8
Use litigation	11	30	8	13	5
Endorse candidates	5	67	4	8	3
Other methods	10	18	9	12	18
(N)	(236)	(55)	(65)	(59)	(29)

The effectiveness of various tactics for achieving successful influence on government decisions is asserted in three propositions from the political economy theory:

Proposition 25: The fewer opponents an organization faces, the greater its success at influencing public-policy decisions.

Proposition 26: Organizations that mobilize resources from their members for political effort have greater success at influencing public-policy decisions.

Proposition 27: The more coalitions that an organization builds with other groups, the greater its success at influencing public-policy decisions.

The mobilization of organization members for external influence activity was discussed above in extensive detail. From the viewpoint of an association's leaders, member mobilization is aimed at impressing public officials with the depth and intensity of a constituency's feelings. It is designed to convince politicians and bureaucrats that great risks are courted by daring to thwart the organization's interests. Member mobilization also validates the association's claims to significantly represent certain policy domains.

The coalition-building approach constitutes a contrasting influence tactic. Coalitions are "action sets," temporary alliances for limited purposes (Aldrich 1979, pp. 280–281; see also Knoke and Burleigh 1989). They are constructed primarily by negotiations among organization leaders to pool limited resources and coordinate strategies. Coalitions aim to impress official policymakers with the breadth and diversity of the constituencies arrayed behind a proposal. As an elite tactic, coalitions are subject to destructive internal forces, especially on completion of the policy struggle. "Organizational egos" work against coalition permanency:

> Interest group leaders and lobbyists have a personal stake in working to enhance their reputation and that of their organizations. The broader and more lasting a prospective coalition is, the more difficult it becomes for organizers to overcome this problem (Berry 1984, p. 202).

The more resources a coalition claims from its partners, the less each organization has for its own agenda. As a result, most coalitions tend to be short-lived, issue-specific networks.

Both member mobilization and coalition formation tactics are much more prevalent when a collective action organization encounters significant opposition to its national policy influence efforts. A study of four Washington policy domains found that large majorities of interest groups identified both allies and adversaries (Salisbury *et al.* 1987, p. 1224). In the National Association

Study, only a third of the organizations active at the federal policy level said they sometimes or regularly face opponents. Among these controversial groups, 87% frequently (i.e., sometimes or regularly) stimulate their members' letters and phone calls, and 90% frequently form coalitions. Among those organizations that rarely or never confront opposition, only 42% frequently mobilize their members or participate in coalitions. During the preceding three years, the controversial associations were three times more likely to ask their members to contact their representatives in Congress regarding national issues of concern to the group (an average of 13 times compared to 4.3 times by the noncontroversial associations).

How important are such tactics to the success of a collective action association's policy influence efforts? A definitive answer to this question requires a different research design than the National Association Study, which did not collect data on specific policy decisions nor on the governmental and for-profit participants in the organizational state. Nevertheless, a few measures can address the issue in an exploratory manner and suggest directions for future research. At the end of the informant interview, each leader was asked to rate how effective he or she felt the organization was in reaching each of the eight basic goals mentioned at the beginning of the interview. Using a scale where 1 meant "totally ineffective" and 10 "totally effective," the mean rating for associations active in the federal system on the goal of "influencing public policy decisions of the government" was 4.18 (standard deviation = 2.53). This policy influence effectiveness rating is used as the dependent measure in a causal path analysis depicted in Figure 10.2. [For a discussion of path analysis methods, see Bohrnstedt and Knoke (1987, pp. 439–458).]

In this diagram, both coalition-building and member-mobilizing tactics are depicted as causes of policy effectiveness; they are affected by two predetermined variables: the frequency with which opposition is encountered, and its agenda scope, the number of policy domains in which it is active. The agenda scope measure was constructed from a factor analysis of the frequency (from "never" to "regularly") with which an association "attempted to persuade each of [28 different] federal government organization to adopt policies that it favors." The factor analysis uncovered five distinct national policy domain clusters:

1. Economic policy (e.g., Departments of Treasury, Commerce, Transportation)

2. Human services policy (e.g., Departments of Education, Labor, Health & Human Services)

3. General policy (White House, Senate, and House of Representatives)

4. Extractive industries policy (Departments of Agriculture, Interior, Energy)

5. Legal policy (Departments of Justice, State)

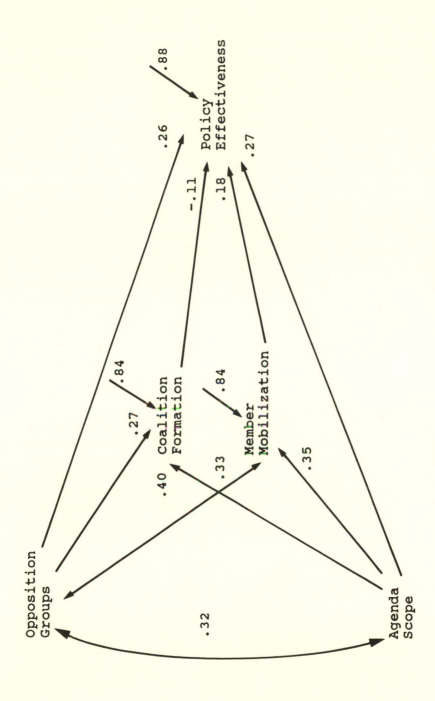

Figure 10.2 Path Diagram of Association Policy Influence Effectiveness

An association was considered active in a policy domain if it tried "regularly" or "sometimes" to influence policies of one or more domain agencies. A low score on the agenda scope variable means that an association is a policy specialist, a high score means that it is a policy generalist. The mean for all associations was 2.50 domains (standard deviation = 1.54), reflecting an average of 5.7 federal target organizations per association.

The path coefficients (standardized regression b^*) in Figure 10.2 denote the direct causal effects of each variable in the recursive structure. The antecedent opposition structure and number of policy domain variables both affect membership mobilization about equally (path coefficients of .33 and .35, respectively). Reliance on coalition formation depends somewhat more on the number of domains in which an association operates (.40) than on the experience of significant opposition (.27). That is, controversial groups and generalist groups tend to use both types of policy influence tactics often. The effect of the two antecedent variables on policy effectiveness are only weakly filtered through the choice of the two influence tactics. Their direct paths are almost identical (.26 and .27, respectively). Thus, associations that operate in many policy domains and those that encounter frequent opposition are considered by their leaders to be more effective in influencing government policy decisions. This result contradicts Proposition 25. Apparently, having enemies in the fight for policy objectives helps much more than it hurts.

A sharp difference emerges regarding the impact of the two influence tactics on policy-making. Consistent with Proposition 26, more frequent member mobilization efforts result in greater policy impact (path coefficient = .18). However, contrary to Proposition 27, reliance upon coalition partners is not only unhelpful, but might even reduce chances for policy success (path coefficient = −.11, not statistically significant). Berry's observations about the fragilities of coalition efforts seems to be borne out in the quantitative analysis. In conclusion, controlling for broad agenda scope and external opposition, an American collective action organization that calls upon its members to help achieve its political goals is much more likely to succeed than are groups that fail to use this important resource and instead seek strength in collaboration with other organizations (see Smith 1988, p. 245).

Conclusion

American collective action organizations are extensively involved in political influence activities at the federal level. Half of the NAS sample associations informed the federal government about their positions on national policy issues. The recent rapid expansion of advocacy groups in Washington has been accompanied by a proliferation of influence tactics. The national associations make extensive use of member mobilization efforts that channel collective resources toward authoritative targets. Association political capacity, organizational governance structures, environmental conditions, member interest in policy issues, and frequent internal communication are critical factors in this mobilization process.

Elements of all three problem paradigms are implicated in this chapter. Members who are strongly integrated into their associations are most accessible for mobilization to attempt policy influence at the system level. Lobbying incentives and extensive communication networks are just as critical for member engagement in external activities as they are for internal involvements (see Chapter 9). Organizational governance structures promote mobilization in an unexpected fashion: associations with major political goals develop greater capacity to fight politically when they have *fewer* democratic structures. Apparently, democratic structures and political capacity are alternative rather than complementary elements. Both these features are conducive to member mobilization, although the latter is substantially more important than the former. Although environmental complexity facilitates member mobilization, uncertainty impedes it.

At the policy system level, an exploratory analysis indicates that an association's success at policy influence (as measured by informants' self-ratings) is increased by mobilizing its members' resources, operating in a large number of policy domains (generalist agenda), and facing opposition groups, though it is unaffected by coalition formation. The importance of member mobilization underscores the attention to intraorganizational processes paid by the political economy theory.

PART V

CONCLUSION

CHAPTER

11

ALL THE ADVANTAGES OF CIVILIZATION

My mail recently brought densely argued appeals from the three groups soliciting contributions for campaigns (1) to prevent the repeal of a handgun control act, (2) to permit contraceptive advertisements on TV, and (3) to make English the official United States language. Each association used classic appeals to potential constituents. Hair-curling alarms were raised ("The gun lobby has held a political pistol to the head of the Congress"; "Over one million teenagers will become pregnant this year—3000 this week."). Normative appeals were framed ("English has long been the main unifying force of the American people"). And dramatic policy breakthroughs were promised ("We must be able to reach the general public with our message and mobilize their support in a broad-based, grassroots citizen movement to change the policies of the three major TV networks"). In form, if not in substance, these appeals for contributions differed little from countless recruitment efforts by liberal, conservative, apolitical, and plain loony American collective action organizations. Their appearance in my mailbox attests to a persistent optimistic streak in our civic culture that individual support can make a difference in changing entrenched public policies.

Collective action associations are a fundamental form of social organization whose principles of formation and behavior are less well understood than more familiar markets, bureaucracies, status groups, and social classes. The objective of this book was to illuminate some basic features of association political economies. Financially, they aggregate and redistribute substantial resources, primarily from members and external constituencies. Politically, they enable the accumulation of power resources and their application to collectively decided tasks. Their internal governance structures serve as important socializing arenas for inculcating democratic norms and procedures. Externally, associations compete and cooperate with other organizations for legitimate influence with public authorities. In this process, collective action organizations help to construct local and national civic cultures of societal constitutionalism (Sciulli 1986). By enabling citizens to recognize and accept their joint responsibilities for conducting a portion of our collective social life, associations promote the nonauthoritarian integration of modern society. As reservoirs of the procedural norms of participativeness and collegial regard, they restrain the arbitrary exercise of power. The voluntaristic nature of collective action organizations resists the drift toward private and governmental bureaucratic domination of public life.

Summary of the Results

The preceding chapters of this book report the results of empirical tests of the propositions in a new synthetic political economy theory of collective action associations. This section summarizes the basic results of those analyses.

The National Association Study interviewed 459 leaders from a representative sample of 13,000 national associations, including labor unions, trade associations, professional societies, recreational organizations, and others. Properly weighted, the sample data reflect the distributions and covariations among variables for the entire population. The membership mail questionnaires from 8746 members of 35 associations are more restrictive in their scope, representing only professional, recreational, and women's organizations, and notably excluding labor unions and trade associations. Almost all the information comes from self-reports and thus is limited to leaders' and members' perceptions and recall of activities. Some data, such as membership size and budget expenditures, are based on "harder" evidence that can be considered fairly reliable. Other measures, such as environmental uncertainty or organizational commitment, are derived from subjective judgments and may be more susceptible to errors. Thus, the quality of data span considerable ranges of both internal and external reliability and validity. Accordingly, the conclusions drawn from the tests of theoretical propositions vary in the degree of credibility that can be attributed to them.

External Environments

Collective action organizations' abilities to acquire useful resources are related to the environmental conditions within which they operate. Most important is the availability of discretionary resources under the control of their members and constituents (sympathizers). Larger groups acquire more revenues than smaller groups, and members with larger family incomes tend to contribute more money to their associations. Having a bureaucratic administrative structure helps to generate more revenues, although the relationship is undoubtedly reciprocal (that is, a wealthier association can afford to maintain a more elaborate administrative apparatus). But wealthier, more bureaucratized organizations diversify in their search for resources: they draw a smaller percentage of their revenues from their memberships and a larger share from external constituents, foundations, and government agencies. A complex interaction effect was discovered: exceptionally high levels of external support are obtained by organizations that pursue societal change goals without attempting to influence government policies *if* they are bureaucratically structured. This relationship is consistent with the institutional perspective that sponsoring groups interpret a bureaucratic form as evidence that an association is accountable and professional in its use of the sponsor's funds.

The major theoretical expectations not supported by the analyses are the effects of environmental uncertainty and complexity on resource contributions. Neither measure of information flow is significantly related to organizational revenues or monetary contributions, once other factors are held constant. Nor are associations that operate in complex and uncertain environments more likely to establish a bureaucratic administrative structure to deal with these conditions. Thus, American collective action organizations seem to be buffered from the negative impacts of unstable environments on the flow of funds into their treasuries. However, as subsequent analyses show, environmental conditions do affect some internal association operations. An important theoretical relationship that could not be tested was Proposition 6, which asserts that the greater the similarities between current members and constituents, the stronger the latter's support, contributions, and rates of joining. Because the National Association Study collected data only on current members, no basis for comparisons with constituents was possible. Nonetheless, this congruence proposition is an important theoretical expectation that awaits future confirmation with an appropriate research design.

Internal Economy

American collective action organizations operate a wide variety of incentive systems, designed to induce their members to provide resources for collective use. Factor analyses disclose six underlying dimensions at both the organizational and individual level of analysis. The majority of national associations offer combinations of utilitarian, normative, and social inducements, rather than concentrating on a single type. The incentives that an organization provides tend to be congruent with its goals. For example, utilitarian incentives are most prevalent in associations that stress member income goals; lobbying incentives are most common in organizations that seek to influence government policies; and groups whose objectives are altruistic and societal value change provide normative inducements. Social-recreational and public-policy lobbying goals appear to have modest cross-modality effects: social groups lobby and lobbying groups socialize. Diverse incentive systems are encouraged by heterogeneous goals, and to a lesser extent by bureaucratic administrative structure and greater association size. However, incentive diversity is unrelated to external environmental conditions.

At the individual level, members clearly respond to diverse organizational incentive offerings. The Olsonian notion that only selective inducements can stimulate member contributions to collective action organizations is inaccurate. Members recall joining for a variety of selective and public-goods reasons (lobbying, normative), which remain fairly stable motives for continuing to contribute (insofar as retrospective reports are reliable). The congruence between members' interests in incentives and organizations' incentive offerings ranges from strong to insignificant, but is not noticeably biased by the public–private goods distinction.

The effects of incentives on participation are consistent with organizational goals. Members of highly political associations say they would be likely to continue participating if their organization emphasized only lobbying inducements. Members of the less political organizations would be more likely to remain if only services were provided. Actual contributions of money and time are greater when members highly value the normative and social-recreational incentives. Normative inducements are especially important for member contributions in highly political associations. However, the four other types of incentives either have no impact or actually reduce members' time and money contributions. Olson's hypothesis that members of smaller organizations are likely to contribute more resources is correct.

Contrary to theoretical expectations, the diversity of organizational incentive systems does not generate higher amounts of member resource contributions. Indeed, diversity appears to depress monetary donations. Thus, although most American collective action organizations emphasize complex incentive packages, those specialist associations that concentrate on relatively few incentives actually seem to acquire more resources from their members. On the other hand, the theoretical expectation that the greater the congruence between organizational incentive offerings and member incentive interests, the larger the amount of monetary resources contributed, is supported.

Internal Polity

The governance structures of a collective action organization—its arrangements for making collective decisions—consist of authority (constitutional requirements) and influence (actual decision making) components. Multiple indicators of these dimensions are only moderately intercorrelated. Most organizational structural, environmental, and goal variables only weakly and inconsistently predict the presence of governance structures. Most notable is that bureaucratic administration covaries with smaller authority role systems, centralization, and less total influence by members and leaders, but with more numerous democratic structures. Environmental complexity also modestly increases democratic governance.

Policy-oriented communication between association leaders and members is the key that links organizational governance structure and members' policy interests to their participation. Members intensely interested in their associations' internal policy issues are much more likely to communicate frequently with other participants. Similarly, associations that maintain democratic governance structures encourage high rates of policy discussion. And, while member interest in normative and social incentives promotes frequent policy communication, high levels of environmental uncertainty and political goals reduce policy interactions. These factors all seem to operate internally: neither member interest in external issues nor in lobbying incentives encourages greater policy communication.

In turn, policy communication strongly promotes members' psychological involvement with and participation in internal organizational activities. Other factors—particularly incentive interest (normative, social, lobbying), organizational governance, and issue interests—also affect member involvements, both directly and indirectly, through their effects on increasing communication rates. Environmental uncertainty consistently depresses members' communication, psychological attachments, and activity participation. These relationships occur in a fairly complex contextual fashion that is not well understood. In several instances, variables that enhance involvements at the individual level operate contrarily at the aggregate (organizational) level. The exact contributions of interpersonal influence, comparison, climate, and selection processes remain to be determined.

External Polity

About half of all American national collective action organizations have goals that require them to interact with organizations outside their boundaries—most notable are group efforts to influence the policy decisions of the government. A key to these organizations' ability to mobilize their members for external action is the creation of political capacity—specialized roles and functions that allow an association to coordinate collective influence actions. Theses components include staff members who monitor national policy domains, legal counsel, lobbyists, political action committees, and programs to contact federal officials. Political capacity is strongly related to political goals and large annual revenues, and weakly related to complex environments. However, having more democratic structures promotes political capacity among less political groups, and reduces it among highly political organizations. For these latter groups, staff-directed political activity is possibly a substitute for member-controlled actions.

Political capacity is the central factor in efforts to mobilize members for collective external influence actions. Environmental complexity also promotes mobilization efforts by highly political organizations, though environmental uncertainty reduces participation. At the individual member level, such mobilization efforts—along with interests in external issues, lobbying incentives, and frequent communication—explain a large proportion of the variation in external influence actions by members. Effects of these factors are more pronounced among the highly political associations. Again, complex individual- and organizational-level relations occur, most notably involving contrasting effects of communication rates.

Finally, among those collective action organizations that try to influence federal policies, a path analysis of their leaders' self-imputed policy success implies that the scope of issue agenda (a large number of policy areas), the presence of organized opposition groups, and efforts to mobilize members all enhance the probability of perceived success. Hence, the leaders see that influence resources obtained from members are significant factors in goal attainment. This result warrants the central importance attached to member resource contributions in the political economy theory of collective action organizations.

Implications

The National Association Study gives strong support to the political economy theory of collective action organizations. Although a few propositions were rejected and some were untestable, the large majority of the results are consistent with the expected relationships. As no theory can rise or fall on a single empirical test, the best conclusion at this time is provisional acceptance. Although no single proposition in itself reveals a startling insight into association behavior, their cumulative and combined quality is impressive. Until new data can be brought to bear on these theoretical issues, the results of the present study must stand as the current state of knowledge about this type of social organization.

The results underscore the multimotivational assumptions about individual choice behavior that guided construction of the political economy theory. In positing that individual decisions are affected by rational, normative, and affective components, the theory rejects as overly simplistic the utility-maximizing assumption embraced by economists and positive political scientists. The Olsonian logic of collective actions as solely self-interested utilitarian calculi is not wrong, merely incomplete. The analyses of association incentive systems and members' incentive interests in this book reveal great heterogeneity at both levels. Many members express substantial interest in both normative benefits and the collective goods produced by organizational lobbying of government public policies. Material inducements evoke little enthusiasm, although many seek the social-recreational rewards that are available only through active involvement. The great diversity of member incentive interests and organizational inducements argues for grounding the analysis of collective action organization behavior in a complex, multimotivational conceptualization of human decision making. Association leaders, struggling with the problems of managing their collectivities with scant resources, have long recognized the diversity of constituent and member claims and have had to respond accordingly. Research scholars likewise must incorporate diversity into their formulations of member–organization interaction.

Above all, American national associations are complex formal organizations. Their internal and external dynamics are shaped by the same economic and political forces that confront corporations and government agencies: every organization must acquire and allocate resources under constraints from its external environment and its internal governance structures; the distributions of authority and influence among collective action organization participants is generally less concentrated than in work organizations; the cultural ethos of democratic control is more pervasive in associations than in firms and bureaus. However, bureaucratic administration has penetrated the larger national associations, creating an uneasy coexistence between these contrary modes of organizational operation. The inclusiveness and openness of democratic governance is fundamentally at odds with the hierarchy and exclusiveness of bureaucratic management. These tensions can never by completely resolved in any organization, for each contributes importantly to the functioning of the collectivity: democracy by building member commitment and involvement, bureaucracy by improving coordination and effective resource usage. In a national society that increasingly distributes its rewards of money, prestige, and power on the basis of institutional affiliations, the inherent conflict between democracy and bureaucracy is likely to intensify. As sites within which these conflicts are most visible, collective action organizations reflect processes that infuse every institutional sector of our nation.

A large proportion of national collective action organizations tries to influence government decisions. In other words, they act as interest groups in the national polity, or pressure group system. The repertoire of tactics designed to influence government targets greatly expanded during the past 25 years with the substantial changes in federal legislative and regulatory processes. But collective action organizations continued to rely heavily on mass membership mobilization to bring pressures upon elected officials to act favorably to the associations' interests. In the leaders' views, mass mobilization holds the key to successful influence, surpassing interorganizational coalitions and rivaling organized opposition in importance. This intimate bond between member participation and organizational influence knits together the internal and external political economy at both levels of analysis. Successful influence enhances organizational resources and attracts more supporters. In turn, larger resources raise the probability of success for future influence efforts. A negative cycle can leave an association poor and ineffective. For confirmation of both dynamics, one need look no further than the struggle by women's organizations to pass the Equal Rights Amendment. At bottom, any theoretical analysis that separates organizational politics from organizational economics is doomed to an inaccurate explanation of either dynamic.

Directions for Future Research

The analyses reported in this book should be seen as only an initial step in a larger program of theory construction and empirical assessment necessary to improve our understanding of collective action organizations. To the extent that the present results lay a solid foundation, future research can proceed in several directions. This section briefly describes some of these opportunities.

Theoretical Formalization

The political economy theory of collective action organizations is presented as an interrelated set of conditional (if-then) propositions written in ordinary language. It lacks the rigor of an axiomatic system in which some primitive terms and relations are assumed true and testable theorems are derived by application of a logical calculus (Freese 1980). The potential benefits of such an approach lie in its conceptual precision and rules of truth-preserving transformation that permit the cumulation of knowledge in ways made impossible by conventional theories that are grounded in the real world of inexact equivalences. However, to develop such a theory requires a formal language and deductive calculus that removes it from the experiential world of social phe-

nomena. This fundamental incompatibility between axiomatic theories and ordinary languages makes a translation difficult to accomplish. The payoff from
using axiomatic theory to understand real-world phenomena is unclear. The
axiomatic road is followed by few social analysts and I do not advocate it
lightly. Still, formalization remains attractive as a potential source of insight
and inspiration in focusing substantive research attention on key relationships.
The alternative to axiomatic formalization is to extend the ordinary language
system of theoretical propositions in directions of greater specificity and complexity. By elaborating the propositions, the present theory can be rendered
more realistic and precise in its depiction of collective action organization behaviors. The following paragraphs suggest several directions:

Ecological Perspectives

Collective action organizations are embedded in communities consisting of
populations of individuals and other formal organizations. Environmental constraints select for the reproduction or attrition of certain characteristics. Human ecologists have adapted biological concepts such as resource competition,
symbiosis, niches, and carrying capacity to explain rates of organization formation, change, growth, decay, and dissolution (McPherson 1983; Bidwell and
Kasarda 1985; Staber and Aldrich 1983, 1986). The political economy theory
in this book could benefit from an integration with ecological principles at the
aggregate level. By reconceptualizing a collective action organization's external environment as organizational populations for the provision of essential
resources, a temporal dimension is introduced to the analysis.

The major limitation to the present analysis lies in the purely cross-
sectional nature of the data collection. Many of the relationships proposed by
the political economy occur dynamically for both members and organizations.
That is, cause and effect stretch across extended time. What is observed at a
given moment may not reflect genuine equilibrium. For example, the analysis
of the sources of association governance in Chapter 8 accounted for very little
of the variation among associations. Conceivably, initial environmental conditions at the time of an organization's creation may better explain its current
form of governance. As conditions change and the governance process remains
unaltered, the fit between environment and structure weakens. The only realistic test of this process is to observe associations across their full life cycles,
a research design entailing considerable cost.

Cross-Cultural Applications

The political economy theory and its empirical assessment are an entirely
Americo-centric construction. Assessing relevance to other cultural settings is
a necessary step for determining the theory's scope. The most obvious candi-

dates for replication are other mature capitalist industrial democracies, particularly the two dozen nations that share the American system of competitive electoral parties and parliamentary and executive branch policy-making. Many of these polities exhibit high degrees of corporatism in their interest groups' involvement with government authorities. These contrasting regime characteristics could reveal features of the American pressure group process that uniquely condition collective action organizations' interest group behaviors. A more ambitions comparison would assess the theory's relevance for societies that lack the democratic traditions of advanced capitalist nations. Voluntary associations operate in many less developed countries, particularly organizations designed for self-help by ethnic or class populations. The limitations of the political economy theory for these situations remain to be determined.

The Micro-Macro Linkage

Associations are ideal sites for investigating the micro-macro links of complex social behaviors. Global, contextual, and individual properties interesh in ways that defy simple statistical separation into aggregative and reducive terms. Conventional models of contextual relationships mask the intervening mechanisms by which social actors shape one another's attitudes and behaviors. Although the analyses reported in this book uncover contrasting individual- and group-level effects upon psychological commitment and participation, the precise connections between these phenomena are obscure, leaving great opportunities to explain how individual and group relationships arise. The solution must be pursued at both the macro- and the microlevels.

At the macrolevel, collective action organizations present participants and constituents with opportunities and constraints for the realization of interests. As bundles of private- and public-goods incentives, associations confront potential supporters with valued objectives that they may enjoy under certain conditions. Typically, members must relinquish control over some of their personal resources—money, time, effort, psychological engagement—to receive the benefits they seek. In the short run these inducements are givens which the participants may take or leave. But in the longer perspective, members can shape organizational structures to fit their changing interests and tastes.

At the microlevel, collective action organizations are susceptible to alteration under influences exerted upon leaders by the members. Given the voluntary nature of associations, disgruntled participants can always exercise the exit option when collective performance proves unsatisfactory. The threat of defection is the ultimate influence that individuals can exert to reconstitute the organization. For example, the American Medical Association experienced massive defections among its youngest physicians during the 1970's, primarily because of its failure to support progressive health legislation. However, voting with one's feet may be less effective than staying in the organization to fight for reform (Hirschman 1970). At present, we do not understand the microconditions under which defection and loyalty occur among participants, nor how such decisions affect the macrostructural performance of the group. Undoubtedly, the reciprocal influences of individuals and organizations are complex and will require ingenious research designs.

Network Structures

One promising approach to specifying the micro-macro connection is an explicit network perspective, examining the concrete ties among positions within organizations (Burt 1980; Berkowitz 1982; Knoke and Kuklinski 1982; Knoke 1990). The underlying principle is that attitudes and actions are, in part, functions of people's locations in global configurations of relationships. A network explanation of members' motivations for joining, remaining, and participating in collective action organizations would emphasize interpersonal bonds among equivalently situated individuals. For associations, the most important type of relationship is clearly communication. Even the crude measure of policy communication frequency used in this book reveals robust effects of individual and group communication on member involvements. A more refined analysis would specify the precise information linkages among particular individuals, especially the vertical (member-leader) and horizontal (member-member) exchanges. A similar treatment of resource exchanges (people's money, time, and effort for organizations' incentives) would expand the analysis to multiplex networks. Recent developments in the survey interview collection of egocentric network measures offer promising procedures for sampling social relationships in large social systems (Burt 1984, 1985; Marsden 1987). However, their suitability for mail questionnaires remains untested. The alternative—complete network mapping—is both extremely costly and potentially feasible only for small organizations (see Erickson and Nosanchuk 1984 for an example using a local bridge club). Nevertheless, the extension of social network analysis approaches to collective action organization research seems a promising next step in unfolding the micro-macro relationships.

Interorganizational Conflict

The unexpected finding that opposition groups promote an association's success in its public-policy influence goals requires further verification and explication. Member mobilization is clearly important, but facing opposition seems more critical than alliance formation. These findings were based on informants' subjective evaluations, with all their potential unreliability and noncomparability. A more systematic comparison must examine specific policy events in which interest groups attempt to influence government decisions. The impact of coalitional and oppositional action sets among the power triads of producers, countervailing interests, and government agencies on the outcome can be measured. The mobilization and application of resources, the interorganizational strategies of bargaining and negotiation, and the ultimate resolution of conflict can be assessed. The policy processes are likely to vary across time and issue domains, being more pluralistic in some contexts and elite-dominated in others (Laumann and Knoke 1987; McFarland 1987). Uncovering the sources of interdomain variation will require systematic comparisons of numerous policy domains, a fairly costly and long-term project. But without concerted efforts to test propositions about the interorganizational dynamics of collective action, our understanding of the role that collective action associations play in national policy-making will remain limited.

To Civilize Our Public Life

In this concluding section, it is important to step back from the immediacy of data details and to consider how the research reported in this book alters our understanding of the three paradigmatic problems of collective action organizations. As described in Chapter 1, these loose, broad perspectives deal with individual integration into social institutions, the governance of organizations, and the making of public policy. The results of the National Association Study give some answers to each of these problems:

Individual Integration into Social Institutions

Durkheim, Simmel, and Tocqueville each expressed trepidation that nineteenth century industrialization had eroded social self-controls and exposed individuals to manipulation that threatened their loss of freedom. Voluntary affiliation in organizations, especially occupationally based associations, could be antibodies against the atomization inherent in democratic leveling and against the implacable weight of state bureaucracy. From the vantage point of late twentieth century hindsight, we see that these theorists had much to fear. The sad, agonized history of modern political struggle reveals recurrent breakdowns in public order, where unscrupulous opportunists incite popular emotions to acts destructive of the commonweal. But for every Hitler or McCarthy who briefly tramples the stage, numerous uncelebrated citizens toil collectively to tighten the sinews of community responsibility in churches, schools, fraternal and service groups, professional societies, unions, and leisure clubs. The dismal picture painted by economistic scholars—of cynical, self-centered actors seeking to maximize personal gains—vanishes under a closer look at the motivations propelling real people into collective action organizations.

These flesh-and-blood participants represent a variety of needs, from altruistic service to the less fortunate, to hungers for social contacts, to hopes for fair and equitable sharing of collective goods. Those organizations that have wisely fashioned their incentives to respond to these heterogeneous concerns will reap the benefit of a devoted membership, attached by diverse bonds of affiliation. The members become strongly disposed to contributing their time and treasure to the collective enterprise, to identifying the organization's fate with their own, and to resisting demagogic manipulation, whether from within or outside the association. The simple answer to the problem of social integration is a robust organizational community that offers citizens numerous opportunities to join with others sharing common concerns while still responding to their diverse individual needs. By striving to satisfy many motives, both organizations and their members learn the toleration necessary for a viable pluralistic society.

The Internal Governance of Organizations

Michels was wrong. American collective action organizations are not oligarchies, not even rigid bureaucracies. Given their predominant professional and middle-class, college-educated members, it could hardly be otherwise. The pervasive cultural biases favoring democratic self-governance assure that self-perpetuating leadership cliques seldom take root. Instead, institutional safeguards assure that leaders remain accountable to the members for their actions. That relationship is not the same as no power differentials between officials and members. Indeed, leaders must be authorized to act as agents of the collectivity, or activities would grind to a halt in the unworkable machinery of participatory democracy. Rather, the power enjoyed by association leaders is delegated power, where members retain sufficient control through meetings, committees, and elections to assure that majority sentiments prevail. Ultimately, the voluntary nature of membership (whereby voicing dissatisfaction is backed up by the threat to disaffiliate) holds leaders' decisions hostage to members' interests. The celebrated cases of racket-ridden unions are infrequent counterexamples that prove the rule: oligarchs can only entrench themselves when members are legal captives compelled to supply financial support and lacking the possibility of exit. For the vast majority of American associations, the vulnerability of the organization to members' withholding of commitment ensures that leaders' interests align with the members. The more opportunities that an organization gives its members to participate in collective decision making, the stronger the support it acquires. When members experience personal responsibility for governance, they cannot lightly cast it aside.

The persisting dilemma is the inherent tension between the legitimacy of constitutional democracy and the efficiency of administrative bureaucracy. Large associations can more effectively pursue their collective goals because they gather greater pools of resources from members and constituents. But sheer size necessitates coordination that can be more readily achieved by use of a paid staff. The trick for many organizations is to walk the fine line between democratic paralysis and bureaucratic arrogation. Progressive social movements have long recognized that democratic governance encompasses ends as well as means. To win collective goals by a bureaucracy that usurps member involvement is a hollow triumph. Civic and political associations can best promote their members' interests by serving as laboratories for learning and practicing the methods of democracy. The development of a mature citizenry within organizational confines spills over to the contest for collective influence in the policy system, both in elections of public officials and in pressing for preferred public policies.

Formulating Public Policies

The American polity changed dramatically over the past generation. Political parties were eclipsed by the pressure group system as major players at the federal level. Half of all national associations now seek to influence the outcomes of public policy debates in legislative, judicial, and regulatory domains. A highly competitive pluralism prevails, where interest groups mobilize their collective resources and contend against opposing groups to impose their alternative agendas on the government. Some interests are incredibly narrow, but others span broad arrays of occupational, industrial, religious, ethnic, racial, gender, and other sociodemographic categories. In this cacophony of voices clamoring for attention, access, and impact, harried government officials need dependable cues on which to base their decisions. Some cues are given in the structure of policy demands made by interest groups. They reveal which population segments will be harmed and which benefited by policy decisions, and what consequences the policymakers are likely to bear.

From the perspective of association leaders, three factors seem especially vital to policy success. Groups able to play in several policy domains typically have large memberships, many resources, and much durability. Government policymakers are more likely to be familiar with them, having encountered them on numerous occasions and developed trusted working relations, perhaps resembling quasi-corporatist arrangements. Because the associations that are broad in scope play in several policy games, they are more likely to succeed in some arenas than are groups that put their entire effort into one game. Associations that can demonstrate mass backing for their policy proposals can better persuade public officials that something important is at stake. Flooding congressional offices with bags of mail or stacking district meetings with constituent supporters can effectively convince vote- and dollar-conscious legislators to treat demands seriously. Finally, the greater importance attributed to opposition than to allies is an unexpected conundrum. Although notoriety may be gained by making enemies, the reason success should also come to those who fight frequently is not clear. Perhaps public officials take dust raised by policy battles as a sign that fundamental values are at stake, and that resolution requires concessions by all sides. Every participant can come away feeling that significant strides were made, that the ground was prepared for the next battle, and that certain obligations are owed to the public officials that helped to arrange the compromise solution. While much more remains to be learned about the role of collective action organizations in national policy-making, pluralist combat is the essential process.

In conclusion, national membership organizations nourish our best hopes for fate control in a society whose state is increasingly dominated by powerful institutions that are unaccountable to the citizenry. As this is written, daily television broadcasts dramatically reveal the privatization of national power. A band of patriotic ideologues working out of the White House basement systematically thwarted constraints on the conduct of foreign policy imposed by the elected people's representatives. The Iran-Contra scandal—a web of secret fund raising, hostage deals, arms smuggling, profiteering, and official lying—dramatically testifies to the isolation of national power from popular control. This is not an aberration but only a vivid instance of the corruption of public power that is multiplied many times over in the environmental degradation, industrial malfeasance, educational ineptitude, urban decay, and military adventurism that impoverishes and threatens our society. Government and private bureaucracies alike pursue agendas whose consequences seriously harm the commonweal and its citizenry.

What can be done? As in Tocqueville's day, collective action organizations remain a viable social formation for humanizing our public life. For more than two centuries, Americans have refined their uses of association. Associations can bring alienated citizens into the political process, teaching them the principles of democratic discourse. They can coordinate common sentiments and mobilize puny individual resources into potent devices for voicing grievances and desires to public officials. They can press demands for public choices that reflect neither partisan nor special interests but broad public values. The use of collective action organizations to achieve popular objectives is both widely understood and accepted as a legitimate basic right. The ongoing struggle is to make them effective in the face of large social forces that would degrade them. That struggle will not end until, in the words of our French visitor, the continual exercise of association makes America truly a nation "where all the advantages of which civilization can confer are procured by means of it" (Tocqueville 1945 Vol. II, p. 115).

BIBLIOGRAPHY

Ajzen, Icek and Martin Fishbein (1980). *Understanding Attitudes and Predicting Social Behavior.* Englewood Cliffs: Prentice-Hall.

Aldrich, Howard E. (1979). *Organizations and Environments.* Englewood Cliffs: Prentice-Hall.

Alexander, Jeffrey (1978). "Formal and Substantive Voluntarism in the Work of Talcott Parsons: A Theoretical and Ideological Reinterpretation." *American Sociological Review,* 43:1771–198.

Alfano, G. and Gerald Marwell (1981). "Experiments on the Provision of Public Goods III: Non-divisibility and Free Riding in 'Real' Groups." *Social Psychology Quarterly,* 43:300–309.

Alford, Robert R. and Roger Friedland (1985). *Powers of Theory: Capitalism, the State, and Democracy.* Cambridge: Cambridge University Press.

Alwin, Duane (1973). "The Use of Factor Analysis in the Construction of Linear Composites in Social Research." *Sociological Methods and Research,* 2:191–214.

Anderson, Paul A. (1983). "Decision Making by Objection and the Cuban Missile Crisis." *Administrative Science Quarterly,* 28:201–222.

Argote, Linda (1982). "Input Uncertainty and Organizational Coordination in Hospital Emergency Units." *Administrative Science Quarterly,* 27:420–434.

Arrow, Kenneth J. (1974). *The Limits of Organization.* New York: Norton.

Bacharach, Samuel B. and Edward J. Lawler (1980). *Power and Politics in Organizations.* San Francisco: Jossey-Bass.

Barber, Benjamin (1984). *Strong Democracy: Participatory Politics for a New Age.* Berkeley: University of California Press.

Barnard, Chester I. (1947). *The Functions of the Executive.* Cambridge, MA: Harvard University Press.

Bayes, Jane H. (1982). *Ideologies and Interest-Group Politics: The United States as a Special-Interest State in the Global Economy.* Novato, CA: Chandler & Sharp.

233

Becker, Gary S. (1976). *The Economic Approach to Human Behavior.* Chicago: University of Chicago Press.

Becker, Howard S. (1960). "Notes on the Concept of Commitment." *American Journal of Sociology,* 65:32–40.

Bendix, Reinhard (1962). *Max Weber: An Intellectual Portrait.* New York: Anchor Doubleday.

Bendor, Jonathan and Dilip Mookherjee (1987). "Institutional Structure and the Logic of Ongoing Collective Action." *American Political Science Review,* 81:129–154.

Benson, Herman (1986). "The Fight for Union Democracy." Pp. 323–70 in *Unions in Transition: Entering the Second Century,* edited by Seymour Martin Lipset, San Francisco: ICS Press.

Bentley, Arthur (1908). *The Process of Government.* Chicago: University of Chicago Press.

Berkowitz, Steven D. (1982). *An Introduction to Structural Analysis: The Network Approach to Social Research.* Toronto: Butterworths.

Berry, Jeffrey M. (1977). *Lobbying for the People: The Political Behavior of Public Interest Groups.* Princeton: Princeton University Press.

Berry, Jeffrey M. (1984). *The Interest Group Society.* Boston: Little, Brown.

Biddle, B. J. (1986). "Recent Developments in Role Theory." *Annual Review of Sociology,* 12:67–92.

Bidwell, Charles E. and Jack D. Kasarda (1985). *The Organization and Its Ecosystem: A Theory of Structuring in Organizations.* Greenwich, CT: JAI Press.

Blalock, Hubert M., Jr. (1969). *Theory Construction: From Verbal to Mathematical Formulations.* Englewood Cliffs, NJ: Prentice-Hall.

Blalock, Hubert M. (1984). "Contextual-Effects Models: Theoretical and Methodological Issues." *Annual Review of Sociology,* 10:353–372.

Blau, Peter M. (1964). *Exchange and Power in Social Life.* New York: Wiley.

Blau, Peter M. and Richard A. Schoenherr (1971). *The Structure of Organizations.* New York: Basic Books.

Blau, Peter M. and W. Richard Scott (1962). *Formal Organizations.* San Francisco: Chandler.

Bohrnstedt, George W. and David Knoke (1987). *Statistics for Social Data Analysis,* 2nd ed. Itasca, IL: Peacock.

Boyd, Lawrence H. Jr. and Gudmund R. Iversen (1979). *Contextual Analysis: Concepts and Statistical Techniques.* Belmont, CA: Wadsworth.

Braithwaite, Richard Bevan (1955). *Scientific Explanation: A Study of the Function of Theory, Probability and Law in Science.* Cambridge: Cambridge University Press.

Brewer, John (1971). "Flow of communications, expert qualifications, and organizational authority structure." *American Sociological Review,* 36:475–484.

Brodbeck, May (1958). "Methodological Individualism: Definition and Reduction." *Philosophy of Science,* 29:1–22.

Browne, William P. (1976). "Benefits and Membership: A Reappraisal of Interest Group Activity." *Western Political Quarterly,* 29:258–273.

Brubaker, Earl R. (1975). "Free Ride, Free Revelation, or Golden Rule?" *Journal of Law and Economics,* 147–261.

Buchanan, James M. (1968). *The Demand and Supply of Collective Goods*. Chicago: Rand McNally.

Burgess, Philip M. and Richard Conway (1973). *Public Goods and Voluntary Associations*. Beverly Hills: Sage.

Burstein, Paul (1985). *Discrimination, Jobs, and Politics: The Struggle for Equal Employment Opportunity in the United States Since the New Deal*. Chicago: University of Chicago Press.

Burt, Ronald S. (1980). "Models of Network Structure." *Annual Review of Sociology*, 6:79–141.

Burt, Ronald S. (1984). "Network Items and the General Social Survey." *Social Networks*, 6:293–339.

Burt, Ronald S. (1985). "General Social Survey Network Items." *Connections*, 8:119–123.

Cafferata, Gail Lee (1979). "Member and Leader Satisfaction with a Professional Association: An Exchange Perspective." *Administrative Science Quarterly*, 24:472–483.

Chamberlain, J. P. (1978). "The Logic of Collective Action: Some Experimental Results." *Behavioral Science*, 23:441–445.

Child, John (1972). "Organizational Structure, Environment and Performance: The Role of Strategic Performance." *Sociology*, 6:1–22.

Chubb, John (1983). *Interest Groups and the Bureaucracy: The Politics of Energy*. Palo Alto: Stanford University Press.

Cigler, Allan J. and John M. Hansen (1983). "Group Formation through Protest: The American Agricultural Movement." Pp. 84–109 in *Interest Group Politics*, edited by Allan J. Cigler and Burdett A. Loomis, Washington: CQ Press.

Clark, Peter B. and James Q. Wilson (1961). "Incentive Systems: A Theory of Organizations." *Administrative Science Quarterly*, 6:129–166.

Clark, Terry N. (1968). *Community Structure and Decision-Making: Comparative Analyses*. San Francisco: Chandler.

Cloward, Richard A. and Lloyd E. Ohlin (1960). *Delinquency and Opportunity: A Theory of Delinquent Gangs*. New York: Free Press.

Cohen, Albert K. (1955). *Delinquent Boys: The Culture of the Gang*. New York: Free Press.

Coleman, James S. (1957). *Community Conflict*. Glencoe, IL: Free Press.

Coleman, James S. (1973). "Loss of Power." *American Sociological Review*, 38:1–17.

Coleman, James S. (1974). *Power and the Structure of Society*. New York: Norton.

Coleman, James S. (1975). "Social Structure and a Theory of Action." In *Approaches to the Study of Social Structure*, Peter M. Blau, ed., p. 76–93. New York: Free Press.

Coleman, James S. (1986a). "Social Theory, Social Research, and a Theory of Action." *American Journal of Sociology*, 91:1309–1335.

Coleman, James S. (1986b). *Individual Interests and Collective Action*. Cambridge: Cambridge University Press.

Conway, Margaret M. (1983). "PACS, the New Politics, and Congressional Campaigns." Pp. 126–44 in *Interest Group Politics*, edited by Allan J. Cigler and Burdett A. Loomis, Washington: CQ Press.

Dahrendorf, Ralf (1959). *Class and Class Conflict in Industrial Society.* Stanford, CA: Stanford University Press.

Denzin, Norman K. (1983). "A Note on Emotionality, Self, and Interaction." *American Journal of Sociology,* 89:402–409.

Dess, Gregory G. and Donald W. Beard (1984). "Dimensions of Organizational Task Environments." *Administrative Science Quarterly,* 29:52–73.

DiMaggio, Paul J. and Walter W. Powell (1983). "The Iron Cage Revisited: Institutional Isomorphism and Collective Rationality in Organizational Fields." *American Sociological Review,* 48:147–160.

Domhoff, G. William (1978). *The Powers That Be: Processes of Ruling Class Domination in America.* New York: Random House.

Domhoff, G. William (1983). *Who Rules America Now? A View for the 80's.* Englewood Cliffs, NJ: Prentice-Hall.

Duncan, Robert B. (1972). "Characteristics of Organizational Environments and Perceived Environmental Uncertainty." *Administrative Science Quarterly,* 17:313–327.

Durkheim, Emile (1933). *The Division of Labor in Society.* New York: Free Press.

Durkheim, Emile (1951). *Suicide: A Study in Sociology.* New York: Free Press.

Durkheim, Emile (1958). *Professional Ethics and Civic Morals.* New York: Free Press.

Edelstein, J. David and Malcolm Warner (1976). *Comparative Union Democracy: Organization and Opposition in British and American Unions.* New York: Wiley.

Erickson, Bonnie H. and T. A. Nosanchuk (1984). "The Allocation of Esteem and Disesteem: A Test of Goode's Theory." *American Sociological Review,* 49:648–58.

Etzioni, Amatai (1968). *The Active Society.* New York: Free Press.

Etzioni, Amatai (1975). *A Comparative Analysis of Complex Organizations.* New York: Free Press.

Etzioni, Amatai (1986). "The Case for a Multiple-Utility Conception." *Economics and Philosophy,* 2:159–183.

Fireman, Bruce and William A. Gamson (1979). "Utilitarian Logic in the Resource Mobilization Perspective." Pp. 8–44 in *The Dynamics of Social Movements: Resource Mobilization, Social Control and Tactics,* edited by Mayer N. Zald and John D. McCarthy, Cambridge, MA: Winthrop.

Fishbein, Martin (1967). "Attitude and the Prediction of Behavior." In *Readings in Attitude Theory and Measurement,* Martin Fishbein, ed., p. 477–492. New York: Wiley.

Freeman, Jo (1979). "Resources Mobilization and Strategy: A Model for Analyzing Social Movement Organization Actions." Pp. 167–89 in *The Dynamics of Social Movements: Resource Mobilization, Social Control and Tactics,* edited by Mayer N. Zald and John D. McCarthy, Cambridge, MA: Winthrop.

Freese, Lee (1980). "Formal Theorizing." *Annual Review of Sociology,* 6:187–212.

Friedman, Milton (1953). "The Methodology of Positive Economics." Pp. 3–43 in *Essays in Positive Economics,* Chicago: University of Chicago Press.

Frohlich, Norman, Joe A. Oppenheim, and Oran R. Young (1971). *Political Leadership and Collective Goods.* Princeton, NJ: Princeton University Press.

Gais, Thomas L., Mark A. Peterson, and Jack L. Walker (1984). "Interest Groups, Iron Triangles, and Representative Institutions in American National Government." *British Journal of Political Science*, 14:161–185.

Galaskiewicz, Joseph (1979). "The Structure of Community Interorganizational Networks." *Social Forces*, 57:1346–1364.

Galbraith, Jay (1977). *Organization Design*. Reading, MA: Addison-Wesley.

Galenson, Walter (1986). "The Historical Role of American Trade Unionism." In *Unions in Transition: Entering the Second Century*, Seymour Martin Lipset, ed., p. 39–73. San Francisco: ICS Press.

Gamson, William A. (1975). *The Strategy of Social Protest*. Homewood, IL: Dorsey.

Godwin, R. Kenneth and Robert C. Mitchell (1982). "Rational Models, Collective Goods and Nonelectoral Political Behavior." *Western Political Quarterly*, 35:161–181.

Godwin, R. Kenneth and Robert C. Mitchell (1984). "The Implications of Direct Mail for Political Organizations." *Social Science Quarterly*, 65:829–839.

Gordon, C. Wayne and Nicholas Babchuk (1959). "A Typology of Voluntary Associations." *American Sociological Review*, 24:22–29.

Gouldner, Helen (1960). "Dimensions of Organizational Commitment." *Administrative Science Quarterly*, 69:468–490.

Greenstone, J. David (1979). "Group Theories." Pp. 243–318 in *Handbook of Political Science*, edited by Fred I. Greenstein and Nelson W. Polsby, Reading, MA: Addison-Wesley.

Gronn, Peter C. (1983). "Talk as the Work: The Accomplishment of School Administration." *Administrative Science Quarterly*, 28:1–21.

Hage, Jerald (1965). "An Axiomatic Theory of Organizations." *Administrative Science Quarterly*, 10:289–320.

Halaby, Charles N. (1986). "Worker Attachment and Workplace Authority." *American Sociological Review*, 51:634–649.

Halebsky, Sandor (1976). *Mass Society and Political Conflict: Towards a Reconstruction of Theory*. Cambridge: Cambridge University Press.

Hall, Richard H. (1987). *Organizations: Structures, Processes and Outcomes*, 4th ed. Englewood Cliffs, NJ: Prentice-Hall.

Hansen, John Mark (1985). "The Political Economy of Group Membership." *American Political Science Review*, 79:79–96.

Harre, Rom (1976). "The Constructive Role of Models." Pp. 16–43 in *The Uses of Models in the Social Sciences*, edited by Lyndhurst Collins, Boulder, CO: Westview.

Harrison, Paul (1959). *Authority and Power in the Free Church Tradition*. Princeton: Princeton University Press.

Harsanyi, John C. (1955). "Cardinal Welfare, Individualistic Ethics, and Interpersonal Comparisons of Utility." *Journal of Political Economy*, 63:309–321.

Harsanyi, John C. (1969). "Rational-choice Models of Political Behavior vs. Functionalist and Conformist Theories." *World Politics*, 21:513–538.

Hayes, Michael T. (1978). "The Semi-sovereign Pressure Groups: A Critique of Current Theory and an Alternative Typology." *Journal of Politics*, 40:134–161.

Hayes, Michael T. (1983). "Interest Groups: Pluralism or Mass Society?" Pp. 110–225 in *Interest Group Politics,* edited by Allan J. Cigler and Burdett A. Loomis, Washington: CQ Press.

Heath, Anthony (1976). *Rational Choice and Social Exchange: A Critique of Exchange Theory.* Cambridge: Cambridge University Press.

Heclo, Hugh (1978). "Issue Networks and the Executive Establishment." Pp. 87–124 in *The New American Political System,* edited by Anthony King, Washington: American Enterprise Institute.

Heirich, Max (1977). "Change of Heart: A Test of Some Widely-Held Theories of Religious Conversion." *American Journal of Sociology,* 83:653–680.

Heise, David (1975). *Casual Analysis.* New York: Wiley.

Hemingway, J. (1978). *Conflict and Democracy: Studies in Trade Union Government.* Oxford: Oxford University Press.

Hempel, Carl G. (1966). *Philosophy of Natural Science.* Englewood Cliffs, NJ: Prentice-Hall.

Hershey, Margaret R. and Daryl M. West (1983). "Single-issue Politics: Pro-life Groups and the 1980 Senate Campaign." Pp. 31–59 in *Interest Group Politics,* edited by Allan J. Cigler and Burdett A. Loomis, Washington: CQ Press.

Hickson, David J., Robert Hinings, C. A. Lee, R. E. Schneck, and Johannes M. Pennings (1971). "A Strategic Contingencies Theory of Intra-Organizational Power." *Administrative Science Quarterly,* 16:216–229.

Hirschman, Albert O. (1970). *Exit, Voice and Loyalty.* Cambridge, MA: Harvard University Press.

Hochschild, Arlie (1979). "Emotion Work, Feeling Rules, and Social Structure." *American Journal of Sociology,* 85:551–575.

Homans, George C. (1961). *Social Behavior: Its Elementary Forms.* New York: Harcourt and Brace.

Homans, George C. (1964). "Bringing Men Back In." *American Sociological Review,* 29:809–818.

Hougland, James G., Jr. and James R. Wood (1979). "Determinants of Organizational Control in Local Churches." *Journal for the Scientific Study of Religion,* 18:132–145.

Hougland, James G., Jr. and James R. Wood (1980). "Control in Organizations and the Commitment of Members." *Social Forces,* 59:85–105.

Hsu, Cheng-Kuang, Robert M. Marsh, and Hiroshi Mannari (1983). "An Examination of the Determinates of Organizational Structures." *American Journal of Sociology,* 88:975–996.

Huckfeldt, Robert (1983). "Social Contexts, Social Networks, and Urban Neighborhoods: Environmental Constraints on Friendship Choice." *American Journal of Sociology,* 89:651–669.

James, S. (1984). *The Content of Social Explanation.* Cambridge: Cambridge University Press.

Janowitz, Morris (1978). *The Last Half Century: Societal Change and Politics in America.* Chicago: University of Chicago Press.

Jennergren, L. Peter (1981). "Decentralization in Organizations." In *Handbook of Organizational Design, vol. 2,* Paul C. Nystrom and William H. Starbuck, eds., p. 39–59. New York: Oxford University Press.

Jurkovich, Ray (1974). "A Core Typology of Organizational Environments." *Administrative Science Quarterly,* 19:380–394.

Kahneman, D., P. Slovic, and A. Tversky, eds. (1982). *Judgment Under Uncertainty: Heuristics and Biases.* New York: Cambridge University Press.

Kalton, Graham (1983). *Introduction to Survey Sampling.* Beverly Hills, CA: Sage.

Kanter, Rosabeth Moss (1968). "Commitment and Social Organization: A Study of Commitment Mechanisms in Utopian Communities." *American Sociological Review,* 33:499–517.

Kanter, Rosabeth Moss (1972). *Commitment and Community.* Cambridge: Harvard University Press.

Kanter, Rosabeth Moss (1977). *Men and Women of the Corporation.* New York: Basic Books.

Katz, Daniel and Robert L. Kahn (1966). *The Social Psychology of Organizations.* New York: Wiley.

Kemper, Theodore D. (1981). "Social Constructionist and Positivist Approaches to the Sociology of Emotions." *American Journal of Sociology,* 87:336–362.

Kerr, Clark (1957). *Unions and Union Leaders of Their Own Choosing.* New York: Fund for the Republic.

Key, V. O., Jr. (1964). *Politics, Parties, and Pressure Groups,* 5th ed. New York: Crowell.

Kim, Jae-on and Charles W. Mueller (1979a). *Introduction to Factor Analysis.* Beverly Hills: Sage.

Kim, Jae-on and Charles W. Mueller (1979b). *Factor Analysis.* Beverly Hills: Sage.

Kingdon, John W. (1984). *Agendas, Alternatives, and Public Policies.* Boston: Little, Brown.

Knoke, David (1981a). "Commitment and Detachment in Voluntary Associations." *American Sociological Review,* 46:141–58.

Knoke, David (1981b). "Power Structures." Pp. 275–332 in *The Handbook of Political Behavior,* edited by Samuel L. Long, New York: Plenum.

Knoke, David (1982). "Political Mobilization by Voluntary Associations." *Journal of Political and Military Sociology,* 10:171–182.

Knoke, David (1983). "Organization Sponsorship and Influence Reputation of Social Influence Associations." *Social Forces,* 61:1065–1087.

Knoke, David (1985). "The Political Economies of Associations." *Research in Political Sociology,* 1:211–242.

Knoke, David (1986). "Associations and Interest Groups." *Annual Review of Sociology,* 12:1–21.

Knoke, David (1988). "Incentives in Collective Action Organizations." *American Sociological Review,* 53:311–329.

Knoke, David (1989a). "The Mobilization of Members in Women's Associations." In *Women in 20th Century Politics,* Patricia Gurin and Louise A. Tilly, eds. New York: Russell Sage.

Knoke, David (1989b). "Resource Acquisition and Allocation in U.S. National Associations." Forthcoming in *Organizing for Change: Social Movement Organizations in Europe and the United States. Vol. 2 of International Social Movement Research*, Bert Klandermans, Hanspeter Kriesi, and Sidney Tarrow, eds. Greenwich, CT: JAI Press.

Knoke, David (1990). *Political Networks: The Structural Perspective*. New York: Cambridge University Press.

Knoke, David and Richard E. Adams (1987). "The Incentive Systems of Associations." *Research in the Sociology of Organizations*, 5:285–309.

Knoke, David and Frank Burleigh (1989). "Collective Action in National Policy Domains: Constraints, Cleavages, and Policy Outcomes." *Research in Political Sociology*, 4:187–208.

Knoke, David and Ronald S. Burt (1982). "Prominence." Pp. 195–222 in *Applied Network Analysis: A Methodological Introduction*, edited by R. S. Burt and M. J. Minor, Beverly Hills: Sage.

Knoke, David and James H. Kuklinski (1982). *Network Analysis*. Beverly Hills: Sage.

Knoke, David and Edward O. Laumann (1982). "The Social Organization of National Policy Domains: An Exploration of Some Structural Hypotheses." Pp. 255–270 in *Social Structure and Network Analysis*, edited by Peter V. Marsden and Nan Lin, Beverly Hills, CA: Sage.

Knoke, David and Edward O. Laumann (1983). "Issue Publics in National Policy Domains." Presented at Annual Meetings of the American Sociological Association, Toronto.

Knoke, David and David Prensky (1984). "What Relevance Do Organization Theories Have for Voluntary Associations?" *Social Science Quarterly*, 65:3–20.

Knoke, David and James R. Wood (1981). *Organized for Action: Commitment in Voluntary Associations*. New Brunswick: Rutgers University Press.

Knoke, David and Christine Wright-Isak (1982). "Individual Motives and Organizational Incentive Systems." *Research in the Sociology of Organizations*, 1:209–254.

Koek, Karin E. and Susan Boyles Martin, eds. (1987). *Encyclopedia of Associations 1988*. Detroit: Gale Research Company.

Kornhauser, William (1959). *The Politics of Mass Society*. New York: Free Press.

Lakatos, Imre (1970). "Falsification and the Methodology of Research Programmes." In *Criticism and the Growth of Knowledge*, edited by Imre Lakatos and Alan Musgrave, London: Cambridge University Press.

Lasswell, Harold D. (1977). *Psychopathology and Politics*. Chicago: University of Chicago Press.

Latham Earl (1952). *The Group Basis of Politics: A Study in Basing-Point Legislation*. Ithaca: Cornell University Press.

Laumann, Edward O. and John P. Heinz (1985). "Washington Lawyers—and Others: The Structure of Washington Representation." *Stanford Law Review*, 37:465–502.

Laumann, Edward O. and David Knoke (1987). *The Organizational State: A Perspective on National Energy and Health Domains*. Madison, WI: University of Wisconsin Press.

Laumann, Edward O., David Knoke, and Yong-Hak Kim (1985). "An Organizational Approach to State Policymaking: A Comparative Study of Energy and Health Domains." *American Sociological Review,* 50:1–19.

Laumann, Edward O. and Franz Urban Pappi (1976). *Networks of Collective Action: A Perspective on Community Influence Systems.* New York: Academic Press.

Lawrence, Paul R. and Jay W. Lorsch (1967). *Organization and Environment.* Cambridge, MA: Harvard University Press.

Leblebici, Huseyin and Gerald R. Salancik (1981). "Effects of Environmental Uncertainty on Information and Decision Processes in Banks." *Administrative Science Quarterly,* 26:578–596.

Lehmbruch, Gerhard, and Phillippe C. Schmitter, eds. (1982). *Patterns in Corporatist Policy-Making.* Beverly Hills: Sage.

Leibenstein, Harvey (1980). "On the Basic Proposition of X-Efficiency Theory." *American Economic Review,* 68:328–334.

Levitan, Sar and Martha R. Cooper (1984). *Business Lobbies: The Public Good & the Bottom Line.* Baltimore: Johns Hopkins University Press.

Likert, Rensis (1967). *The Human Organization.* New York: McGraw-Hill.

Lincoln, James R. (1982). "Intra- (and Inter-) Organizational Networks." *Research in the Sociology of Organizations,* 1:1–38.

Lipset, Seymour Martin, Martin Trow, and James Coleman (1956). *Union Democracy.* New York: Anchor Doubleday.

Lipsky, Michael (1970). *Protest in City Politics: Rent Strikes, Housing and the Power of the Poor.* Chicago: Rand McNally.

Loomis, Burdett A. (1983). "A New Era: Groups and the Grass Roots." Pp. 169–190 in *Interest Group Politics,* edited by Allan J. Cigler and Burdett A. Loomis, Washington: CQ Press.

Lowi, Theodore J. (1979). *The End of Liberalism,* 2nd ed. NY: Norton.

McAdam, Doug (1982). *Political Process and the Development of Black Insurgency 1930–1970.* Chicago: University of Chicago Press.

McCarthy, John D. (1983). "Social Infrastructure Deficits and New Technologies: Mobilizing Unstructured Sentiment Pools." Unpublished manuscript, Catholic University, Washington, D.C.

McCarthy, John D. and Mayer N. Zald (1977). "Resource Mobilization and Social Movements: A Partial Theory." *American Journal of Sociology,* 82:1212–1241.

McConnell, Grant (1966). *Private Power and American Democracy.* New York: Random House, Vintage.

McConnell, Grant (1969). "The Public Values of the Private Association." Pp. 147–160 in *Voluntary Associations,* edited by J. Roland Pennock and John W. Chapman, New York: Atherton Press.

McFarland, Andrew S. (1976). *Public Interest Lobbies: Decision Making on Energy.* Washington: American Enterprise Institute.

McFarland, Andrew S. (1983). "Public Interest Lobbies Versus Minority Faction." Pp. 324–353 in *Interest Group Politics,* edited by Allan J. Cigler and Burdett A. Loomis, Washington: CQ Press.

McFarland, Andrew S. (1984). *Common Cause.* Chatham, NJ: Chatham Press.

McFarland, Andrew S. (1987). "Interest Groups and Theories of Power in America." *British Journal of Political Science,* 17:129–147.

McKelvey, Bill and Howard Aldrich (1983). "Populations, Natural Selection, and Applied Organizational Science." *Administration Science Quarterly,* 28:101–128.

McNeil, Kenneth (1978). "Understanding Organizational Power: Building on the Weberian Legacy." *Administrative Science Quarterly,* 23:65–90.

McPherson, J. Miller (1977). "Correlates of Social Participation: A Comparison of the Ethnic and Compensatory Theories." *Sociological Quarterly,* 18:197–208.

McPherson, J. Miller (1982). "Hypernetwork Sampling: Duality and Differentiation Among Voluntary Organizations." *Social Networks,* 3:225–250.

McPherson, J. Miller (1983). "An Ecology of Affiliation." *American Sociological Review,* 48:519–532.

McPherson, J. Miller and William Lockwood (1980). "The Dynamics of Voluntary Affiliation: A Multivariate Analysis." *Journal of Voluntary Action Research,* 9:74–84.

McPherson, J. Miller and D. Lynn Smith-Lovin (1982). "Women and Weak Ties: Differences by Sex in the Size of Voluntary Associations." *American Journal of Sociology,* 87:883–904

McPherson, J. Miller and D. Lynn Smith-Lovin (1986). "Sex segregation in voluntary associations." *American Sociological Review,* 51:61–79.

Malbin, Murray J., ed. (1980). *Parties, Interest Groups, and Campaign Finance Laws.* Washington: American Enterprise Institute.

Mansbridge, Jane J. (1980). *Beyond Adversary Democracy.* Chicago: University of Chicago Press.

Mansbridge, Jane J. (1986). *Why We Lost the ERA.* Chicago: University of Chicago Press.

March, James G. and Herbert A. Simon (1958). *Organizations.* New York: Wiley.

Marradi, Alberto (1981). "Factor Analysis as an Aid in the Formation and Refinement of Empirically Useful Concepts." Pp. 11–50 in *Factor Analysis and Measurement in Social Research,* edited by David J. Jackson and Edgar F. Borgatta, Beverly Hills: Sage.

Marsden, Peter V. (1987). "Core Discussion Networks of Americans." *American Sociological Review,* 52:122–131.

Marsh, David (1976). "On Joining Interest Groups: An Empirical Consideration of the Work of Mancur Olson, Jr." *British Journal of Political Science,* 6:257–271.

Marwell, Gerald and Ruth E. Ames (1979). "Experiments on the Provision of Public Goods. I. Resources, Interest, Group Size, and the Free Rider Problem." *American Journal of Sociology,* 84:1335–1360.

Marwell, Gerald and Ruth E. Ames (1980). "Experiments on the Provision of Public Goods. II. Provision Points, Stakes, Experiences, and the Free-Rider Problem." *American Journal of Sociology,* 85:926–937.

Marwell, Gerald and Ruth E. Ames (1981). "Economists Free Ride, Does Anyone Else?: Experiments on the Provision of Public Goods IV." *Journal of Public Economics,* 15:295–310.

Mayhew, Bruce H. (1980). "Structuralism vs. Individualism." *Social Forces,* 59:355–375.

Meister Albert (1984). *Participation, Associations, Development, and Change*. New Brunswick, NJ: Transaction Books.

Menzies, Ken (1977). *Talcott Parsons and the Social Image of Man*. London: Routledge.

Messinger, Sheldon (1955). "Organizational Transformation: A Case Study of a Declining Social Movement." *American Sociological Review*, 20:3–10.

Meyer, John and Bryan Rowan (1977). "Institutional Organizations: Formal Structure as Myth and Ceremony." *American Journal of Sociology*, 83:340–363.

Michels, Robert (1949). *Political Parties: A Sociological Study of Oligarchical Tendencies in Modern Democracy*. Glencoe, IL: Free Press.

Mills, C. Wright (1956). *The Power Elite*. New York: Oxford University Press.

Mintzberg, Henry (1983). *Power In and Around Organizations*. Englewood Cliffs, NJ: Prentice-Hall.

Mitchell, Robert C. (1979). "National Environmental Lobbies and the Apparent Illogic of Collective Action." Pp. 187–221 in *Collective Decision-Making*, edited by C. Russell, Baltimore: Johns Hopkins University Press.

Moe, Terry M. (1980). *The Organization of Interests: Incentives and the Internal Dynamics of Political Interest Groups*. Chicago: University of Chicago Press.

Morris, Aldon (1984). *The Origins of the Civil Rights Movement: Black Communities Organizing for Change*. New York: Free Press.

Muller, Edward N. (1979). *Aggressive Political Participation*. Princeton: Princeton University Press.

Muller, Edward N. and Karl-Dieter Opp (1986). "Rational Choice and Rebellious Collective Action." *American Political Science Review*, 80:471–487.

Namboodiri, N. Krishnan, Lewis F. Carter, and Hubert M. Blalock, Jr. (1975). *Applied Multivariate Analysis and Experimental Designs*. New York: McGraw-Hill.

Neal, Arthur G. and Melvin Seeman (1964). "Organizations and Powerlessness: A Test of the Mediation Hypothesis." *American Sociological Association*, 25:216–226.

Nisbet, Robert (1953). *The Quest for Community*. New York: Oxford University Press.

Nuttall, Ronald L., Erwin K. Scheuch, and Chad Gordon (1968). "On the Structure of Influence." Pp. 349–380 in *Community Power and Decision-Making*, edited by Terry N. Clark, San Francisco: Chandler.

Nyden, Philip W. (1985). "Democratizing Organizations: A Case Study of a Union Reform Movement." *American Sociological Review*, 90:1179–1203.

Oliver, Pamela (1980). "Rewards and Punishments as Selective Incentives for Collective Action: Theoretical Investigations." *American Journal of Sociology*, 85:1356–1375.

Oliver, Pamela (1984). " 'If You Don't Do It, Nobody Else Will': Active and Token Contributors to Local Collective Action." *American Sociological Review*, 49:601–610.

Oliver, Pamela and Gerald Marwell (1988). "The Paradox of Group Size in Collective Action: A Theory of the Critical Mass. II." *American Sociological Review*, 53:1–8.

Oliver, Pamela, Gerald Marwell and Ruy Teixeira (1985). "A Theory of Critical Mass. I. Interdependence, Group Heterogeneity, and the Production of Collective Goods." *American Journal of Sociology*, 91:522–556.

Olsen, Marvin E. (1982). *Participatory Pluralism: Political Participation and Influence in the United States and Sweden*. Chicago: Nelson-Hall.

Olson, Mancur, Jr. (1965). *The Logic of Collective Action*. Cambridge, MA: Harvard University Press.

Olson, Mancur, Jr. (1982). *The Rise and Decline of Nations*. New Haven: Yale University Press.

Opp, Karl-Dieter (1986). "Soft Incentives and Collective Action: Participation in the Anti-Nuclear Movement." *British Journal of Political Science*, 16:87–112.

Ornstein, Norman J. and Shirley Elder (1978). *Interest Groups, Lobbying and Policymaking*. Washington DC: CQ Press.

Panitch, Leon (1977). "The Development of Corporatism in Liberal Democracies." *Comparative Political Studies*, 10:61–90.

Parker, Robert Nash (1983). "Measuring Social Participation." *American Sociological Review*, 48:864–873.

Parsons, Talcott (1937). *The Structure of Social Action*. New York: Free Press.

Parsons, Talcott (1969). *Politics and Social Structure*. New York: Free Press.

Parsons, Talcott and Edward A. Shils (1951). "Values, Motives, and Systems of Action." In *Toward a General Theory of Action*, p. 47–275. Cambridge: Harvard University Press.

Pateman, Carole (1970). *Participation and Democratic Theory*, Cambridge: Cambridge University Press

Pennings, Johannes M. (1976). "Dimensions of Organizational Influence and Their Effectiveness Correlates." *Administrative Science Quarterly*, 21:688–699.

Perrow, Charles (1970). "Members as Resources in Voluntary Organizations." Pp. 93–116 in *Organizations and Clients*, edited by Mark R. Rosengren and Mark Lefton, Columbus, OH: Merrill.

Pertschuk, Michael (1986). *Giant Killers*. New York: Norton.

Pfeffer, Jeffrey (1978). *Organizational Design*. Arlington Heights, IL: AHM Publishing.

Pfeffer, Jeffrey (1981). *Power in Organizations*. Marshfield, MA: Pitman.

Pfeffer, Jeffrey and Gerald R. Salancik (1978). *The External Control of Organizations*. New York: Harper and Row.

Piven, Frances Fox and Richard A. Cloward (1977). *Poor People's Movements: Why They Succeed, How They Fail*. New York: Vintage.

Pope, Whitney (1986). *Alexis de Tocqueville: His Social and Political Theory*. Beverly Hills, CA: Sage.

Popper, Karl R. (1959). *The Logic of Scientific Discovery*. New York: Basic Books.

Powell, Walter W. (1985). *Getting Into Print: The Decision-Making Process in Scholarly Publishing*. Chicago: University of Chicago Press.

Price, James L. and Charles W. Mueller (1986). *Handbook of Organization Measurement*. Marshfield, MA: Pitman.

Pugh, Derek, David Hickson, and Robert Hinings (1969). "The Context of Organizational Structures." *Administrative Science Quarterly*, 14:91–114.

Riker, William H. (1982). *Liberalism Against Populism: A Confrontation Between the Theory of Democracy and the Theory of Social Choice*. San Francisco: Freeman.

Riker, William H. and Peter C. Ordeshook (1973). *An Introduction to Positive Political Theory.* Englewood Cliffs, NJ: Prentice-Hall.

Ripley, Randall B. and Grace A. Franklin (1976). *Congress, the Bureaucracy, and Public Policy.* Homewood, IL: Dorsey Press.

Rogers, David L. and Gordon L. Bultena (1975). "Voluntary Associations and Political Equality: An Extension of Mobilization Theory." *Journal of Voluntary Action Research,* 4:172–183.

Rogers, David L., Gordon L. Bultena, and Ken H. Barb (1975). "Voluntary Association Membership and Political Participation: An Exploration of the Mobilization Hypothesis." *Sociological Quarterly,* 16:305–318.

Rogers, Everett M. and David L. Kincaid (1981). *Communication Networks: Toward a New Paradigm for Research.* New York: Free Press.

Rogers, Mary F. (1974). "Instrumental and Infra-Resources: The Bases of Power." *American Journal of Sociology,* 79:1418–1433.

Rose, Arnold (1967). *The Power Structure.* New York: Oxford University Press.

Rossides, Daniel W. (1978). *The History and Nature of Sociological Theory.* Boston: Houghton-Mifflin.

Runge, Carlisle Ford (1984). "Institutions and the Free Rider: The Assurance Problem in Collective Action." *Journal of Politics,* 46:154–181.

Salisbury, Robert H. (1969). "An Exchange Theory of Interest Groups." *Midwest Journal of Political Science,* 13:1–32.

Salisbury, Robert H. (1975). "Interest Groups." Pp. 171-228 in *Handbook of Political Science,* vol. 4, edited by Fred I. Greenstein and Nelson W. Polsby, Reading, MA: Addison-Wesley.

Salisbury, Robert H. (1979). "Why No Corporatism in America?" In *Patterns in Corporatist Policy-Making,* Gerhard Lehmbruch and Phillippe C. Schmitter, eds., p. 213–230. Beverly Hills: Sage.

Salisbury, Robert H. (1984). "Interest Representation: The Dominance of Institutions." *American Political Science Review,* 78:64–76.

Salisbury, Robert H., John P. Heinz, Edward O. Laumann, and Robert L. Nelson (1987). "Who Works with Whom? Group Alliances and Opposition." *American Political Science Review,* 81:1217–1234.

Samuelson, Paul A. (1954). "The Pure Theory of Public Expenditure." *Review of Economics and Statistics,* 36:387–390.

Santee, R. T. and T. L. Van Der Pool (1976). "Actors' Status and Conformity to Norms: A Study of Student's Evaluations of Instructors." *Sociological Quarterly,* 17:378–388.

Savage. L. J. (1954). *The Foundation of Statistics.* New York: Wiley.

Scheff, Thomas (1983). "Toward Integration in the Social Psychology of Emotions." *Annual Review of Sociology,* 9:333–354.

Schlozman, Kay L. (1984). "What Accent the Heavenly Chorus? Political Equality in the American Pressure System." *Journal Politics,* 46:1006–1032.

Schlozman, Kay L. and John T. Tierney (1983). "More of the Same: Washington Pressure Group Activity in a Decade of Change." *Journal Politics,* 34:351–377.

Schlozman, Kay L. and John T. Tierney (1986). *Organized Interests and American Democracy.* New York: Harper and Row.

Schmidt, A. J. (1973). *Oligarchy in Fraternal Organizations*. Detroit: Gale Research.

Schmitter, Phillippe C. (1981). "Interest Intermediation and Regime Governability in Contemporary Western Europe and North America." Pp. 287–330 in *Organizing Interests in Western Europe*, edited by Suzanne D. Berger, Cambridge: Cambridge University Press.

Schulman, D. C. (1978). "Voluntary Organization Involvement and Political Participation." *Journal of Voluntary Action Research*, 7:86–105.

Schumpeter, Joseph A. (1943). *Capitalism, Socialism and Democracy*. London: Allen & Unwin.

Schwartz, Shalom (1977). "Normative Influences on Altruism." Pp. 221–279 in *Advances in Experimental Social Psychology 10*, edited by Leonard Berkowitz, New York: Academic Press.

Sciulli, David (1986). "Voluntaristic Action as a Distinct Concept: Theoretical Foundations of Societal Constitutionalism." *American Sociological Review*, 51:743–766.

Scott, W. Richard (1983). "The Organization of Environments: Network, Cultural, and Historical Elements." Pp. 155–175 in *Organizational Environments: Ritual and Rationality*, edited by John W. Meyer and W. Richard Scott, Beverly Hills: Sage.

Scott, W. Richard (1987). *Organizations: Rational, Natural and Open Systems*, Sec. Ed. Englewood Cliffs, NJ: Prentice-Hall.

Scott, W. Richard and John W. Meyer (1983). "The Organization of Societal Sectors." Pp. 129–153 in *Organizational Environments: Ritual and Rationality*, edited by John W. Meyer and W. Richard Scott, Beverly Hills: Sage.

Scott, William G., Terence R. Mitchell, and Newman S. Peery (1981). "Organizational Governance." Pp. 135–151 in *Handbook of Organizational Design, vol. 2*, edited by Paul C. Nystrom and William H. Starbuck, New York: Oxford University Press.

Selznick, Philip (1960). *The Organizational Weapon*. Glencoe, IL: Free Press.

Shott, Susan (1979). "Emotion and Social Life: A Symbolic Interactionist Analysis." *American Journal of Sociology*, 84:1317–1334.

Shubik, Martin (1982). *Game Theory in the Social Sciences: Concepts and Solutions*. Cambridge, MA: MIT Press.

Shye, Samuel, ed. (1978). *Theory Construction and Data Analysis in the Behavioral Sciences*. San Francisco: Jossey-Bass.

Silver, Morris (1974). "Political Revolution and Repression: An Economic Approach." *Public Choice*, 17:63–71.

Simmel, Georg (1950). *The Sociology of Georg Simmel*. New York: Free Press.

Simmel, Georg (1955). "The Web of Group Affiliations." In Georg Simmel, *Conflict and the Web of Group Affiliations*, p. 125–195. New York: Free Press.

Simon, Herbert A. (1965). *Adminstrative Behavior*. New York: Free Press.

Simon, Herbert A. (1983). "Rational Decision Making in Business Organizations." Pp. 281–315 in *How Economists Explain: A Reader in Methodology*, edited by William L. Marr and Balder Raj, Lanham, MD: University Press of America.

Simon, Herbert A. (1985). "Human Nature in Politics: The Dialogue of Psychology with Political Science." *American Political Science Review*, 79:293–304.

Simpson, Richard L. and William H. Gulley (1962). "Goals, Environmental Pressures and Organizational Characteristics." *American Sociological Review*, 27:344–351.

Small, Albion and G. Vincent (1894). *An Introduction to the Study of Society*. New York: American Books.

Smith, Clagett G. and Michael E. Brown (1964). "Communication Structure and Control Structure in a Voluntary Association." *Sociometry*, 27:449–468.

Smith, Hedrick (1988). *The Power Game: How Washington Works*. New York: Random House.

Smith, Jan (1976). "Communities, Associations, and the Supply of Collective Goods." *American Journal of Sociology*, 82:291–308.

Snow, David, Louis A. Zurcher Jr., and Sheldon Eckland-Olson (1980). "Social Networks and Social Movements: A Microstructural Approach to Differential Recruitment." *American Sociological Review*, 45:787–801.

Sprague, John (1982). "Is There a Micro-Theory Consistent with Contextual Analysis?" Pp. 99–121 in *The Nature of Political Inquiry*, edited by Elinor Ostrom, Beverly Hills, CA: Sage.

Staber, Udo and Howard Aldrich (1983). "Trade Association Stability and Public Policy." Pp. 179–194 in *Organization Theory and Public Policy*, edited by R. H. Hall and R. E. Quinn, Beverly Hills: Sage.

Staber, Udo and Howard Aldrich (1986). "Government Regulation and the Expansion of Trade Associations: An Exploration of Some Ecological Propositions." Paper presented at the annual meetings of the American Political Science Association, Washington, DC.

Starbuck, William H. (1976) "Organizations and Their Environments." Pp. 1069–1123 in *Handbook of Industrial and Organizational Psychology*, edited by M. D. Dunnette, Chicago: Rand McNally.

Stark, Rodney and William S. Bainbridge (1980). "Networks of Faith: Interpersonal Bonds and Recruitment to Cults and Sects." *American Journal of Sociology*, 85:1376–1395.

Stigler, George J. (1950). "The Development of Utility Theory." *Journal of Political Economy*, 58:307–327, 373–396.

Stinchcombe, Arthur L. (1965). "Social Structure and Organizations." Pp. 142–193 in *Handbook of Organizations*, edited by James G. March, Chicago: Rand McNally.

Stinchcombe, Arthur L. (1968). *Constructing Social Theories*. New York: Harcourt, Brace, World.

Stoltzenberg, Ross M. (1979). "The Measurement and Decomposition of Causal Effects in Nonlinear and Nonadditive Models." Pp. 459–488 in *Sociological Methodology 1980*, edited by Karl F. Schuessler, San Francisco: Jossey-Bass.

Streeck, Wolfgang and Philippe C. Schmitter (1985). *Private Interest Government: Beyond Market and State*. Beverly Hills, CA: Sage.

Tannenbaum, Arnold S. (1968). *Control in Organizations*. New York: McGraw-Hill.

Tannenbaum, Arnold S., Bogdan Kavcic, Menachem Rosner, Mino Vianello, and Georg Wieser (1974). *Hierarchy in Organizations: An International Comparison*. San Francisco: Jossey-Bass.

Taub, Richard P., G. P. Surgeon, S. Lindholm, P. B. Otti, and A. Bridges (1977). "Urban Voluntary Associations, Locality Based and Externally Induced." *American Journal of Sociology,* 83:425–442.

Thelen, M. H., N. M. Frautschi, M. C. Roberts, K. D. Kirkland, and S. J. Dollinger (1981). "Being Imitated, Conformity, and Social Influence: An Integrative Review." *Journal of Research in Personality,* 15:403–426.

Thurow, Lester C. (1980). *The Zero-Sum Society.* New York: Basic Books.

Tillock, Harriet and Denton E. Morrison (1979). "Group Size and Contribution to Collective Action: A Test of Mancur Olson's Theory on Zero Population Growth, Inc." *Research in Social Movements, Conflict, and Change,* 2:131–158.

Tilly, Charles (1978). *From Mobilization to Revolution.* Reading, MA: Addison-Wesley.

Tocqueville Alexis de (1945). *Democracy in America.* New York: Knopf.

Truman, David B. (1971). *The Governmental Process: Political Interests and Public Opinion,* 2nd Ed. New York: Knopf.

Ullman-Margalit, Edna (1977). *The Emergence of Norms.* Oxford: Clarendon Press.

Useem, Michael (1984). *The Inner Circle: Large Corporations and the Rise of Business Political Activity in the U.S. and U.K.* New York: Oxford University Press.

Verba, Sidney and Norman H. Nie (1972). *Participation in America.* New York: Harper and Row.

Vroom, Victor (1969). "Industrial Social Psychology." Pp. 196–268 in *The Handbook of Social Psychology* (2nd ed.), edited by G. Lindzey and E. Aronson, Reading, MA: Addison-Wesley.

Walker, Henry A. and Bernard P. Cohen (1985). "Scope Statements: Imperatives for Evaluating Theory." *American Sociological Review,* 50:288–301.

Walker, Jack L. (1983). "The Origins and Maintenance of Interest Groups in America." *American Political Science Review,* 77:390–406.

Walker, Jack L. and Frank Baumgartner (1989). "Survey Research and Membership in Voluntary Associations." American Journal of Political Science (Forthcoming).

Warner, R. Stephen (1978). "Toward a Redefinition of Action Theory: Paying the Cognitive Element its Due." *American Journal of Sociology,* 6:1317–1349.

Weber, Max (1947). *The Theory of Social and Economic Organization.* New York: Free Press.

Weber, Max (1968). *Economy and Society.* Totowa, NJ: Bedminister Press.

Weber, Max, (1978). *Economy and Society.* Berkeley: University of California Press.

Wicker, A. (1969). "Size of Church Membership and Members' Support of Church Behavior Settings." *Journal of Personality and Social Psychology,* 13:278–288.

Wilensky, Harold (1967). *Organizational Intelligence.* New York: Basic Books.

Willer, David (1967). *Scientific Sociology: Theory and Method.* Englewood Cliffs, NJ: Prentice-Hall.

Williamson, Peter J. (1985). *Varieties of Corporatism: A Conceptual Discussion.* London: Cambridge University Press.

Wilson, Graham K. (1982). "Why is There No Corporatism in the United States?" In *Patterns of Corporatist Policy-Making,* Gerhard Lehmbruch and Phillippe C. Schmitter, eds., p. 219–236. Beverly Hills: Sage.

Wilson, James Q. (1980). *The Politics of Regulation.* New York: Basic Books.

Wilson, Kenneth and Tony Orum (1976). "Mobilizing People for Collective Political Action." *Journal of Political and Military Sociology,* 4:187–202.

Wrong, Dennis H. (1979). *Power: Its Forms, Bases and Uses.* Oxford: Basil Blackwell.

Yuchtman, Ephraim and Stanley E. Seashore (1967). "A System Resource Approach to Organizational Effectiveness." *American Sociological Review,* 32:891–903.

Zablocki, Benjamin (1980). *Alienation and Charisma.* New York: Free Press.

Zald, Mayer N. (1970). *Organizational Change: The Political Economy of the YMCA.* Chicago: University of Chicago Press.

Zald, Mayer N. and David Jacobs (1978). "Compliance/incentive Classifications of Organizations: Underlying Dimensions." *Administration and Society,* 9:403–424.

Zey-Ferrell, Mary (1981). "Criticisms of the Dominant Perspective on Organizations." *Sociological Quarterly,* 22:181–205.

Zucker, Lynne G. (1983). "Organizations as Institutions." *Research in the Sociology of Organizations,* 2:1–47.

INDEX